Shrinking the Earth

Shrinking the Earth

THE RISE AND DECLINE
OF NATURAL ABUNDANCE

Donald Worster

OXFORD
UNIVERSITY PRESS

OXFORD

UNIVERSITY PRESS

Oxford University Press is a department of the University of Oxford. It furthers the University's objective of excellence in research, scholarship, and education by publishing worldwide. Oxford is a registered trade mark of Oxford University Press in the UK and certain other countries.

Published in the United States of America by Oxford University Press
198 Madison Avenue, New York, NY 10016, United States of America.

First issued as an Oxford University Press paperback, 2018

Cataloging-in-Publication Data is on file at the Library of Congress.
ISBN 978–0–19–984495–1 (hardcover); ISBN 978–0–19–084985–6 (paperback)

For my newest generation

Mattia, Emma, and Leo

CONTENTS

Epilogue

LIST OF IMAGES OF EARTH

Color plates appear between pages 114 and 115.

ACKNOWLEDGMENTS

MANY WONDERFUL INSTITUTIONS, AND many individuals within them, made this book possible, and I want to offer humble thanks to all. First in time were the Yale University Institute of Biospheric Studies and School of Forestry and Environmental Studies, which offered me their Strachan Donnelley Visiting Professorship and allowed me to initiate this research and writing project. In particular I want to thank Peter Crane, Jeffrey Park, John Wargo, Stephen Kellert, Mary Evelyn Tucker, John Grim, Michael Dove, and Paul Sabin for their hospitality and advice, along with all those who attended lectures and seminars I gave during my stay. Special mention should go to Vivian Donnelley and the late Strachan Donnelley for their commitment to the environmental humanities.

The Rachel Carson Center for Environment and Society in Munich, affiliated with the Ludwig-Maximilians-Universität and the Deutsches Museum, gave me a Carson Fellowship, which allowed more than a year of residency. It was an incomparable opportunity to read, think, and compare notes with colleagues from many countries and disciplines. I am most grateful to the RCC's director, Christof Mauch, for his invitation and for his inspired leadership, and also want to thank Codirector Helmuth Trischler, the Center's able and cheerful staff, Germany's Federal Ministry of Education and Research, and all the other fellows. Jon Mathieu of the University of Lucerne deserves particular mention for introducing me to the Swiss heritage of "balancing on an alp," or practicing the art of ecological sustainability. The RCC experience helped me see the broader international significance of my themes and to overcome, at least partially, my American provinciality.

Renmin University of China, located in Beijing, has now become my home for much of the year, and I am very grateful for the warm reception I have found there. Various parts of this book took shape on that campus, and many audiences there have helped shape my ideas and research. In particular I want to give credit to Mingfang Xia, director of the Center for Ecological History, and Xingtao Huang, dean of the School of History. Above all, I want to say *xie xie* to my dear friend and former student Shen Hou, associate professor of History and Deputy Director of the CEH, for her untiring efforts to make my Renmin visits so smooth and rewarding. She has been an indispensable interpreter, facilitator, coteacher, and guide. Other friends, colleagues, and students across the breadth of China have also made a large difference in the way I think about the history presented in this book.

Back home in the United States, I was privileged for more than two decades to be a part of the University of Kansas. Here I want to praise the librarians, administrators, students, and faculty there who enabled this book, especially in its early stages, to take shape and who provided financial and intellectual support over that long span of years.

Susan Ferber, my esteemed friend and editor at Oxford University Press, along with the whole OUP production team, have once again given me their wise and skilled guidance, for which I am grateful. My longtime advisor Gerry McCauley, now happily retired after a highly successful career as literary agent, also has my heartfelt gratitude for all his efforts on my behalf over the years. Not least I want to express appreciation to my trusted friends and critics Adam Rome, Ted Steinberg, and Angus Wright, who gave various parts of the manuscript the benefit of a close reading, and above all to my wife Bev, who for many years has borne cheerfully the many burdens that make my writing life possible. I am always grateful for all their encouragement, support, and intelligent counsel, without which I could never have brought this project to a finish.

Finally, this book is dedicated to my grandchildren, whose future on earth has been much on my mind throughout their young lives.

Shrinking the Earth

Prologue

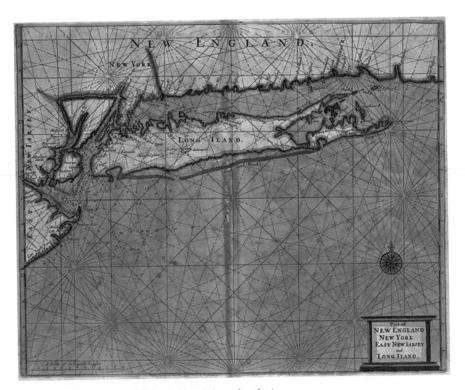

Eighteenth-century map of Long Island (*see color plate*)

Gatsby's Green Light

HE WAS THE MOST SYMPATHETIC rich man in America's literary history, a generous idealist despite his vast material possessions, starry-eyed and dreaming of the immaterial things he could never have. In the end he died ingloriously, shot dead in his own swimming pool for a crime he did not commit.

No one would choose Jay Gatsby (aka Jimmy Gatz) to represent the inner life of those born to wealth and privilege, for he did not descend from that pampered elite. He was the son of poor prairie farmers. While the ruling class asserted power, smashed everyone around them, and walked away unscathed from their ruinous ways, he was merely one of their casualties.

The Minnesota novelist F. Scott Fitzgerald created this compelling figure in 1925, in his ironically named *The Great Gatsby*, a book that many have regarded as the finest American novel ever.[1] Made popular again and again by Hollywood, it tells the story of an aspiring but obscure youth falling in love with a gorgeous, wealthy woman, who proves impervious to all his efforts to woo her. Despite acquiring a grandiose palace on New York's Long Island, his fate is to be rejected. Both the rich and the poor treat Gatsby badly, and his virtuous innocence, although hidden under a superficially corrupt exterior, shines through for only one of his acquaintances, his self-effacing neighbor and the story's narrator, Nick Carraway.

Fitzgerald's novel is considered by some to be too lush in flourish, too improbable in incident, and too nebulous in argument to be altogether satisfying. Yet it evokes poignant empathy for dreamers—particularly dreamers from the meager, bleak side of American life who try to transcend their insufficiency by dreaming even harder. Nick Carraway wisely understands that there is a bit of Jimmy Gatz in everyone, and always exemplifies the caring observer even toward the less deserving. Most readers probably dislike Daisy Buchanan, the woman Gatsby falls hopelessly in love with, for she is shallow and unaware, but Carraway is her friend and cousin and doesn't blame her for her suitor's failure to succeed. He blames Gatsby's personal tragedy on fate and circumstance. Here is a man whom life has put in an impossible situation, promising more than could ever be redeemed.

Aspiring Jay Gatsby lacks any insight into what drives him or any realistic sense of his own or nature's limits. In the night, vulnerable and alone, he stands on his magnificent lawn sweeping down to the Long Island Sound, arms outreached toward a mysterious green light that shines far away in the mist. He is enchanted by something he cannot understand or articulate. Carraway is shrewd enough to know that the light is merely a navigation aid installed at the end of Daisy's boat dock, no more magical than a light bulb. Later on, however, the narrator begins to realize that the green light has intense symbolic energy. It is what remains of the rich aura that once suffused the shores along the sound, and beyond those shores suffused an entire continent—nature's green light of infinite promise.

Somewhere in Gatsby's and America's past lay the dream of a land unspoiled and fertile with possibilities. The modern world seems by contrast an impoverished, polluted wasteland on the one side, and rows of empty, soulless mansions on the other. Once the land offered much more than that. Why has that failure happened? Why has nature become so diminished—so bankrupt?

By the story's end the narrator begins to see how his flawed hero's dreams began and why they have turned out badly. "Gradually," he says, "I became aware of the old island here that flowered once for Dutch sailors' eyes—a fresh, green breast of the new world. Its vanished trees, the trees that had made way for Gatsby's house, had once pandered in whispers to the last and greatest of all human dreams; for a transitory enchanted moment man must have held his breath in the presence of this continent, compelled into an aesthetic contemplation he neither understood nor desired, face to face for the last time in history with something commensurate to his capacity for wonder."[2]

Like those awestruck sailors, Gatsby was possessed by a vision of infinite natural abundance and the radiant grandeur it would make possible for every boy or girl raised in deprivation. The dreamer, however, had come to the wrong place. "He did not know that it was already behind him, somewhere in that vast obscurity beyond the city, where the dark fields of the republic rolled on under the night."[3]

How strange that those melancholy words came out of the fabulous Jazz Age of the 1920s, the birth years of the consumer society, when Americans seemed sure of getting rich, when capitalism was in its heyday. Why in such giddy times did a leading writer feel so disillusioned? Although not recognized as such, F. Scott Fitzgerald wrote one of the country's earliest environmental laments. Later generations would add to his impression that America's natural legacy, which once had awakened so much ambition, was fading fast where it had once been strong, dying under the weight of too much demand and exploitation. And with its demise must come for many a shattering of hope.

Novels tell stories about people who have never actually lived or carried out any of the things ascribed to them. Their readers step out of reality into a different universe, where effects still follow causes but where none of them truly occurred. What novels can do, and do wonderfully, is provide an escape from reality that our deepest feelings seem to require now and then. They can teach us how to observe more carefully and prepare us to understand better the flesh-and-blood people we encounter. From novels we can learn how to be more open, tolerant, and sympathetic toward others, and they can also confirm our prejudices and fears. Either way, they are the product of an artist at work, who creates intriguing characters, invents intricate stories, touches our full range of emotions, and plays on our imaginations as skillfully as any musician or painter.

Now and then a novel like *The Great Gatsby* can lead us toward insight into human behavior, the workings of the natural world, or the shape of the past that can be examined and tested. Testing the truthfulness of such an insight need not be dull or prosaic work.

Let us call Nick Carraway's concluding insight the "theory of the green light." Briefly, the theory holds that the discovery around 1500 A.D. that the earth has an entire Western Hemisphere of immense continents and oceans marked a watershed in human experience, perhaps the most extraordinary ever. Then began the modern era, a time when humans living in the more socially advanced civilizations—and eventually other parts of the human population—enjoyed an unprecedented natural abundance. That wealth of nature, when appropriated and turned to use, touched off a multifaceted revolution in society, economy, politics, and culture, which swept over the entire globe. It stimulated a shift in perception, but it also changed people's material conditions. For a while the perceptual change was congruent with the material one, but then perception outran reality. During the twentieth century, however, it became increasingly clear that the modern era of extraordinary natural abundance was coming to an end, and that neither scientific knowledge, innovations in technology, or hard work could bring it back. Humankind, consequently, faced an adjustment of ideas, institutions, and ecologies of global proportions.

The aim of this book is to explore the theory of the green light using the tools and methods of the historian. It is not an altogether new theory, but it needs to be taken seriously and examined in detail. Doing so requires setting aside some deeply entrenched and familiar perspectives. The first of them is the "sympathy for losers" view that has dominated postimperial, postcolonial historical writing. In recent decades increasing numbers of historians, within the United States and other privileged nations, have expressed disillusionment with the outcomes of the past few centuries and outrage over the sad plight of the unsuccessful. From this point of view the most important result of Gatsby's Dutch sailors arriving in America was a genocidal war against native peoples and the transportation and enslavement of African peoples. For those who strongly advocate that highly critical perspective on modern history this book may seem insufficiently sympathetic, although by no means does it minimize the tragic human consequences of the new world conquest or the importation of slavery.[4]

A second interpretation of history that this book competes with is the "good habits and institutions" school.[5] Contrary to the first perspective, this one tries to explain the rise of the United States and the West as the result of Westerners' learning how to be industrious and develop the right institutions, not their ruthless immorality. Here the moral lesson drawn from the past is not that the United States should feel guilty because of its rise to power, but rather that it should understand the cultural roots of its success and try to transplant them to more backward parts of the world. Once again, this argument contains a measure of truth. But like the first school, this one is too simple: it ignores the fact that North Americans and Western Europeans did not simply make the nature of the Americas pay off handsomely, thanks to their ingenuity and hard work. They were also lucky. For reasons beyond their control, such as the vulnerability of Indians to the white man's diseases, they managed to gain access to an abundance of resources that others did not. That they profited from that abundance cannot be explained merely by their intelligence, ethics, and institutions. The windfall of nature's abundance contributed significantly to their success.

A third and newer perspective on modern history, which has not yet become so widely established among mainstream historians, lies in the concept of the "Anthropocene." This term has been given to the past two centuries by natural scientists Eugene Stoermer and Paul Crutzen, who suggest that a new geological epoch of the earth began in the late eighteenth century with large-scale burning of coal, leading to fundamental changes in the planet's atmosphere.[6] The Anthropocene has subsequently been expanded to become the very name of the modern. The modern age, some argue, is that time when the human species began to dominate the planet and alter the earth's biogeological composition—not only changing the planet's crust and atmosphere but also its climate, oceans, global ecosystems, and the very rocks under their feet. Humankind has achieved, scientists and historians declare, an unprecedented influence over the processes and cycles of nature with profound social consequences. The only limits we face are those we choose to impose on ourselves. This view, I think, ignores the persistence of natural limits that no human power can wholly overcome. It also ignores that watershed moment when the Western Hemisphere first entered into the minds of Europeans, dazzled their imaginations, enriched their material lives, and revolutionized their way of life.

Like the concept of the Anthropocene, the green light theory focuses on human relations with the natural world over a long period of time. Like the effort to see through the eyes of those who lost to the invading Europeans their power and autonomy, it acknowledges that the past five hundred years have been a time of brutal conquest. Like the good habits and institutions school of thought, the theory acknowledges that the conquerors succeeded to some extent by their own hard work and because of enlightened social support. But it goes further than any of those views to emphasize that the earth has been a powerful agent in human history, both when it was replete with resources and when it could no longer offer the old abundance.

The modern period of human ecology, which began with the European discoveries of the Americas (along with Australia, Oceania, and southern Africa), was global in scope and triggered profound changes in almost every society on earth. But the green light theory is not simply about a long period of successful niche expansion; it is also about a subsequent period of contraction and disappointment. Just as Western civilization's sense of the earth once opened to a sweeping new horizon, so too it eventually began to shrink, until today we find ourselves living on a planet that is no longer as big as it once was.[7]

What lesson can we draw from this alternative view of the past? Not necessarily the lesson that Carraway drew at the end of Fitzgerald's novel. The narrator ends up wracked by gloom, with Gatsby dying and he himself abandoning his job and going back home to the Midwest, with little hope for the future. We need not accept a similar conclusion. We can respond to the fading green light in more hopeful, constructive ways.

This book offers a story of Americans seeking hope in the face of disappointment. Beginning in the mid-nineteenth century a growing number of citizens began taking their country's ecological shrinkage seriously and launched an ambitious and successful movement to conserve natural resources, reduce their waste, and preserve natural beauty. They too believed in the green light and were determined to preserve some of its glow for future generations. Even those who, as the decades rolled on, increasingly came to accept the decline of the new world did not always sink into a mood of despair or defeat.

The Great Gatsby is a fatalist's fable. Readers are often irresistibly drawn to it and may feel that success in life is completely predetermined, and that tragic loss is inevitable and irreversible. Many readers expect Gatsby to die, just as they expect the earth to die. But fatalism has not always been the only or the dominant reaction to change. In many times and places people have managed to come to terms with a diminished plenty and face up to natural limits and their own vulnerability.

What will be the future for those real people who live in the once new world that has become an old world? What will it be for those who always had to experience that world from afar, never directly and close up? The work of history offers no prophecies about what comes next. The theory of the green light leads us only toward a better explanation of how we arrived at where we are.

PART I

Second Earth

Map based on Mercator's Second Earth (*see color plate*)

CHAPTER 1

The Discovery of Natural Abundance

DUISBURG, A CITY IN NORTHERN Germany, is a green and peaceful place, favorably located at the junction of the Rhine and Ruhr rivers. Five hundred years ago, however, it bristled with military fortifications. The city surrounded itself with high walls and star-shaped battlements to protect against the cannons of enemy forces. It was a city wracked with fear. All foreign objects had to pass through its narrow gates. What the city's elaborate star fort defended was not freedom of the mind or freedom to trade or freedom to travel the rivers. Instead, it defended a cathedral spire that soared above everything else and dominated the city's skyline and its view of the world. The Church then ruled over Duisburg. Although in another German city of the same period the same religious establishment was waging war against an upstart priest named Martin Luther, here its authority was still intact. The spire, the thick city walls, the gates that could be locked at night all expressed entrenched attitudes: a commitment to religious orthodoxy, along with intellectual and economic restraint, deference to traditional authority, and a view of the natural world as firmly ordered by God and limited in resources and opportunities.

Yet this walled city would soon become the home and workplace of two of the greatest, most innovative cartographers in early modern Europe, Gerard Mercator and his son Rumold. Their visual images of the world, produced in this formidably barbed porcupine of a city, would mark a profound change in Western thinking. The Mercators were part of an emigrant family from Flanders, now called Belgium—a family that fell into dispute with the Catholic authorities and left to find freedom and success someplace else. What they saw in Duisburg that was so promising is hard to say. But after their coming the city would never be the same. The Mercators were leaders of a movement that began breaking down, intellectually and physically, the formidable walls of an old order.

The father Gerard was the most famous member of the family. He was a brilliant mathematician, instrument maker, calligrapher, and cartographer. He was also a free thinker who did not accept the Church and its Pope as the only legitimate source of knowing the mind of God. Arriving in Duisburg in 1552, he was already well known for having produced a comprehensive map of the entire world, based on reports from early navigators and explorers of the newly discovered Western Hemisphere. Gerard was among the first to depict the shimmering immensity of the Americas, and he was the first cartographer to use the phrase "North America." Making maps of that amazing new world to the west became his way of asserting his own freedom and of enlarging his private fortune.

The senior Mercator was well known, and highly controversial, for his embrace of the Polish scientist Nicolas Copernicus's model of the universe—the theory that started the modern scientific revolution by arguing that the sun, not the earth, stands at the center of the celestial system. Mercator followed Copernicus in rejecting the ancient authority on the heavens and the earth, the Roman-Egyptian geographer, astronomer, and mathematician Claudius Ptolemy. A man of uncommon brilliance, Ptolemy was born a few decades after the death of Jesus Christ. Seeing the universe as a set of fixed, nested spheres with the earth as their center, Ptolemy became Western civilization's chief guide to the cosmos for a millennium and a half and its dominant cartographer of Planet Earth. His world map, which he called "Ecumene," included only Europe, Asia, and the northern part of Africa. Although the Americas were already inhabited by millions of people, none of them entered Ptolemy's or his followers' consciousness. Around his Ecumene flowed a world-circling ocean, like a constraining frame to the picture. The earth, along with the universe, thus had a center—the lands surrounding the Mediterranean Sea. But then came Copernicus—and along with him came Gerard Mercator. Together, they began to envision the earth and cosmos in radically enlarged terms.

But it was Gerard's shadowy third son Rumold who created, in 1587, out of his father's global perspective and the data coming from voyages to the west, the most striking new image of the planet. We can call the picture "Second Earth." The son re-imagined the earth not as a single sphere but as a *pair* of spheres, coequal in size and conjoined in a celestial embrace, the old world and the new. It was as though a wandering body from outer space had gently approached the earth, edging closer and closer, until the two planets touched and kissed somewhere off the coast of Brazil. Happy union of the old and accomplished with the young and fertile—the beginning of a long and grand romance.

The image of two gently colliding orbs seems clearly to suggest that out in the western sea lay an immense windfall of untapped natural resources. Unmistakably the map promised at least a *doubling* of Ecumene's natural resource base. So the vision, and so the reality. The material foundations of Europeans were enriched and yet shaken to their core. And with that revolution in material reality, in human ecology and economy, came profound changes in perceptions, values, institutions, and ways of behavior. The discovery of Second Earth ushered in an age of unprecedented material abundance, eventually flooding the older civilizations with new natural resources and the freedom those resources made possible. That age has now lasted more than five centuries.

Rumold's grandiose vision of Second Earth looms so large on his world map that it tends to overbalance the old world. South America, for example, bulges far into the Atlantic, swelling to a size almost as large as Africa (though it is only half as big). North America, although accurately drawn around the Caribbean and up the Atlantic coast where the navigators had gathered the most data, begins to swell fantastically as the eye follows its outlines far into the Arctic. The continent appears to extend over the North Pole, becoming a single gargantuan landmass that overshadows Eurasia although Eurasia is actually twice as large as North America. Speculating where he did not have sufficient data, Rumold got some of his geography wrong. There was not really quite that much new land. But the exaggerations suggest how impressed he was with the new prospects. Such exaggerated hopes would animate Europeans and others for centuries to come, whether they were immigrants leaving their old homes, capitalists seeking profits, scientists awakening to the fecundity and diversity of nature, or politicians seeking to expand their national power.

Remember how it all began. In August 1492, Christopher Columbus set sail from Spain in search of the fabled Indies and ran into unsuspected continents, islands, and oceans. The sailor from Genoa had launched his little fleet with no reliable chart and only an amateur's theory, mistaken as it turned out, about the width of the span of open water separating Europe from Asia. His motive was to find a quicker way to wealth—the wealth that derives from trading shiploads of finished goods, like silks and woolens, clocks and knives, between two parties. For centuries Europe had struggled against its ecological limits and recently had begun seeking a release through trade with those glittering empires of the East, China and India. Unwittingly, Columbus found that release. But he came upon a far greater and more fundamental kind of wealth than anyone could have imagined—not merely man-made goods but the wealth of nature. He opened to western eyes an unexpected abundance of space, land, soil, forests, minerals, and waters, an abundance that was almost free for the taking. With that surprising windfall, civilization's growing sense of privation and limits seemed finally over.

Although Columbus never realized the full extent of those new lands, extending like a single golden mountain ten thousand miles long and as much as four thousand miles wide, he came home with a personal fortune, collecting enough gold to die, in 1506, a rich man. The monarchs of Spain, his grateful sponsors, dubbed him "Admiral of the Ocean Sea, Viceroy and Governor of the Islands and Mainlands in the Indies." He died believing he was now the boss of Asia. A good map would have ruined the blind arrogance he took to his grave.[1]

Columbus was followed by Ferdinand Magellan, who not only sailed to the shores of America but managed to sail around them, surviving treacherous Cape Horn and emerging into the Pacific Ocean, then crossing that ocean too, despite being plagued by mutiny and starvation, until ingloriously he lost his life in the Philippines. Other western explorers—John Cabot, Giovanni da Verrazzano, Martin Frobisher, Jacques Cartier, and Francis Drake—added important bits and pieces to fill in Europe's picture of Second Earth.[2]

The Mercators rightfully belong to that pantheon of discoverers, although they never left the valley of the Rhine. They brought the many new discoveries together and made them comprehensible to their contemporaries. Reverently, Rumold painted Gerard's white-bearded visage down in the lower left-hand corner of his Second Earth map, along with lush border images of paradise. In 1587 the revolutionary new map was published in Isaac Casaubon's edition of Strabo's *Geographica*. Merchants bought many copies printed by copperplate engraving to hang on their walls. Through the rest of the sixteenth century and throughout the seventeenth it became the most popular projection among maps of the world, and many rival versions appeared in Amsterdam, Rome, Cologne, Frankfurt, Nuremberg, Venice, and Paris (see Plate 2 for perhaps the most beautiful of those many versions).[3]

Centuries, however, would go by before that newly discovered abundance could be more fully measured, mapped, and exploited. In Rumold's time the abundance was mainly a leap of faith. No one yet knew much about the interior, only the coastlines and the mouths of incredible rivers. They knew little about where those rivers—newly named the Amazon, the Plata, the Orinoco, and the St. Lawrence—originated or what kinds of forests and meadows grew along their banks or who their human inhabitants might be. A hundred years after Columbus, most Europeans had no understanding of the mountains or plains lying deep in the interior of North America, although the mountains of Central and South America had quickly established a reputation for furnishing precious gold and silver. Nor had anyone from Europe realized the full variety of animals roaming across the interior of the Americas. The soils too were a complete mystery: How fertile were they, how many acres did they cover, and how many people could they support?

Nor could Mercator and his contemporaries, along with early naturalists, have realized the unique position that Second Earth occupies in the cosmos. It was nothing like its neighboring planets. Fortunately, it did not actually come from outer space, given how little that infinite space offers to the human species as a place to live. Second Earth was promising precisely because it was another earth, so like the first in offering all the resources needed to survive. Once the old world had been home to the Garden of Eden, but that garden had become lost in distant mists of mythology. Suddenly in the Western Hemisphere appeared a real place that invited people to come and begin anew. The potential for the species had to be incalculable.

To be sure, farms, villages, even a few cities, and a large number of human residents were already there. Every report told of people living in the Americas, although their numbers and the strength of their arms no one could calculate. Whether those native people were the offspring of the biblical Adam and Eve or whether they owed their existence to a separate divine creation, the Indians (to use their conventional name) by their presence demonstrated that the Western Hemisphere might be a good place for Europeans to live too.

The Indians themselves had no idea of how numerous they were. They could count their own families and tribes, and even estimate the numbers of close neighbors, but they could not describe the full dimensions of the Western Hemisphere or calculate the density of Indian peoples inhabiting its lands. Despite impressive local knowledge, they had no broad maps or comprehensive understanding of the continents on which they lived.

The Europeans were for a long time equally unprepared to estimate the native population or get an accurate sense of their ecological impact. Only scholars working centuries later would attempt to do so, although the evidence would always be scanty and open to conflicting interpretations. Some aboriginal population estimates have been extremely high, some extremely low, the difference owing much to contrasting views about whether the native peoples were "primitive races" who were not very successful in exploiting nature, or whether they too were "highly civilized" nations, turning natural resources into substantial wealth that could support multitudes.

In the 1970s the *Atlas of World Population History* calculated that the human population of North and South America at the time of Columbus was 14 million. One third of that number, according to the authors, was living in what is now Mexico, where civilization reached one of its hemispheric peaks. For comparison, Europe in that year had an estimated population of 81 million, France alone counting 15 million, while Asia was populated by 280 million people, and Africa, according to the *Atlas*, was home to 46 million.[4]

Fourteen million Indians might seem like a big increase since the point when tiny bands of Asian migrants first crossed the Bering land bridge or paddled down the Pacific coast. Those bands had first arrived thousands of years earlier—some said around 13,000 years before the present. In any case, 14 million human inhabitants would have been enough to make a substantial impact on some of the hemisphere's major ecosystems. But these days that population estimate for the Americas is widely rejected as too low. Some even insist that Second Earth was as heavily populated as Europe or China, with 80 to 100 million inhabitants. Where did all those extra numbers come from? The "low counters" say they come from nowhere—that they are fantasy figures created by white guilt. In defense, the "high counters" say that because as many as nine out of ten Indians died from diseases inadvertently introduced by the Europeans, and usually in advance of their actual presence as epidemics spread like vapors on the wind, no Europeans could have seen them. The Indians died of smallpox, measles, typhus, influenza, and other diseases, for they were highly vulnerable after millennia of geographical isolation.[5]

This much is undeniable: the loss of Indian life in the aftermath of the European discoveries was tragic. The scale of that loss, however, remains largely a matter of speculation and dispute. It seems safe to say that the *Atlas* was wrong, but so too are the extremely high estimates. In 1988 the Smithsonian Institute's demographic expert, Douglas Ubelaker, came up with what seemed like an educated compromise—he estimated 1.9 million natives living north of Mexico at the first point of contact with Europeans—twice the estimate given ten years earlier in the *Atlas,* but well below some contending estimates. More recently anthropologist Shepard Krech has raised that number to 4 to 7 million.[6] Raising all the *Atlas* estimates by a factor of two or four leads to a tentative conclusion that 30 to 60 million Indians were living in the Americas. But that is all guesswork, an extrapolation and not an actual census.

Numbers cannot alone explain the ecological impact that people make. Different modes of production and consumption can have substantially different impacts, and among the Indians a wide diversity of such modes existed. Some were hunters and gatherers, with a relatively small impact, while others were primitive farmers (really horticulturalists), while still others were much more advanced farmers and city dwellers, raising food on elaborately terraced, artificially watered, or otherwise highly manipulated lands. The most densely impacted regions were, obviously, those that practiced a more intensive agriculture. Yet by no means was every part of the hemisphere such a managed landscape supporting heavy numbers.

All of Native Americans' agricultural fields in what is now the United States could have fit into one corner of Kansas. To be sure, farms were never concentrated like that; they were scattered through forests, along riverbanks, and in a few desert oases watered by irrigation. Most commonly, agriculture was practiced where people cleared land by burning patches in the forests and then planting seeds among the blackened tree trunks where the sunlight could penetrate, or it was practiced in bottomlands wherever spring floods helped keep the landscape open, or in the case of the Hohokam of present-day Arizona it was practiced by diverting water from the Salt River. In those various and scattered fields, Indians, outfitted with simple digging sticks and the shoulder blades of game animals fashioned into hoes, planted and weeded their crops. Lacking plows or draft animals, they could not exploit the fertile soils of the immense grasslands. Other areas were beyond cultivation, as they still are today; for example, the short growing seasons and poorly drained and nutrient-poor, shallow soils of the boreal forests did not allow farming across most of Canada and Alaska. By setting fires Indians could affect a wider swath of vegetation, but then lightning-set fires may have been more common than human-set ones so that ecosystems were already naturally adapted to fire. Thus much of Second Earth was only lightly touched, and the natives were by no means harvesting the full bounty of the land that Europeans would later call "virgin."

The main food crops developed in the Americas, nonetheless, were abundant in species variety and rich in nutritional value. Corn, potatoes, beans, sunflowers, peppers, squash, and other vegetables dominated north of the Rio Grande. Further south the diversity of staples and minor crops was even more impressive, although only now is that diversity becoming fully known and appreciated. Cultivars included manioc (cassava), yucca, peanuts, and sweet potatoes, along with amaranth, quinoa, tomatoes, cocoa, pineapples, cactus tunas, vanilla, pecans, black walnuts, Brazil nuts, cashews, and cotton. Turkeys, llamas, and alpacas were domesticated among the native fauna.[7]

Production from those foods was enough to allow, during times of favorable climate, many millions to survive (although for short life spans). We should admire that achievement and acknowledge that those cleared lands and productive crops eventually became part of the bounty that the Europeans took possession of and made their own, filling their bellies and setting off the modern world population explosion. Without that Native American gift of knowledge and economic development, the peoples of Africa and Asia—as well as Europe and its settler societies—today would live more hungry, impoverished lives.

But whether the new world's bounty came from man or nature, Europeans from the earliest days of contact began exaggerating it, sometimes wildly and fantastically. Often they could not imagine any limits to so great an abundance. They dreamed of a paradise of plenty wherever they ventured. From the sixteenth century on tales of lost ancient civilizations producing wealth far beyond what Europe had achieved stirred the white man's ambitions. The Spanish conquistador Vasquez de Coronado went off in hot pursuit of the fabled cities of Cibola, which turned out to be a few dusty villages on the Great Plains. Amateur archaeologists once mistakenly imagined that the mound builders of the Middle West had represented a powerful civilization that could rival those of Europe or Asia. The mound builders' Cahokia—the largest city in North America before contact, situated near present-day St. Louis, Missouri—was often described as a glittering metropolis, although its average population turns out to have been a mere 20,000, and it was no Athens or Rome. Then there were the Incas, who were reputed to have created, by 1492, the greatest empire on earth. Perhaps their empire was greatest in terms of territory claimed—thanks to the quality and extent of their road network and centralized system of power—but it was not the greatest in wealth or inventions, literature or science.[8]

More recent fabulists talk about lost cities buried in the Amazonian jungle but now coming into view as deforestation lays bare the landscape. Golden kingdoms, we are told, once sprawled across the river's wide basin, before the rainforests took over in the aftermath of European invasion and native depopulation. At one time those lost kingdoms are said to have raised immense crops from soils that scientists later dismissed as infertile or easily degraded. Just how big those cities and fields really were, however, or how much impact they had on the overall ecology of Brazil, remains to be determined. Likely the truth will turn out to be less impressive than the fabulists want to believe.[9]

The once romanticized "noble savage," who supposedly lived in simple harmony with nature, has disappeared and been replaced by the Indian as a paragon of "sustainable" wealth creation. One myth chases another. In the past as in the present, it was always easy to exaggerate the power and significance of any and all *Homo sapiens* in the landscape, to see everywhere the hand of man rather than the hand of nature. Through our evolutionary history we have become wired to look for evidence of our species' presence in the environment and then to ask, "Are those other peoples our friends or our enemies? Are they dangerous to our interests or not?"[10]

Where the interests of the Spanish, Portuguese, French, Dutch, or British (to name the most prominent nations in the European scramble to possess the Western Hemisphere) focused on getting an abundance of furs or other resources across the ocean and into the London or Paris markets, the Indians seemed potential partners who could aid the newcomers in exploiting the bounty. They could be induced to bring the natural wealth of pelts or hides into trading posts, and thus a peaceful exchange could occur to everyone's advantage. Where those European interests were intent on extracting gold or silver from the ground, a more difficult challenge,

Indians could be enslaved as a labor force. They could be whipped and beaten by the armed guards of foreign empires to make them dig up the loot. Then they would be regarded not as partners but as savage brutes. So too would be the fate of Indians who occupied soils that European farmers or planters wanted. Then they would be seen as encumbrances to be driven off and replaced by African slaves, indentured white servants, or children forced to work under a white farmer's parental command. Whatever the Europeans came to exploit, the indigenous peoples often became part of the labor force, and a contemptible part at that, unworthy of a fair share.

Nature's new world offered a richness that had been partly exploited, partly left wild and unmanaged. In either state, the Europeans were prepared and eager to seize it all. On a personal level, their motives may have been little different from those earlier immigrants who first crossed into the Western Hemisphere from Siberia or Scandinavia, and their discovery just as accidental and just as blind to global significance. But the modern Europeans, we can be sure, from the beginning came with grander vision and more inflated expectations than the first waves of immigrants. They came with a greater capacity to imagine wealth on a global scale and to gather facts, make maps, and calculate profits. In their minds, therefore, as much as in hard physical reality, they "discovered" another planet teeming with potential riches, and that abundance, though often exaggerated, was really and truly there.

For an enthusiastic but down-to-earth account of new world abundance we can turn to that neglected classic *A Description of New Netherland*, published in Amsterdam in 1655 by Adriaen Van der Donck. It was not translated into English until two centuries later. Van der Donck was a careful man, not prone to puffery, and he understood clearly the international significance of America. He tried to give his fellow Dutchmen a better sense of what the place offered in terms of natural wealth. "The superabundance of this country," he concluded, "is not equaled by any other in the world."[11] While he had seen only a very small part of Europe or America, he set out to back up that claim by a full listing of assets.

Van der Donck, born in 1618, grew up in the Dutch-speaking town of Breda, in the border country between the Netherlands and Belgium, not far from the ancestral home of the Mercators. At age twenty he entered the prestigious University of Leiden to study law, where the renowned founder of international law, Hugo Grotius, taught. Elegant canals linked that college town to the Rhine River,

and by the seventeenth century a rising devotion to trade was helping it flourish. Here map and book sellers had become plentiful, as
were rowdy taverns and sober Protestant churches, and here in an
emerging atmosphere of tolerance the Pilgrims took refuge before
leaving for New England. But none of that newly acquired Dutch liberalism stimulated by affluence (derived in large part from distant
continents) could induce Van der Donck to stay. Following gradua-
tion he turned his back on Leiden, on the Netherlands, and on any
opportunity he might have had to practice law in a country and time
that was experiencing a golden age of riches. Instead he accepted
the position of *schout*, or bailiff, for a wealthy diamond merchant
in Amsterdam, Kiliaen van Rensselaer, who had acquired, without
ever going there, one million acres along the banks of the Hudson
River. The absentee landowner, or patroon, needed someone to
keep order among his tenants. Van der Donck volunteered for the
job, was hired, and sailed off into a new life.

Once arrived in "the new found land of New Netherlands," he
soon lost interest in his employer's tenant problems and took up the
grievances of ordinary settlers against the colonial governor and the
infamous West Indies Company, a corporate monopoly created to
exploit the wealth of the Americas for the Dutch nation. He became
an agitator for political and economic freedom, for policies encouraging open trade and frontier enterprise. Later returning to the
home country to present settlers' grievances, he was forced to wait
for years for a response from the government. During that time Van
der Donck wrote and published his *Description* to tell what kind of
place he had found.[12]

New Netherlands, first claimed by Captain Henry Hudson sailing aboard the *Half Moon* in 1609, extended from the Delaware River
to the Connecticut River, and was bisected by the Hudson.[13] At the
center of the colony were Manhattan and Long Island. How far inland
the colony extended no one could say, for the Europeans so far had
penetrated merely seventy or eighty miles. They assumed that "the
land stretches for hundreds of miles into the interior, so that the
size of this province is as yet unknown." The Indians with whom
they traded for pelts were "not aware of any end, limit, or boundary, and appear amazed when questioned concerning it." Unlike
the colonists, the natives had actually seen some of that interior, but
their seeing or even using the place, its inland forests or well-watered
islands or clean, sandy shores did not, in the eyes of the Dutch, constitute a claim to ownership. Van der Donck was concerned only with
the claims of contending Europeans. Since there was "no sign that

Christians had ever been there before," he declared, the country properly belonged to the Dutch. And what a magnificent piece of real estate it was.[14]

Predictably, a Dutchman would begin by emphasizing the abundance of water in the landscape—the local rivers and seas, what they offered in transportation, mill sites, and fisheries. Here no expensive canals had to be dug or land drained and reclaimed by pumps and windmills. Here land did not have to be hard wrestled from the sea. Then Van der Donck turned to the soil—so rich, deep, and black. Covered with a green tapestry of thickets, trees, brushwood, and vines, the soil was "a marvel to behold." When cleared of vegetation and plowed and planted with imported crops, it proved "fertile beyond compare," yielding such excellent returns that the farmer could "share with all the world." Even after so much forest clearing had gone on, there were still plenty of mature oak trees, growing as high as seventy feet and as thick as twelve feet around. The remarkable hickory, with its tough grain and annual crop of edible nuts, grew so quickly and densely that "there will be no shortage of it for a hundred years to come, even if the population were to grow appreciably." Then there were the pines, chestnuts, birches, beeches, hornbeams, cedars, and alders, all festooned with grapevines, and under them a forest floor redolent with berries, wild onions, and mushrooms. Europeans followed Indian practices by selective fall burning, but the native trees survived all the fires. The trees grew so closely that one could hardly walk, let alone ride a horse, through them.[15]

Bears were common, along with wolves, otters, and elk. "The whole country is full" of deer, "with no signs of decrease" despite heavy hunting by both whites and Indians. Even more remarkable creatures were reportedly living in the interior. The native Mohawks claimed there was an animal with a horn growing squarely in the middle of its forehead, a possibility that Van der Donck thought might be real but never actually saw. And the birds! Bald eagles, gray-feathered geese, hooting owls with catlike faces, wild turkeys, woodcocks and woodpeckers, grouse winging through the air, and pigeons roosting so thickly that a single gunshot could bring down twenty-five at once. And the fish—salmon, bass, pike, and trout! In the waters on and around Manhattan, one could catch them easily, and lobsters growing five or six feet long. Seals thronged the shores, and whales now and then ventured upriver.[16]

Compared to the dank Netherlands, the American climate was salubrious; the air was dry and light, as "wholesome as could be desired," and the place would quickly make a sick man well again. To be sure, the winters were cold, but nature "very providently relieves the discomforts that accompany" freezing temperatures by providing easily collectable firewood and warm furs. One could wrap oneself in the luxuriant pelt of the beaver (Van der Donck devoted an entire chapter to the "amazing ways" of this animal, whose skin was the most profitable commodity the colony shipped back to Europe, to be made into coats and hats.) The old country may have boasted great universities, artists like Rembrandt and Vermeer, and smart burghers who were learning how to organize global corporations, but New Netherlands offered the common man a better deal.[17]

This colonial lawyer's purpose was not to drum up customers for real estate, but to argue that such abundance could become a vital asset for the Dutch people. The colony needed happy, hardworking emigrants to tap its bounty. Those who emigrated and those who stayed home could alike profit from the transoceanic flow of resources. But that enrichment could be realized only if the heavy hand of concentrated power were loosened and more individual liberty and a more egalitarian land ownership were allowed to flourish.

Van der Donck did not persuade his government to change its still tenacious hierarchical policies. Immigrants remained few—too few to hold the colony firmly. In 1664 Great Britain seized control, and New Amsterdam became New York. The Dutch had, despite Van der Donck's warnings, let a treasure slip through their fingers. But then so did the French, the Swedes, and the Russians (the latter probing along the Alaskan and California coasts) eventually lose most or all of their colonies. In contrast, the Spanish and Portuguese managed to hold on to Central and South America, while Britain gained control over North America and with that abundance created the world's greatest empire, vastly overshadowing the Incas or the Aztecs. North America, not India, was the real jewel in Britain's imperial crown.

As for Van der Donck, he returned dejectedly to claim a mere 24,000-acre estate on the Hudson River. The locals called him the *Jongkeer,* the young squire who fought for their rights while appropriating for himself some of the "superabundance." He built a sawmill for cutting up oaks and pines. But in 1655 he died at the hands of Indians, cut down at the age of thirty-seven. All that plenty in the end provided no lasting advantage for him. But then no one ever promised that possessing the newfound land would be easy or secure.[18]

Other immigrants found a more lasting prosperity, until today the population of the Americas is approaching one billion. A third of that number live in the United States, making it one of the most densely populated countries in the hemisphere. Nowhere is that density higher than in the heart of Van der Donck's land of plenty, which we now call the New York Metropolitan area. Its soils have become home to more than 22 million people. Sixty-one percent of them are white, 17 percent are black, and many others are Asian or Hispanic. Only one half of one percent of modern-day New Yorkers are Native North Americans. From this place an incredible wealth has been extracted, and it has flowed out to every corner of the globe, though mostly to Europeans and Euro-Americans.

At the same time, the transition from native America to commercial metropolis and a more intensified consumption of resources have left little that the Jongkeer would recognize. Gone are most of the natural assets he reported—depleted, degraded, and changed. Ecologically, no place on earth has been more altered than this one. These days, natural resources tend to flow into the New York harbor rather than out. Meanwhile, the outflow of waste and pollution has increased excessively, becoming in fact monumental, turning the nearby seas into toxic dumps.[19]

Who today would not want to acquire another New Amsterdam or another Second Earth? Finding such a bonanza would make the next five hundred years so much easier—affording so much material stuff for manufacturers, energy companies, and homebuilders—and also add so much beauty and adventure to our lives. Like our ancestors, we too, whatever our ethnic or class identity, might be tempted to brush away any rival claims and ignore those who might have arrived there first, unless their guns and armies were bigger than ours. And if we could ever be so lucky again, how would the discovery of that "Third Earth" change *us*?

The coevolution of nature and culture has been going on since the first hominids. A new planet, if it came drifting our way, would throw that evolutionary process into disequilibrium, upsetting all that seemed solid and forever. Like Van der Donck, people would seek to exploit the new environment, although some would prove more adept than others at doing so. Minds would begin to innovate and experience a burst of adaptive creativity. People would develop new technologies, invent new economies, and think new thoughts. A radical change in resource abundance might encourage a radical change in the structure of the human community, the organization of industry, the distribution of political power, and the relations between rich and poor. Religion might take a new direction. Ethics might be upended and revised.

Above all, people might learn once more the old lesson that nature matters in human life. Land, water, soil, organisms, and climate are all vital to our well-being. They can change who we are. They can limit our possibilities, or they can expand them. But what are the odds of finding another nature, another hemisphere of such easy abundance? Zero. It happened once long, long ago before writing existed, and it happened once again at the beginning of the modern age. It can never be repeated.

CHAPTER 2

Many Revolutions Follow

GUILLAUME-THOMAS RAYNAL, A FRENCH PRIEST dismissed by his parish for radical thoughts, sits poised with quill in hand. He is ready to begin writing a searing indictment of European violence toward the Americas, not only violence toward the Indians but also toward the colonists who have gone out with hope in their hearts but are now growing increasingly restive and resentful toward their oppressive mother countries. The indictment will be published anonymously in Amsterdam in 1770 in four volumes. But before laying out all the hideous details and atrocities committed by his fellow Europeans, Raynal steps back to assess the age of revolution in which he lived. These are his dramatic opening words:

> There has never been an event as interesting for the human species in general and for the peoples of Europe in particular as the discovery of the new world and the passage to the Indies by way of the Cape of Good Hope. Then began a revolution in commerce, in the power of nations, in the way of life, the industry and government of all peoples.[1]

These bold words, sweeping claims, and powerful insights into modern history have been ignored, taken for granted, or forgotten by many.

The discovery of the Americas, Raynal argued, along with the finding of a sea route around Africa to southern and eastern Asia, touched off an epoch of revolutions. It was like a bomb with a very long fuse that continued to detonate. During the three centuries stretching between Columbus and the priest, many revolutions went off again and again. First, an explosion occurred in economic relations within and among nations—helping create what Raynal called the commercial revolution, but what might more accurately be called the capitalist revolution, since commerce was an old idea whereas capitalism as a ruling ideology was a new innovation. Then the discovery and appropriation of Second Earth shifted the international balance of wealth and power decisively away from Asia and toward Europe. After that, with the Abbé cheering in anticipation, would come a political independence movement among the French and British colonies of North America, followed by a tumultuous revolution against feudalism in his native country—the French Revolution. New nations would emerge, some of them eventually overshadowing the nations of Europe, while the latter would be shaken and changed beyond recognition.

Raynal preferred a peaceful transition to the chaos of bloody guillotines and mob action, but in general he liked the idea of revolution. Despite all their dangers of terror and injustice, revolutions were necessary to achieve a future free of absolute monarchs, exploitation, poverty, bigotry, and superstition. Like his sometime coauthor Denis Diderot, he belonged to France's famous circle of liberal *philosophes*. Unlike the rest of them, however, he reached back to understand historically when the explosions had first begun. Thus he discovered the Americas, and thus he realized that his revolutionary era could only have begun through an unprecedented collision of First Earth with Second Earth and its untold riches.

Much has been written on early modern Europe's age of revolution and its global impact, yet seldom do historians focus on their ultimate cause. Like Raynal, writers and scholars talk of radical changes taking place in commerce and capital, technology and industry, politics and culture—changes that continue right down to the present, until the phenomenon of big change regularly occurring over short periods of time has come to be normalized. They conceive of revolution as part of ordinary life, almost as a matter of course. Some powerful force, everyone seems to agree, punctured the world's equilibrium around 1500. What was it? Some see revolutions exploding only within Europe's boundaries, but in doing so they overlook that distant impact of Second Earth.

To be sure, the Abbé Raynal, for all his perspicacity, did not see the full picture and missed some of the most important aspects of the intellectual and material explosion that began going off in the old world. He saw revolutions occurring in commercial networks and state relations, in social thought and social order, but he did not see how a simultaneous revolution in science and technology might have been another important consequence, changing the world forever. Perhaps the most basic of modern revolutions, essential to all the rest, was the astonishing rise of modern science in the seventeenth and eighteenth centuries. Henceforth, Europe's leading thinkers would turn away from traditional views of man and nature, grounded in religion and mythology, and instead look to human reason and empirical research as the best foundation for knowledge. That radical shift in thinking would bring a new intellectual openness that began to shatter longstanding assumptions about every aspect of life.

The first great leader of the scientific revolution was the man that Gerard Mercator looked to for leadership, Nicolas Copernicus (or Mikolaj Kopernik in his native Polish), who in 1543 published *On the Revolutions of the Celestial Spheres*. The book—which Copernicus long delayed, fearing the hostile reception he might get, especially from the Catholic Church—punctured the Ptolemaic perspective on the earth and cosmos. But why did the Copernican revolution happen just at the time it did? Why not a hundred or five hundred years earlier?

Born in 1473, Copernicus was nineteen years old when Columbus made landfall in the Caribbean and fifty-two years old when Magellan died from multiple stabbings on Mactan Island in the Philippines. When he sat down to write his masterpiece in astronomy, Copernicus almost certainly had the Americas on his mind. How could any informed man or woman in those heady days not do so? In 1517, for example, he wrote a short memorandum on the destabilization of European currencies caused by the influx of precious metals from Peruvian and Mexican mines. Such a rapid increase in the money supply, he argued, must lead to long-term price inflation, which could cause family hardship. All that gold did not always glitter.[2] Economists have been debating ever since the effects of changes in the money supply, but Copernicus was asking more specifically how the sudden influx of American wealth might be upsetting European life.

Likewise, Copernicus seems to have been thinking about Second Earth as he pursued his investigations into the heavens. He traveled and studied extensively across Europe before reaching his disturbing conclusion about the relative position of the sun and earth. But

it is generally overlooked that it was not fellow European astrono-
mers and mathematicians alone who shaped his imagination. A hint
of other influences appears in the second chapter of his famous
book, where he introduces the notion that the earth is "spherical,"
a fact that he admits is not readily apparent to the casual observer.
Christopher Columbus had known it was so, of course, as did many
others, but apparently not everyone thought so. Copernicus took the
trouble to point out that an observant sailor knows that land invisible from the deck of a ship may be seen clearly from the top of
its mast. The earth, therefore, must be round. In his third chapter
Copernicus refers to "the islands discovered in our time under the
rulers of Spain and Portugal, and especially America, named after
the ship's captain who found it." While he was wrong that Vespucci
Americus discovered the new world, the Polish astronomer did see
that hemisphere vividly, at least in his mind's eye. From the great
explorers he had learned to see the earth as a round ball floating
through space, and understood that old fixed notions of the earth
and cosmos were no longer tenable.[3]

Pre-Copernican and pre-Columbian views that had put the
Mediterranean at the center of the earth had begun to crack. The
biggest chisel making those cracks was an awareness of strange new
worlds populated by strange new peoples and biota. Eventually, that
strangeness offered to a rising group of scientific observers many
startling comparisons of life forms, copious new climate and geological data to be absorbed and explained, disturbing questions about
the deep past, and any number of anthropological opportunities.

After Copernicus, the single greatest achievement of the scientific revolution occurred in 1859, when Charles Darwin's *On the
Origin of Species* appeared in print. Darwin shattered the colossally
wrong notion that humans had always lived at the pinnacle of a fixed
and predetermined chain of being. Even more than Copernicus,
Darwin owed his scientific theory to the discovery of Second Earth.
He first glimpsed the process of biological evolution by means of
natural selection during a voyage he made aboard the H.M.S. *Beagle*,
a British exploring vessel that sailed from 1831 to 1836 around
South America and into the Pacific Ocean. It was in the Galápagos
Islands, located about six hundred miles off the coast of Ecuador,
that Darwin's most important observations about natural history
took place.

Darwin, like Copernicus and other modern scientists, insisted
on forming hypotheses and then testing them by empirical observation. How much that shift in thinking owed to the discovery and

exploration of the Americas, along with their adjoining seas, is not a widely asked question, and it should be. The discovery of Second Earth does not explain everything, of course. Yet so much of modern scientific inquiry, with its devotion to collecting new facts and organizing them into theories, came in the wake of that extraordinary event.[4]

Another revolution that the Abbé Raynal missed was industrialization. He might be forgiven that one, for at the time he wrote no economy anywhere was based on mass production by machines, and the transition now called the Industrial Revolution had barely begun in England and Scotland. Machines were not new on the earth; many had appeared over the centuries and changed the processes of work and production, but previous upheavals had never before been so sweeping and sustained. A pivotal machine in that new economy was the Glasgow inventor James Watt's steam engine, developed during the years 1763 to 1775. By increasing the efficiency of burning coal to make steam (which drove pistons that could drive other machines), Watt touched off a cacophony of clattering, rumbling, roaring innovation. But even before the steam engine, textiles were the first big product of the new manufacturing, and they used water power before they used steam. Machines spun cotton fibers into yarn and wove that yarn into cloth. Long before steamships, sailing vessels brought cotton to the textile mills and carried machine-made garments to customers all over the world.

Was the Industrial Revolution completely independent of Second Earth, or was it another detonation from a slow-burning fuse? Scholars have assumed that industrialization was an internal European development, a shining example of human rationality overcoming the limits of land and labor. Supposedly, it owed nothing to the expansion of Europe's resource base—nothing to the beneficence of nature but only to the contriving hand of Western man. Yet without the long-fibered cotton imported from the Americas, the manufacture of textiles by machines would never have worked.[5]

Before there was an industrial revolution, there had to be Raynal's commercial (or capitalist) revolution. To understand the connection would require tracing the origins of the great private trading corporations that were created to exploit Second Earth and examining the great commercial plantations set up in the Americas, growing monocultures of sugar and cotton and transporting millions of Africans across the Atlantic to work as slaves. In other words, grasping the importance of the Western Hemisphere would focus attention on the capitalist-led invasion of tropical and subtropical soils, ecosystems, and climates, as well as the invasion of the temperate and even arctic zones. And it would highlight how European capitalists rose to power by promising that they alone, not the old landed aristocracy or the church authorities, were equipped to lead the way west and bring back beaver and cod, forests and grain. Once again, the role of natural resources coming from that newly discovered "planet" would need to be acknowledged as a fundamental part of the rise of the modern West.[6]

But if Raynal failed to include science and industry among his list of revolutions, or understand the full implications of "commerce," he did manage to grasp the essential fact that a profound change in human affairs had commenced around the year 1500 A.D. Until recently, scholars have focused more heavily on tracing the rise and fall of political or political-economic regimes within the borders of nation-states than the larger, more global, ecological changes set in motion. They have tended to focus on local or national institutions and ideologies (political ideologies especially) as the key forces determining the fate of nations. They have reduced Raynal's many revolutions to thinner threads of change: the decisions of this president or that parliament, the cost of labor over time, the appearance of a newfangled loom or locomotive, the impact of this "ism" or that one. But those threads are too fragile to support a complete explanation.[7]

Well after Raynal, a scholar appeared who understood fully the epoch-making significance of finding and taking possession of the Americas. In 1952 Walter Prescott Webb published *The Great Frontier*, a book that remains in print to this day. No doubt it was flawed by weaknesses of evidence, style, and bibliography, but its biggest problem was that it challenged the conventional wisdom. Existing books made the great revolutions creating the modern world simply and purely a self-contained European story free of any influence from the rest of the planet.

Europe, Webb declared, did not make itself great or revolutionary without the help of other lands and peoples. It was jolted out of deep historic ruts of poverty and inequality by the unexpected discovery of faraway resources. Without that discovery, the small, crowded nations strung along Europe's coast would have remained backward for centuries to come. Instead they were jolted into reorganizing their institutions and cultural attitudes, so eager were they to possess the new world's bounty. Webb called the bounty "a windfall." Like peasants living in the lord's forest, Europeans woke up one morning to find the ground littered with sticks and fruits that the wind had knocked down in the night. Those resources, unlike others tied up in property rights and ancient usages, were free for them to seize and use. Quickly, they prepared to go out and collect.

Echoing generations of white frontier settlers, Webb called the new world "a vast body of wealth without proprietors." What he meant was that in the eyes of the invaders, "practically nobody" lived there, only "primitive inhabitants, whose rights need not and will not be respected." The invaders, who on average were poor and primitive too, were intensely hungry for land. Leaving Europe, they escaped the direct, daily oversight of governments or elite classes. The modern quest for personal freedom, egalitarian rights, and self-promotion were all, according to Webb, stimulated by a huge expansion in physical space and material resources. Freedom meant a cabin by the river, a farm in the grasslands, or a herd of cattle that no one else could own. Or it meant a mine located far away from the taxman or regulators. Or a forest that lay outside the control of aristocratic owners. The unexploited hemisphere to the west appealed as a place where rules were unformed or weakly enforced. "Individuals," Webb wrote, "obtained recognition of their freedom by fighting and bargaining, or—failing in this—they could run away. This running away was possible because they had somewhere to go."[8]

Webb's name for that "somewhere to go" was "the Frontier," a metaphor for a place of abundant natural resources that lay beyond the overcrowded, depleted Old World. Mainly, the Frontier lay in the Americas, but it also included on its margins Australia and the southern tip of Africa, for they too were places where white settlers could go, dispossess the natives, and assert ownership. He referred to what they sought to own by the simple term "land," a narrow word reflecting the mentality of farmers. The Frontier, however, offered more than land; it promised untapped seas, minerals hidden in underground seams and veins, wild-growing and domesticated plants and animals, and all the forms of energy latent in the earth's crust. But whatever the resource on offer, the immigrant asked, "What can I get out of it?" And the answer was, in Webb's words, "you can get everything of a material nature you want, more than you ever dreamed of having."[9]

On the other side of the "Great Frontier" stood the "Metropolis": that is, Europe with its civilization, laws, and culture, but also a declining resource endowment. One way of measuring how much that endowment was suddenly enhanced—doubled, tripled, and sextupled by Second Earth—was to look at the land–people ratio. "To the 100 million people of the Metropolis was suddenly made available nearly 20,000,000 square miles of fabulously rich land practically devoid of population, an area more than five times as great as all Europe."[10] Instead of twenty-four acres per European, the average shot up to 148 acres for every man, woman, and child across Europe, from the Atlantic Coast to the Urals. Many would never own an estate that large, but everyone, even paupers, would benefit from the overseas wealth flooding from foreign estates into their ports and factories.

That influx of wealth touched off a "business boom such as the world had never known before and probably never can know again." Webb formalized this argument as the "boom hypothesis of modern history." The boom began when Columbus returned to Spain from his first voyage, and it continued right down to the twentieth century.

But a boom always ends in bust. Webb was convinced that the bubble of modern resource expansion was beginning to burst, although he was not sure exactly when that moment might occur. His first notion was to identify it with the closing of the American frontier in "1890 or 1900," when a long, discrete line of settlement advance in the United States disappeared. The census of 1890, which inspired Wisconsin historian Frederick Jackson Turner to write his famous essay "The Significance of the Frontier in American History," published in 1893, had identified that date as pivotal.[11] From a more global perspective, the year 1890 was a parochial choice. What about all those other parts of the Great Frontier—Canada, Mexico, Brazil, New Zealand, and the rest? Had they also at that moment reached the end of their boom days?

Webb, to his credit, was not content with Turner's parochial thinking about the US frontier. Thus instead of asking when did an abundance of arable land become no longer available in the American West, he asked, what were the international people–land ratios? When all the Americas became densely populated, the boom would begin to fail. That point, he calculated, began sometime during the 1920s and 1930s, when F. Scott Fitzgerald published *The Great Gatsby*. By 1940, there were 34.8 people per square mile living in what had been the new world, compared to the 26.7 people per square mile who were living in Europe before Columbus. Second Earth's population had increased much more dramatically than Europe's: "The big house was fuller than the small house had been four centuries earlier."[12]

Fixing an exact point when the boom began to fail was not easy, and getting others to accept that date harder still. When Webb wrote, during the 1950s, Americans were enjoying an exuberant time of consumer shopping and shining automobiles rolling down well-paved highways. Abundance seemed to many of his fellow citizens more endless than ever. Webb, nonetheless, was making the big and hard-to-deny point that Nature puts limits on humans—not absolute or rigid limits, but limits of great consequence. The limits of Second Earth must at some point be reached, just as other lands had seen their limits reached. "The land," Webb wrote, "has only so much to offer ... There is a limit beyond which we cannot go; and if our techniques speed up the process of utilization and destruction, as they are now doing, they hasten the day when the substance on which they feed and on which a swollen population temporarily subsists will approach scarcity and exhaustion." Webb acknowledged that an "acquisitive instinct" and "skills and techniques" were necessary to exploit resources, but he could not see how acquisitiveness, skills, or capital alone could generate an endless supply of wealth.

The consequences of ending the five-hundred-year boom would be immense. The end would bring a challenge to unprecedented personal freedoms and laissez-faire policies, a demand for government-enforced redistribution of riches, and a more sober view of the future. But pessimism was not where Webb ended up. He was not writing a panegyric to the boom or fearing its end. "The fact that we cannot find a new frontier comparable to the one we have had need not make us feel that we are now bereft of a challenge and an opportunity. It does mean that we have a different challenge and perhaps an even greater opportunity for achievement." The challenge would not be how to grow and expand infinitely, but how to manage and sustain "what we have so eagerly taken."[13]

Those views did not come from one who had personally benefitted much from nature's gifts, who had grown up wealthy and secure. On the contrary, Webb had experienced considerable disappointment in the land of riches. Born in 1888, he spent his boyhood not in a highly endowed environment but in the poor, hardscrabble Cross Timbers region of Texas, a land of droughty prairie and stunted oak trees that never had much economic value. They were among the sorriest agricultural lands on the Great Plains. In his middle years he had witnessed the Dust Bowl years of wind erosion and land abandonment. Like his father, he ended up teaching school as an alternative to farming. Despite heavy odds, he eventually found success in a university position and enjoyed many honors in his professional life.[14]

Even after his own condition had improved and he had achieved success, he never forgot that history must "always deal with man in an environment." Sometimes the environment was favorable, and sometimes, he knew in his bones, it was not. The environment did not determine everything, but it was a powerful force in a person's or a society's fate. "I shall doubtless be charged," he acknowledged, "with attributing too much to the environment." He granted that culture, education, and sheer effort were all potent in personal outcomes. Yet he always felt that for some individuals success came easier than for others, thanks to a richer endowment and more opportunity, and likewise for some societies or ages success came easier than for others, or it didn't come at all. There were two sides to the street that runs through human history, he insisted, culture and environment, and "the historian should have the choice of working the side of the street he sets out to work."[15]

Among Webb's critics was the British medievalist Geoffrey Barraclough, who complained about what he took to be a lament for "frontier values." The future was brighter than ever, Barraclough wrote, because of the promise of modern Communism and what it offered the underprivileged of Asia, Africa, and Europe as a solution for "the problems of a frontierless society." Communism would usher in an even more abundant age as the proletariat assumed control of the factories and began to produce goods not for the capitalists but for the masses, lifting everyone out of poverty. Webb, he charged, exaggerated the role of natural resources in creating wealth and paid "too little attention to economic developments within Europe since the Industrial Revolution." But exactly how the proletariat, any more than the capitalists, could run their factories without natural resources, or without clean water or clean air, was left unanswered.[16]

Whether or not they agreed with the Marxist theory that the working class would find a way to unlimited abundance, historians have commonly assumed that industrialization represented a self-contained source of wealth, independent of nature. Most have ignored or dismissed Webb's environmental argument. But a recent exception to that conventional thinking is Kenneth Pomeranz, who like Webb has acknowledged the significance of the Americas' resources for European economies and cultures. Pomeranz brings into the discussion Asia, particularly China and Japan. What, he asks, did the new world give to Europe but not to Asia?

Pomeranz's *The Great Divergence*, published in 2000, rejects the notion that Asia has needed Western economic theory, capitalist or communist, to become prosperous. On the contrary, before 1700 A.D.

it was Europe that lagged behind Asian nations in almost every way; only in the eighteenth and nineteenth centuries did Europe begin to surge ahead. The usual explanation for that reversal of power and fortune has been that Europe—initially Great Britain—surpassed the East through hard work and inventiveness, or through probusiness institutions and good political governance. Pomeranz dismisses this self-congratulatory view as "Euro-centric" and proposes instead a "polycentric" view that understands Europe's long backwardness and then its unique and fortunate access to America's resources. From a Chinese perspective, the economic superiority of Europe looks quite recent and highly contingent on that fact that it was an Italian sailing under a Spanish flag, not a Chinese navigator, who took home the gold and Europeans who gathered in the bonanza.[17]

Pomeranz, like Webb, calls the "extraordinary ecological bounty" of the new world a "windfall." His writing, however, offers comparative data from the East and provides a more complex storyline. Pomeranz compares the economic conditions of the most advanced parts of Europe with those of China and concludes that prior to 1800, there was little difference in standard of living, longevity of life, or technological sophistication. Around 1900, however, the gap had become immense. By that point the once Celestial Kingdom had become weak and disorganized, trampled on by the Europeans and struggling to feed its exploding population. Why did that large gap between East and West begin to open up? The most convincing answer begins with the fact that it began before 1800, which means before the full impact of industrialization—that it began as early as 1500, which means that a gap appeared only after the Europeans became the primary beneficiaries of the new world windfall.[18]

Pomeranz assembles a persuasive argument about the historic significance of the Western Hemisphere's resources. These can be divided into precious metals, such as gold and silver, and "real" resources, including food and wood—real because they were more important for supporting populations and inducing long-term economic change. Spain, the nation profiting most from metals from American mines, did not maintain its early lead in economic growth. Rather it was England, and, to a lesser extent, the Netherlands, neither of which benefited much from America's gold and silver mines, that led the way. They concentrated on acquiring "real" resources, which led to more lasting changes that eventually engulfed all of Europe, then bounced back to and engulfed America, then spread to other parts of the world, then in the twentieth century touched off a sequence of revolutions in China and other countries that missed out on the first flush of new wealth.

Let us not, however, dismiss too quickly the importance of the new world's precious metals. For thousands of years gold and silver have stood for wealth in people's imaginations. The earliest known coins, alloys of the precious metals, date back to 600 B.C. Unsurprisingly, two thousand years later those metals were the first resource that Europeans went looking for in the wake of Columbus, and they found plenty of them on Second Earth. The total number of Spanish pesos, or "pieces of eight," mined and minted in Potosi, Lima, and Mexico City from 1503 to 1660 has been carefully counted—no fewer than 447,820,932 coins. Add in the amount stolen by pirates and the amount smuggled illegally into Seville, and the total comes to about 500 million coins—a hefty bag of loot indeed.[19] Add in all the gold and silver that came later, during the nineteenth and twentieth centuries, from mines in Brazil, California, Idaho, Colorado, British Columbia, and Alaska, and the total contribution made by the Western Hemisphere to the world's supply of money would be hard to exaggerate.

Whether or not that immense increase in money caused a "price revolution" in early modern Europe, as Copernicus argued, it had global ramifications for transportation, capital investment, labor supply, and the real estate market. It helped pay, as Pomeranz notes, for the establishment and administration of the American colonies. It paid for the ships needed to transport planters, slaves, peasants, and entrepreneurs to those distant lands and bring back a long list of commodities. According to economist Earl Hamilton,

> Treasure drawn from the Indies [he means the Americas] financed the memorable voyage of Magellan. . . . It paid the salaries of such notable servants of Spain as Amerigo Vespucci and Sebastian Cabot; and it provided the means to purchase and to carry to America the seeds, plants, animals, tools, books, and scientific instruments of the Old World.

Some of those ships heavily laden with silver went to China, and they came back with cloth, porcelain, and spices. Thus American bullion flooded into East Asia as well as Europe and unsettled more than one national currency, financed more than one government, and for the first time in history facilitated trade on a global scale.[20]

But in the end, as Pomeranz rightly says, it was those "real" resources from the Americas on which people could directly subsist and produce children that mattered most. What did that food, fuel, and fiber make possible in European development? How many additional people have those gifts kept warm and alive over subsequent centuries? What effect did the exploitation of those "real" resources have on entrenched inequalities? Simply put, the nonbullion resources allowed Europeans to overcome their environmental constraints and provided the human work energy on which economic growth depended. Sugar from the slave plantations became an important source of calories, as did dried meat and fish, timber, corn, and wheat taken from the new lands and seas.

Pomeranz calls those fresh sources "ghost acres," for they were invisible to European consumers but vital to their survival. Take Great Britain, for example, which added to its 17 million acres at home millions of ghost acres in the form of thirteen colonies east of the Appalachian Mountains. That was not enough land to qualify the colonies as a Second Britain, but then came "the much larger boom in American imports in the mid-nineteenth century" and then came the contributions of Canada, New Zealand, Australia, South Africa, and India. Out of that overseas territory came the nearly 300 million pounds of cotton that Britain was importing from the American South by 1830, which provided clothes to keep bodies warm and conserve energy, freeing British land from the necessity of raising so much wool, and made the textile mills possible. Great Britain, boldly and sometimes ruthlessly leading the way to modern wealth, grew rich on its ghost acres.[21]

Thanks to that commodity importation, Great Britain experienced an increase in population unlike any nation before. Added resources, especially foods from the Americas, meant that more people could survive infancy. They could not, however, always find work and thrive. So Britons left by the millions to find homes in the overseas territories. There they were joined by the surplus population of Scandinavia, Germany, Italy, Eastern Europe, and over time by large numbers of immigrants (and unwilling slaves) from Africa and Asia too. In the course of a single century, from 1820 to 1930, more than 50 million Europeans migrated overseas, most of them to the United States.[22] Huge numbers went to live on the prairie soils of Illinois, Iowa, Nebraska, and Saskatchewan. When those prairies were all transformed into homesteads, the immigrants moved farther west on to more marginal lands, as Webb's family did. Finally, they were forced to take jobs in factories, sawmills, meatpacking plants, or mines, extracting another kind of "real" wealth from the soil and making it into steel rails, boards and nails for construction, or dressed beef for the urban consumer. Yet despite all that human migration, the population of First Earth kept increasing: in Europe, it went from 81 million in 1500, to 180 million in 1800, to 390 million in 1900.[23]

Canada's supply of arable land was relatively small compared to that of the United States, and so were Mexico's and Chile's, so those countries drew fewer immigrants. Even in the fabulous new world some people had to confront poor soils, short growing seasons, or mountainous terrain. Second Earth was not everywhere a potential garden waiting for the plow, and no amount of ingenuity could make every place bountiful. The poorer lands could not support crops year in and year out or offer rich deposits of oil, silver, or iron ore. Only poor people would go there to stay, people with no other choices, and there they would remain poor.

Among the new nations carved out of the Americas, the United States was the luckiest in assets. Somewhere within its borders, it offered almost everything that people wanted: the world's greatest expanse of prime soils; a supply of fresh water that seemed limitless (until one got to the western deserts); a forest cover that surpassed in quality, diversity, and utility that of any other nation; a vast renewable resource of furs and fish; and almost every mineral known to man. It had *almost* everything—but even the United States did not enjoy infinite resources.

Luxuriating in their bounty, American citizens boasted of their hard work, their moral worthiness, and their openness to risk, innovation, and enterprise. They saw themselves as the people with get-up-and-go, the model that others should admire and follow. Seldom did they reflect on how much nature had contributed to their fortune or worry about what the future might bring. Their third president Thomas Jefferson exulted that they "possessed a chosen country, with room enough for our descendants to the thousandth and thousandth generation."[24] Chosen as in "chosen people"—a land as well as a people chosen by God. By "our descendants" Jefferson meant their offspring and future immigrants. But what did he mean by the "thousandth and thousandth generation?" That's two thousand generations! Allow thirty years per generation, and we are talking about 60,000 years of future growth and increase. Jefferson was extravagantly optimistic, but so the prospects for the United States seemed in his day. Likewise, his fellow citizens could see no limits to their land and no limits to the endless wealth they would extract from it.

CHAPTER 3

Ultimately, Stability

E VENING CONVERSATIONS AT THE LITERARY Club, a self-identified elite among London's intellectuals and politicians led starting in 1764 by the painter Joshua Reynolds and the essayist Samuel Johnson, were apt to ramble from topic to topic. Once every fortnight the group gathered at the Turk's Head Tavern in Gerrard Street for oysters and roast beef, and always the discussions went on long after the dinner plates were cleared away. But with the outbreak of armed conflict in Massachusetts between colonial militiamen and the king's army in April 1775, the talk frequently turned to what the British government should do with those American colonists—crack their heads or give in to their demands for more freedom and self-determination?

During that same year of rebellion leading to the emergence of the United States of America, the club voted to admit a prominent Scottish philosopher, Adam Smith. Formerly of the University of Glasgow, he was living in London to finish a book he had been writing for some time. It would be published in March 1776, just three months before the Americans declared their independence. Appearing in two volumes totalling over one thousand pages, the book bore the ponderous title *An Inquiry into the Nature and Causes of The Wealth of Nations*. Nevertheless, it sold vigorously and would thereafter be regarded as the foundation text for modern economics. Influenced by those dinner conversations, Smith had begun thinking about the new world. His book turned out to be, at least partially, a commentary on that world and on what the discovery of Second Earth might mean for the wealth of nations.

Economics, along with other sciences, owed much to the discovery of Second Earth, but in its early days economics still carried a residue of prediscovery attitudes—an awareness of natural limits that must eventually restrain the accumulation of wealth. Later on that awareness would nearly vanish, as economists confidently began assuming they could make wealth grow forever. But in its "classical" period, the time stretching from Adam Smith to the middle of the nineteenth century, a sense of limits among economists remained potent. While theorists of wealth-making reflected their society's rising expectations of plenty, calling for more economic freedom to realize them, at the same time they cautioned that the wealth could not expand forever, that abundance was only temporary, and that scarcity would one day return. The earth was not an infinite storehouse of riches. The human population would always threaten to exceed the limits. And at least one of those early economists, John Stuart Mill—perhaps the most brilliant of them all—argued that accepting natural limits would not be a bad thing.

The founder of modern economics, Adam Smith, a fleshy man with a bulbous nose and a distracted air, remained on the whole a firm optimist about growth in the immediate future. He felt very much at home around the Literary Club's dining table, where lively, amusing companions shared his enthusiasm for good meals and material progress. Like them, Smith was a city man—not an outdoor sort nor in any way a romantic in his feelings for nature, nor one who knew the land through intimate contact or hard work. Like his companions, he was inexperienced in the practical problems of tracking a deer through the Highlands or constructing a power loom. Even his fellow diner and denizen of London, the urbane Samuel Johnson, had seen more of Britain's marginal lands than he, for Johnson had traveled across moors and mountains all the way to the picturesque but impoverished Hebrides, where he witnessed firsthand the sad departure of surplus people for America. Yet Smith, insulated though he was from nature and poverty, did not lack a sense of the land's limits.[1]

Born in 1723 in the commercial seaport of Kirkcaldy, across the Firth of Forth from Edinburgh, Smith gave up his youthful intention to become a priest and instead turned to lecturing on moral philosophy in Glasgow. Then, after thirteen years in the university, during which time he enjoyed much academic success, he left that prestigious position to serve as private tutor to the stepson of one of the richest landowners in Britain, the Duke of Buccleuch. Although the position was little more than a high-level servant's job, it gave Smith a chance to travel abroad, meet leading French intellectuals, and retire with a substantial annuity. He also used the position and the income it generated to undertake a comprehensive study of how wealth might be maximized.

Wealth in Smith's mind meant the multiplication of "all the necessaries and conveniences of [human] life." He furnished no list of what those necessaries might be, but he did set forth his theory of how to make one's purchasing power multiply. Wealth increases, he argued in the opening pages, as human labor is divided into smaller and smaller parts, making each worker's task more specialized and efficient. The result is a gain in "productivity," and steadily increasing productivity leads to "universal opulence." The process had been going on since the time when humans left the savage state, and it would go on indefinitely. Agriculture, the first major step forward, allowed more productivity than hunting and gathering, while manufacturing allowed even more and therefore was the most promising road to personal and national affluence.[2]

What drove the long process forward, Smith argued, was "a certain propensity in human nature . . . to truck, barter, and exchange one thing for another." No other species showed that tendency. Because it was natural to humans and irrepressible, it did not require any encouragement by those in authority. Governments, however, might thwart the advance of productivity by ill-considered policies, thus doing themselves and their subjects no good. Smith's advice to government was to get out of the way and give people their freedom. In a "system of perfect liberty," he urged, every individual, "as long as he does not violate the laws of justice," should be "perfectly free to pursue his own interest" and to compete with every other individual. An "invisible hand," not visible government, would ensure that the human species kept marching toward greater efficiency and productivity forever.[3]

Yet this happy faith in increasing productivity, which became the core doctrine of modern capitalism and liberal and neoliberal (confusingly known in the United States as conservative) economics, was in Smith's book complicated by factors that had nothing to do with economic efficiency—with dissolving a job into its discrete parts, encouraging specialization, or implementing laissez-faire policies. Those extraneous factors came from the contingencies of nature. Wealth, Smith could not deny, requires more than human labor; it requires land, resources, and the natural world. He became aware of nature's significance following two linked observations: nature in Europe had in the past posed real limits to the economy, while at the same nature in the Americas was opening astounding opportunities. In both places, nature had to be acknowledged as an important factor in making wealth. Conceptually, such an admission turned *The Wealth of Nature* into an intellectual hodgepodge and left future economists with a confused legacy.

Well into the book, for example, Smith unexpectedly wrote that "in a country which had acquired that full complement of riches which the nature of its soil and climate, and its situation with regard to other countries, allowed it to acquire; which could, therefore, advance no further, and which was not going backward," wages and profits would stabilize, albeit at a low level of equilibrium. No future growth could occur. Wealth would reach a stationary state, and no efficiency breakthrough or division of labor could increase it. Reassuringly, he added, "perhaps no country" had yet arrived at that point. But a stationary state was, make no mistake, the inevitable fate of all societies. That much he had gathered from his study of European and Asian history.[4]

On the other side of the globe stood China, a country that Smith knew only from reading travelers' reports. China, he wrote, "seems long to have been stationary, and had probably long ago acquired that full complement of riches which is consistent with the nature of its laws and institutions." The economist allowed that with better laws and institutions, China might make more efficient use of its soil and climate. If its leaders would embrace the principles of free enterprise and allow their people to exercise their "natural liberty," economic stagnation might be overcome for a while. But Smith did not believe that in China or anywhere else it could be overcome forever. Even a reformed China must one day reach "that full complement of riches" that its nature and geography allowed. Nature, though a generous mother, does not permit the endless production of all "the necessities and conveniences" that humans seek.[5]

The other stimulus for Smith's environmental awareness came from the wondrous lands of the Americas. He seems to have begun thinking about them rather late in his career, perhaps not until after he had settled in London, and then he did not quite know what to do with all that vastness of space and richness of natural endowment. It was not until he came to write the latter part of his book that he stuck in an entire chapter (Book IV, Chapter VII) on the colonies. And in that chapter he wrote words that cannot easily be reconciled with his older core philosophy of steady, step-by-step universal progress toward efficiency and productivity.

"The discovery of America," Smith writes emphatically, "and that of a passage to the East Indies by the Cape of Good Hope, are the two greatest and most important events recorded in the history of humankind."[6] The words come almost verbatim from Abbé Raynal's opening sentences in *Histoire Philosophique et Politique* from 1770. Breathlessly, Smith made Raynal's thesis his own and embellished it. The discovery of America and the passage to Asia he ranked greater than any other historical events—greater, he means, than the birth of Jesus, greater even than the creation of Adam and Eve! Those events had been celebrated in churches and in the Bible, but then Smith was not much of a Christian or a Bible reader. He assessed history in secular terms.

What made the "discovery of America" and "a passage to the East Indies" seem so pivotal to Adam Smith was that they excited his imagination with a vision of unexploited natural resources. Despite many dreadful consequences for the dispossessed native peoples, Smith felt in his heart that European access to those resources "in general tendency would seem to be beneficial." Beneficial in economic terms, he meant, beneficial because they increased "the necessaries and conveniences of life." But if the accidental discovery of Second Earth could do that, then what did it reveal about the "nature and causes" of wealth? What did it say about steady, rational progress toward efficiency as the foundation of all wealth?

"The colony of a civilized nation which takes possession either of a waste [uncultivated] country, or one so thinly inhabited, that the natives easily give place to the new settlers, advances more rapidly to wealth and greatness than any other human society."[7] That was the main lesson that Smith gleaned from America. Wealth grows faster in a new country than an old one. Not, however, because of the extraction of gold or silver. Spain, by focusing only on extracting precious metals from the ground and shipping them home, had not seen any lasting improvement in its condition. Britain, according to Smith, had by contrast seen such improvement. It had sent thousands of settlers to the new world, and they had invested their energy in exploiting the fertile soil.

Agriculture, Smith thought, must be the first step in human progress, the foundation on which all further wealth must build. Agriculture required for its success a land rich in organic resources. The British colonists had discovered in America "waste lands of the greatest natural fertility," lands that could be had for a trifle, and

on that fertility they had prospered. The coming together of hitherto untapped natural abundance, skilled labor, and wise imperial
policies allowing immigrants their freedom had generated prosperity beyond compare. Britain had profited from that wealth and now
needed to do everything possible to encourage the American colonists and keep them loyal to the motherland.[8]

Alas, the imperial government failed to take Smith's advice,
and its richest colonies were lost to rebellion. The British Empire
would, in another hundred years or so, Smith predicted, give way
to the American Empire. Differences in natural endowment would
determine that outcome, though Smith kept insisting that economic
freedom was also important. But what then would be the fate of that
future American Empire, if natural limits exist everywhere? Would
liberty or labor alone be sufficient to keep the United States new
and progressive? The answer, Smith suggested, had to be negative.
Economic liberty could offer no panacea to any country, even in the
new world, once it had reached its "full complement of riches."

The optimistic, even revolutionary, tone of *The Wealth of Nations*,
is hard to miss. But his celebration of capitalism was qualified by
Smith's awareness, however muddled, of the limiting factor of natural resources. The European resource base could increase, as it did
dramatically following Columbus, but eventually, no matter how
abundant, it would be consumed and exploited. The best that one
could hope for was not progress forever but progress for a while—
progress that would end with a comfortable stationary state.

Many economists who came after Smith, especially in the United
States, echoed his optimism while ignoring his old-world residue of
pessimism. But not every economist did; some pushed his thinking
about limits to deeper levels. They combined the master's general
faith in progress through laissez-faire policies with his doubts about
the long-term prospects for growth and the promise of infinite
abundance. Thomas Malthus was the most controversial, but David
Ricardo, Stanley Jevons, and John Stuart Mill all understood that
there are limits to wealth and, like Smith, they understood that both
plenty and scarcity depend on what nature will allow.

So much vitriol has been heaped on the head of the Reverend
Thomas Robert Malthus that one suspects he made the cardinal mistake not of offering poor arguments or weak facts, but of calling
into question strongly held beliefs. He was the enemy of what he
regarded as a false new religion—the gospel of infinite abundance
that spread in the wake of Columbus. Although true believers in that

gospel disagreed about what a fair distribution of new wealth might be, one side insisting that businessmen and corporations deserved everything, while the other side complained that the distribution was unfair, they all agreed that abundance is desirable and abundance is eternal. Malthus did not disagree with their desire to find and create more wealth, but he argued that it would never be enough to keep up with the increase in human population. Once again, he represented economic thinking that was inspired by the Americas, while at the same time he was sobered by the old world's long experience with resource limits.

Malthus was only ten years old, living in his parents' country house in Surrey, England, when *The Wealth of Nations* appeared in print. By 1798 he had become a parish priest in his home county, but also the author of a small book entitled *An Essay on the Principle of Population*. Refuting the more giddy enthusiasts of the day, the book asserted "the power of population is infinitely greater than the power in the earth to produce subsistence for man." This is a "fixed law," applicable to England or America.[9] No matter how much wealth people derived from the earth, they would reproduce even faster, so that poverty would always be the lot of many. In later editions of his book Malthus allowed that voluntary birth control might be possible, that poor people could be encouraged to have fewer children and thus be in a position to feed them better. But Mother Nature could never supply all the "necessaries," let alone all the "conveniences," that it is in our nature to demand. Without restraint in reproduction and consumption, he warned, misery would go on plaguing the world as it always had done. Unfortunately for his reputation, he put all the burden of that restraint on poor people.

When Malthus left the church to become a professor of history and political economy at East India Company College in Hertfordshire, his students called him "Pop [short for Population] Malthus." They were poking fun at his obsession with fertility. Yet many agreed with him that despite the riches pouring in from abroad and from the factories of the growing industrial cities, huge numbers of people were seeing no increase in their well-being, and in fact often were experiencing a decline. They were the "unhappy persons who, in the great lottery of life, have drawn a blank." More growth alone would not make them happier. Malthus put the blame for failure on poor people's inability to refrain from sexual intercourse. But it was not only the poor he blamed. He also in effect blamed God. Both nature and human nature were the creations of God, so it had to be God who had decided that the earth would never produce enough resources for the super-prolific species He had created.

This apparent cruelty in the Creator's plan had the benign purpose, argued the economist, of forcing humans to work hard and develop their minds. We were not meant to live idly in a garden: "To urge man to further the gracious designs of Providence by the full cultivation of the earth, it has been ordained that population should increase much faster than food."[10] For a religious believer there could be no other explanation. Although Malthus did not say so, the voyages of Columbus must likewise have been the design of Providence, opening a land of plenty to encourage more work. Then like Smith, Malthus argued that the enjoyment of new resources would last only for a brief time, for the Americas too would become intensely cultivated and unable to keep up with the waves of migrants. Opening more mines or factories without adding more farms and food would not be a solution. The Western Hemisphere would have to either find another uncultivated frontier (although none were floating into view) or cultivate the lands more intensely, with diminishing returns. The implications in Malthus's reasoning led straight back to Adam Smith's stationary state, but this time with a more tragic outcome.

For centuries Jews and Christians had believed that maximizing human numbers was divinely ordained. God, they read in Genesis 1:28, had instructed Adam and Eve to "be fruitful, and multiply, and replenish the earth, and subdue it: and have dominion over the fish of the sea, and over the fowl of the air, and over every living thing that moveth upon the earth."[11] But that was not the belief of Rev. Malthus, who unlike Smith normally read his Bible quite carefully. He simply ignored that passage. As a curate, he might have said to himself that those instructions to multiply came *before* humankind's expulsion from Eden, that original sin had necessitated a change in the instruction manual. He might have added that there would never be a return to Eden, not even in the new world. There would only be work and struggle. Subdue the earth, by all means, but don't expect a paradise in the end. And watch those numbers!

Most citizens of the United States were not inclined to see the world as Malthus did. Generally they were convinced they had rediscovered a perennial Eden. After all, they enjoyed "plenty of rich land, to be had for little or nothing" (as Malthus put it) and, thanks to minimal government, they were making "by far the most rapid progress" in population, "probably without parallel in history." In the back settlements, where land was most free and abundant and few luxuries were available for frivolous consumption, the white population doubled every fifteen years. In more settled areas, the doubling took thirty-five years. Malthus could only conclude that God wanted Americans to become an industrious, prosperous people, but at the same time he had to warn that sexual passion would some day force them, as it had forced others, out of their Eden and into a life of hardship and struggle.[12]

The pioneer economist David Ricardo, the son of a Dutch Jew who settled in London and made a fortune on the stock exchange in 1815, speculating on the outcome of the Battle of Waterloo, reflected a similar mix of optimism and pessimism about growth. He accepted Smith's prescription of "natural liberty" as the best recipe for generating wealth and yet also accepted Malthus's laws of population and food. Like his mentors he seems to have believed that all economies must one day end in the "stationary state," when the land has been fully exploited and material progress comes to an end. What he added to the analysis was the "law of diminishing returns." Increasing inputs, say, from human labor, does not always lead to more output. Plant a field thoroughly with seed, so that those seeds take up all the available nutrients, moisture, and sunlight, and a full harvest appears. Doubling the number of seeds sowed, however, does not double the harvest. Each seed will have less to grow on. Similarly, doubling manure on a field may increase the yield, but laying on more and more manure will not lead to an infinitely greater amount of food. As people move on to more marginal lands, requiring greater inputs of labor and fertilizer, they must expend more energy and harvest less. Always humans run up against nature's limits.

Some have contended, then and now, that this residue of traditional resource thinking in classical economics is wrong and needs correcting. Modern nations, they insist, can always manage to produce more from the land, creating an abundance that will never diminish. This was decidedly the attitude of leading thinkers in the American School, led by Henry Charles Carey, an influential writer and businessman from Philadelphia who summarily rejected Malthus's population arguments, the notion of a stationary state, and the law of diminishing returns.[13] By the twentieth century Carey's way of thinking had become almost universal in the United States, spreading into every region and abroad. Growth without any end in sight became the consensus creed of economics even as Second Earth became more crowded and fought over, more polluted and depleted.

This US-based revision of Smithian-Malthusian thinking occurred in part because experts were sure that they had found something better than a new hemisphere. They had found what seemed like an unlimited source of energy, which would allow nations to do anything they wanted. This was not energy dependent on the daily flux of the sun—energy stored in living organisms like trees, crops, and human bodies. This supposedly inexhaustible source of energy came from long-buried plant and animal remains—the fossil fuels of coal, oil, and natural gas. Adam Smith and his fellows had missed the significance of those fuels; therefore, their warnings about limits, whether far off or near in time, must not be valid.

One prominent spokesman for this view was Edward Wrigley, a twentieth-century historian of industrialization at Cambridge University, who set about to refute classical economics on whether the land imposes limits to growth. Such thinking, Wrigley declared, belonged to "a traditional economy, an economy bounded by the productivity of the land, what I shall term an organic economy." In other words, it belonged to an agrarian past. The Industrial Revolution, he argued, blew that economy apart and set humans free from soil and sun. It discovered a new energy source coming out of the ground but with far more wealth-generating potential than mere soil. That source was the carbon-rich remains of ancient plants. From their dark molecules came an explosive force that revolutionized everything, creating a wholly new productive landscape:

> A world of huge cities and an industrialized countryside; a world that no longer follows the rhythm of the sun and the seasons; a world in which the fortunes of man depend largely upon how he himself regulates the economy and not upon the vagaries of weather and harvest; a world in which poverty has become an optional state rather than a reflection of the necessary limitations of human productive powers; a world increasingly free from major natural disaster but in which human folly can mean utter and total destruction; a world that has gained an awesome momentum of growth but may have lost any semblance of stability. Such has been the legacy of the industrial revolution.[14]

Like the voyages of Columbus, the discovery of coal occurred almost by accident and not by a slow, incremental unfolding of human rationality, technological innovation, or the adoption of a work ethic. Coal was a windfall that no one could have anticipated. Coal made that other windfall, the Americas, superfluous, Wrigley implies, or at least marginal to history. Unlike the Western Hemisphere, coal was distributed around the globe. Thus every place on earth could become potentially a new world.

Coal was indeed a big thing—but it was not that big, not that abundant, and not quite so pivotal to the 500-year-old revolution that is modern history. As a resource, it had been around for a long time and was widely used in China, Germany, and many other places long before industrialization. People found it messy to handle and smelly when burned, so its potential had not been fully pursued until, because of deforestation, it became necessary to do so. Wherever there were alternatives, coal was not the fuel of choice. It did not become so, for example, in the United States until around 1870; before then wood and water power had been the major sources of energy, and they were enough to create an industrial revolution and a powerful nation. "Globally," writes the Canadian environmental scientist Vaclav Smil, "coal began to supply more than 5% of all fuel energies around 1840, more than 10% in the 1850s, more than a quarter of the total by the late 1870s, and one half by the beginning of the twentieth century." That transition was slow, but even more important, it came much later than the discovery of Second Earth. Compared to the Great Discoveries, all of the fossil fuels—coal, oil, and natural gas—were late supplements to the age of abundance.[15]

Without coal there might have been no progressive industrialization, but then the same could be said about cotton or potatoes imported from abroad. Mainly, the black stuff dug from the ground fed machines; it did not feed people. Burning it instead of burning wood did not free up much land for food production, not compared to the ghost acreages of America. Thus, it was a secondary rather than a primary driver of revolution.

Perhaps, as Wrigley says, Smith and the others gave little attention to coal because they could not imagine all the social consequences that an energy transition would bring. More likely, their seeming indifference was due to the fact that they did not think that new sources of energy alone would be enough to prevent a future of stagnation. Coal was just another resource in that "full complement of riches" a country owned and as finite as the rest. If a "resource" as big as Second Earth might one day be filled with people who were extracting all that was possible, then the coal mines of Northumberland and Wales were even more likely to have limited potential and not prevent the inevitable stagnation.

Like the Americas, it is true, the coal mines of Great Britain did inspire visions of infinite wealth. "Our mines are literally inexhaustible. We cannot get to the bottom of them." "The coal we happily possess in excellent quality and abundance is the mainspring of modern material civilization." "We are growing rich and numerous upon a source of wealth of which the fertility does not yet apparently decrease with our demands upon it." "We are like settlers spreading in a rich new country of which the boundaries are yet unknown and unfelt."[16] All those quotations came from one of the last of the great classical economists, William Stanley Jevons, in his book *The Coal Question*, first published in 1865. He was quoting, with considerable irony, his fellow countrymen. Jevons said everything that later scholars like Wrigley would say about coal's importance in creating wealth, and yet Jevons was still worried about Britain's economic future. Only a century had occurred since Watt's steam engine had started burning coal, but in that time the resource had already begun to lose its promise.

Dig down deeper, Jevons admitted, and men would certainly find more coal. For the moment that plenty was easily accessible. Britain mined nearly 100 million tons during the year his book was published. But already the mining of coal was running up against the limits of extraction. Somewhere around four thousand feet below the surface, the difficulty of extracting coal and the cost of that work would become prohibitive; mining would slow down and then cease altogether. Before that point the cost of the fuel would become prohibitive, rising "to a rate injurious to our commercial and manufacturing supremacy." That day, Jevons predicted, would come in about a century—that is, during the 1960s. Before it did, Britain's civilization, once the envy of the world, would begin to falter and give way to other countries. Most likely it would give way to the United States, which contained (Jevons guessed) at least forty times as much coal as Britain. One day the mother country would contract "to her former littleness," and then she would have to learn to take vicarious pride in her offspring fattening on their greater supplies overseas.[17]

The new world imposed itself metaphorically as well as materially in Jevons's treatise on coal: "In the increasing depth and difficulty of coal mining we shall meet that vague, but inevitable boundary that will stop our progress. We shall begin as it were to see the further shore of our Black Indies [referring to the blackness of coal]. The wave of population will break upon that shore, and roll back upon itself. And as settlers, unable to choose in the far inland new and virgin soil of unexceeded fertility, will fall back upon that which is next best, and will advance their tillage up the mountain side, so we, unable to discover new coal fields as shallow as those before, must deepen our mines with pain and cost."[18]

Britain's coalfields were undeniably powerful in their material effects, but those effects were the gift of nature, not of technology alone. Coal proved once again that nature matters in human affairs. All the founding figures of modern economics, even a man as detached from the earth and its web of life as Adam Smith, had to grant that truth. Whether one lived in a traditional society based on farming or an industrial society based on manufacturing, the same reality applied. Natural resources, whether soil or coal, were vital. Multiply human demands, and sooner or later societies must confront the physical fact that the world is finite. And nothing, neither nature nor machine, could make the finite become infinite.

Such warnings of environmental limits have been unwelcome in many corporate offices or among progressive-minded intellectuals, in Malthus's or Jevons's day or our own. Again and again critics have launched a fierce attack on small thinking, modest consumption, and above all on "pessimism." Everyone must be taught to think more hopefully, to see that the earth is inexhaustible and that technological efficiency is leading humankind toward a paradise on earth. All talk of a "stationary state" must be banished because it is depressing—it is too "old world."

The brilliant economist John Stuart Mill, however, refused to become a booster for that kind of thinking. Born in 1806, he was one of the last of the great classical economists, living until 1873, and the most prolific and most widely read. He was a philosopher as well as economist, perhaps the most influential philosopher in the English language during the nineteenth century. A follower of Smith, Malthus, and Ricardo, he was the author of, among other works, *On Liberty* (1859), *The Subjection of Women* (1869), and *The Principles of Political Economy* (running through seven editions, from 1848 to 1871). Like his predecessors in economics, he advocated trade liberalization and competitive markets. But more than his predecessors, he harbored many doubts. He doubted that growth could be sustained forever and doubted that endless growth was good for the human spirit. The latter doubt was especially novel, for it suggested that reaching an end to growth might not be so bad after all. In fact, it might lead toward a more enlightened kind of happiness and satisfaction. The end of growth would free people, Mill argued, from extravagant dreams of material plenty and encourage them to seek other forms of fulfillment. In contrast, the ideology of progress, with its intense drive for wealth, was leading toward a new kind of deprivation. Increasingly, it was depriving men and women of any moral or spiritual purpose, leaving them trapped in a culture of excessive materialism.

The stationary state, when the earth will be full of people and resources everywhere will be thoroughly exploited, Mill wrote, will be "on the whole, a very considerable improvement on our present condition. I confess that I am not charmed with the ideal of life held out by those who think that the normal state of human beings is that of struggling to get on; that the trampling, crushing, elbowing, and treading on each other's heels ... are the most desirable lot of human kind." In the wide-open spaces of North America, he noted in the first edition of *Principles*, an insatiable hunger for wealth had subverted all reason and virtue. The white majority in the northern United States might be living free of historic poverty and injustice, he granted, but "all that these advantages seem to have done for them is that the life of the whole of one sex is devoted to dollar-hunting, and of the other to breeding dollar-hunters." These harsh words would be suppressed in later editions, but they reflected his true, if rather bitter, view of an age that set impossibly high expectations for people.[19]

How, Mill asked, would adding greatly to the human population or the accumulation of capital make life better for anyone? Only the "backward countries" needed more production; the more advanced ones needed "a better distribution" and more constraints on fertility. Mill would not wait until the stationary state abruptly arrived. That would be too late to ease into a more balanced life, in which both nature and the human spirit still had room to breathe. He would protect the natural world from overdevelopment.

> It is not good for man to be kept perforce at all times in the presence of his species. A world from which solitude is extirpated is a very poor ideal. Solitude, in the sense of being often alone, is essential to any depth of meditation or of character; and solitude in the presence of natural beauty and grandeur, is the cradle of thoughts and aspirations which are not only good for the individual, but which society could ill do without. Nor is there much satisfaction in contemplating the world with nothing left to the spontaneous activity of nature, with every rood of land brought into cultivation, which is capable of growing food for human

beings; every flowery waste or natural pasture ploughed up, all quadrupeds or birds which are not domesticated for man's use exterminated as his rivals for food, every hedge-row or superfluous tree rooted out, and scarcely a place left where a wild shrub or flower could grow without being eradicated as a weed in the name of improved agriculture. If the earth must lose that great portion of its pleasant-ness which it owes to things that the unlimited increase of wealth and population would extirpate from it, for the mere purpose of enabling it to support a larger, but not a better or a happier population, I sincerely hope, for the sake of posterity, that they will be content to be stationary, long before necessity compels them to it.[20]

One can hear in that call to preserve nature's wildness a few echoes of William Wordsworth, Henry David Thoreau, and dozens of land-scape painters who were searching through the Americas, north and south, to find and celebrate places of natural beauty before they were destroyed. For Mill and those others, life should offer more than Smith's list of "necessities and conveniences."

Mill was not a mathematically oriented, narrowly technical expert in the moneymaking business. He was, in the broadest sense, a moralist contemplating life's value and worth, concerned not only with the economics of supply and demand but also with "unpriced" values like those so commonly found in the natural world—clean air, good water, and companionship of other forms of life. He lamented the declining value of nature in his home country, and indeed over the whole earth.

Perhaps once again that set of critical thoughts derived from encountering Second Earth through reports and pictures. Distant travelers and explorers had opened his eyes and those of others of his day to the astonishing spectacle of nature—setting off still another revolution, this one ushering in a greater appreciation of the planet's wildness. If Mill, a man of the city and industry, some-how came to value wild natural beauty, so too did many others. In his day men and women began enthusiastically to conserve some of those disappearing natural landscapes, even while the chief motive of the age remained growing richer and richer on a planet of wide-open opportunity.

The awesome beauty of Second Earth has been haunting the human mind for centuries. Millions have gone out to see it for themselves and have been changed by the sight in ways both subtle and obvious. Aesthetic and intellectual revolutions, along with the material and political ones, followed from the encounter, until they became too entangled to separate or isolate.

If the dominant impulse after seeing Mercator's map of Second Earth was to throw off old ideas of constraint and tradition, to go, settle, and possess, another impulse was to see, appreciate, conserve, and preserve. There was something irresistible in both impulses, and together they have made modern thinking far more complicated than Adam Smith's "natural propensity" to barter and trade. Europeans came to kill and eat, to burn and build, but now and then, like Jay Gatsby, they stood in wonder before a hitherto unknown and gorgeous world.

Nantucket Island

A BOAT LEAVES THE PINE-AND-OAK forested shores of Massachusetts and sails into the blue, until the mainland falls out of sight and the world becomes a seamless blend of sky and sea. Thirty miles out a small pancake of earth appears on the horizon, but only barely; the closer one gets the more uninspiring it looks. Some ten by fifteen miles in size, it offers no hills or valleys, only a pygmy forest and swales of spartina grass, and a soil so poor that even a New England farmer would scorn to plant.

The Indians who came here in the wake of the glacier's retreat called this island "Nanticoot," the "far away land," a name that was adopted and handed down as "Nantucket." Neither those Indians nor many generations of white European settlers who came later understood that the island is the work of a melting glacier, which more than ten thousand years ago left behind a sandy moraine on which immigrant plants landed and struggled to take hold. But the human invaders soon realized that this place was no Eden. Farther west the retreating ice sheet created a few more islands, including the fertile garden of Long Island on which Jay Gatsby cultivated his extravagant dreams. No one ever expected so much of Nantucket.[1]

Second Earth offered not just a vast, highly variable, continental landmass but even vaster oceans—the Atlantic, the Pacific, and the polar seas. In fact the new world offered far more water than land. Those seas, mostly unexplored by Europeans until after 1500, covered 100 million square miles, fully half the surface of the whole planet.[2] Although large parts of the newly discovered oceans were desert-like in their inability to support much life, other parts were teeming with fish, krill, mammals, birds, and forests of kelp. The watery new world also included thousands of islands of various sizes, some of which became the sites of very profitable sugar plantations or important sources of guano fertilizer or big timber. Why then come to Nantucket to remember those early encounters?

This little island is a reminder that obvious and immediate ecological limits existed even in the midst of so much untapped abundance. Despite those land limits, people found wealth here by turning to the oceans around them. But when celebrating their burst of enterprise, it should be recalled that their wealth from the ocean was acquired through bloodshed and violence toward both nonhuman and human life—through a frenzy of exploitation. Remember too that the oceanic wealth proved to have its own limits. In the end Nantucket offers a complicated parable of heroic achievement mixed with brutality and failure. Today it lives on lost visions of grandeur. Perhaps it is ready for John Stuart Mill's stationary state, where nonmaterial needs have gained in importance over material ones.

The seas around Nantucket and the rest of New England were, according to the earliest European reports, abounding in life that no longer flourished in the old world: fish, shellfish, and mammals, including cod, striped bass, salmon, lobster, crab, oyster, and whales of several species. William Bradford, the first and longtime governor of the English colony at Plymouth, Massachusetts, founded in 1620, was astonished by that plenty. Although obsessed with his religious mission and dismissive of the land he would colonize as a "desolate and howling wilderness," he took time to note that his Pilgrims had come to "a place of good fishing, for we saw daily great whales of the best kind for oil and bone ... Every day we saw whales playing hard by us, of which in that place, if we had instruments and means to take them, we might have made a very rich return ... Our master and his mate, and others experienced in fishing, professed we might have made three or four thousand pounds' worth of oil. They preferred it before Greenland whale-fishing, and purpose the next winter to fish for whale here." Likely he knew that the Basques, along with the English and Dutch, had been exploiting the waters off Greenland and Labrador for almost a hundred years. His economic imagination was following in a heavy wake stirred by others, but Plymouth Plantation would never make much of an impact on the sea. Other nearby places, however, would.[3]

Clearly, Bradford's is not the Atlantic Ocean of today, where depletion and pollution are the common story all along the New England coast, the Canadian Maritime provinces, and almost everywhere else. A staggering loss of richness in species, populations, and ecosystems has occurred. The Canadian author and environmentalist Farley Mowatt, born in 1921, has observed in his own lifetime "a massive diminution of the entire body corporate of animate creation." But long before the twentieth century, all the way back to the sixteenth, that decline has been going on—not without partial recoveries now and then, but nonetheless a long-term decline in marine life that now, in the twenty-first century, is reaching its nadir, the darkness of mass extinction.[4]

That tragic history of biocide has many land-based chapters in what is now the United States—the disappearance of the heath hen, the ivory-billed woodpecker, the California grizzly, the passenger pigeon. The list of extinct species throughout the rest of the hemisphere is depressingly long. Many aboriginal human communities have also gone extinct, including on Nantucket Island, although in many places Indian numbers have made a remarkable recovery. But extinction is only the most extreme form of loss. More common has been a substantial diminution in populations, with numbers of many nonhuman species permanently falling as low as 10 or 20 percent of pre-1500 levels. Ecological diminution is a critical part of the story that Nantucket tells, and that loss led to a failure of human aspirations and community.

In the fall of 1659 a middle-aged British immigrant and sometime tavern owner from Salisbury, Massachusetts, Tristram Coffin, came to Nantucket seeking freedom from the oppressive religious intolerance of the mainland. With a few other dissidents, numbering twenty-nine in all, he purchased the western half of the island from the resident Wampanoag people, then totaling more than two thousand, and brought sheep there to graze. A more savvy farmer might have chosen someplace farther north, up the Merrimack River Valley, on fertile bottomland fringed by dense forests sufficient for all his needs. Nantucket was a poor choice agriculturally—fifty square miles of mostly open grassland, with a few salt- and freshwater ponds. There was not enough wood to fence land as private property, so the newcomers turned the whole island interior into a sheep commons and, here and there, into an old-fashioned open field system with communal plowing. Soon they realized there was not enough humus to support any form of agrarian economy, collective or individualistic. Even where there was sufficient soil, the crops they sowed were hindered by the salt-laden winds that blew hard and desiccated the land. Consequently, learning from the more experienced Indians, the new immigrants turned primarily to hunting and gathering from the wild.[5]

The best hunting ground turned out to be the seashore and surrounding waters, for, as the Indians knew, they yielded plenty of fish and other food along with energy resources like driftwood or animal oil. The biggest and most profitable resources in the sea were the great whales that migrated seasonally and occasionally washed up on the beaches. By law, stranded whales belonged to the Indians, but live whales swimming in the deep were fair game. The reward for killing one was a large harvest of the animal's insulating blubber that could be rendered into oil and sold in Boston or even London as fuel for lamps. None of the white settlers went after whales for protein, only for their oil and for the "whalebone" (baleen) that lined the animals' mouths and worked as a sieve to collect food, mainly small copepods and other invertebrates. Cash was what the English sought, and with the cash they could buy from the mainland whatever they needed.[6]

The whales they hunted were the North Atlantic "right" whales (*Eubalaena glacialis*, the "right" one to kill), found offshore from Florida to Finland, with dark chunky bodies that could weigh as much as 200,000 pounds. They were gentle giants and easy to catch. They swam slowly, so that a man could aim carefully and bury his harpoon deeply in their flesh. Then in 1712 one of the islanders, Christopher Hussey, managed to kill a whale of another species, one that would turn out to provide a bonanza lasting more than a century. It was the cachalot, or sperm whale (*Physeter macrocephalus*), so called because of the white waxy fluid, called spermaceti, that filled a cavity in the animal's massive head. This whale, like other species, was well wrapped in blubber from its huge blunt nose to its powerful flukes. A single sperm whale could weigh as much as sixty adult bison, another species that became a popular target for North American hunters. It came armed with a set of teeth that could crunch a wooden boat and a brain that was the largest in biological history, weighing seven times more than the human brain. The animal could swim fast and dive as deep as two miles and stay there for well over an hour, eluding its human predators. The payoff in killing one of these formidable creatures was a shipload of spermaceti, which made the finest candles for the parlor or the best lubricant for machines. Nantucket's hunters nearly gave up all other pursuits to concentrate on pursuing the sperm whale wherever it could be found, and happily it was found throughout the world's midlatitudes, from Nova Scotia to the Cape of Good Hope, from Chile to Japan.[7]

During the American Revolutionary War a hostile British navy shut down Nantucket Island, but when the war was over its whaling fleet went back to the slaughter. They combed the Atlantic up and down until they could find few whales of any kind left to kill. The Atlantic gray, once estimated to number 100,000, they hunted to extinction. Whaling crews going out from ports on both sides of the ocean drove the right whale nearly to the vanishing point. Then the sperm whale became harder to find, as whaling crews could not kill enough to make a cruise profitable.

But if the Atlantic had become heavily depleted, other hemispheric possibilities were not yet exhausted. In 1789 a British whaling vessel became the first to sail around Cape Horn in search of a fresh abundance of the animals. Nantucket was not far behind. In 1791, the *Beaver* (aptly named, for this animal was likewise the target of a continental land hunt that nearly decimated it) rounded the same cape and found sperm whales swimming peacefully off the coast of South America. The killing resumed. Seventeen months after setting sail from Nantucket, the *Beaver* brought back 337 barrels of spermaceti, 650 barrels of oil rendered from the sperm whale's blubber, and 250 barrels of other whale oil.[8]

So dedicated to the chase were the whaling captains that they effectively no longer resided on Nantucket Island. The sea was their home. Captain Benjamin Worth spent only seven years with his family out of a career of forty-one years. Another captain traveled more than a million miles in his lifetime, and over a period of thirty-seven years he resided on the island only four years and eight months.[9] In this restless life men in the whaling business—and they were all men, hailing from many New England ports, including New Bedford and Sag Harbor, from New Hampshire or Connecticut farms, from all over the globe and its many races—would invade every part of the Pacific, leaving an impact throughout Polynesia, East Asia, the west coasts of the Americas, and eventually the Bering Sea. Americans, through the whalers' agency, came to dominate the Pacific region, leading to territorial acquisition as well as unintended ecological and social upheaval in the places they touched. With intense competitiveness and at considerable personal sacrifice, they drove their international rivals out of the sea and created one of the most important enterprises in the new American nation, while transforming Nantucket and other ports into busy little hubs of industry.[10]

Capital readily flowed into those hubs for the constructing and outfitting of whaling vessels, and also for making rope and candles and provisioning the ships. At its peak the American whaling fleet counted over 700 vessels with a combined on-board storage capacity of 239,189 tons.[11] A successful voyage was one that killed at least sixty whales. Every pound of blubber had to be boiled down to oil, in the process polluting the air, blackening the rigging, and spreading a rancid slime everywhere. The refined oil was poured into barrels that were stored below decks, while the rest of the carcass was left behind in the sea. Each large whale ship was not only a floating refinery but also a toxic disaster of blood, guts, bone, and stench. Back home, the centers of investment and construction were likewise polluted by the smell of candle works that turned refined oil into illuminants and profit.

As the hunt intensified and spread, the days of success became fewer and fewer. To fill their holds to capacity, ships had to stay out at sea for longer periods of time. Each day the crew would scan the horizon for signs of whales and perhaps once a week would spot one "blowing," or exhaling through its nostril, with the moisture condensing into a fine mist that could sparkle with rainbows and bring a ship's rudder around fast and hard. Down would come the small boats, off would go the harpooner and his rowers, from his hand would fly a steel barbed spear, and perhaps once a month that harpoon would find its mark, going deep into the animal's flesh and tethering its body to the boat. Many whales escaped with severe wounds. Many died and sank into the sea. A few turned on their tormenters and sank the boats, forcing the entire crew to swim for their lives.

The social life aboard a whale ship and the social life of the towns and families left behind drew many curious observers, for a whaling community was in some ways quite unlike other communities that Americans had formed on farms and plantations, or in river-based cities. One of the earliest accounts came from the French-born Hector St. John de Crèvecœur, who included no less than five chapters on Nantucket and its neighboring island Martha's Vineyard in his *Letters from an American Farmer* (1782). He did not make a voyage or witness the killing process, which may explain why he found the whaling industry a pastoral idyll, like farming the sea. "Is it not better," he asked, "to be possessed of a single whale-boat or a few sheep pastures, to live free and independent under the mildest of government, in a healthy climate, in a land of charity and benevolence, than to be wretched as so many are in Europe?" Nantucket seemed happy and prosperous, though he found it unusual in being managed by the women left behind. Women ran the island's businesses as well as its homes. Their managerial burdens, added to their anxiety over the fates of absent husbands, fathers, brothers, and sons, was assuaged by the habit of taking a few grains of opium with their morning coffee, a habit acquired by the local sheriff as well. Although these predominately Quaker citizens of Nantucket were strong advocates of temperance and purity, they were not free of anxiety or addiction, and their source of wealth, though they seldom acknowledged this, thrust them into complicated moral contradictions.[12]

Edward Byers, historian of the island's changing social order, describes Nantucket as an inward-looking "nation" set off from the rest of the country, yet mirroring broader trends in national development. Because of their unusual condition of land-based scarcity, its people exemplified strong communal tendencies, based on collective decision making and mutual aid, while, on the other hand, at sea they were moving fast to embrace the logic and ethos of economic individualism associated with a rising capitalist worldview. They were caught between the land and the sea, the group and the self, the local and the global. But on both sides of that cultural contrariety, they exploited nature relentlessly. Their communal pastures continued to be overstocked with as many as 10,000 sheep. On the sea they set out to grab as many whales as quickly as possible to maximize personal wealth, hoping that nature would always support them. Legal scholar Robert Ellickson concludes that "even if the New Englanders could have created norms to stem their own depletion of world whaling stock, they might have concluded that a quick kill was more to their advantage." The rules they made, the order they created, increasingly assumed an infinity of natural resources, despite growing evidence to the contrary.[13]

Away from the island, the social world aboard a whaling vessel was no training school for philanthropy. The most vivid description, based on firsthand knowledge, comes from Herman Melville, whose novel *Moby Dick* (1851) tells about a single voyage of the whaling ship *Pequod*, manned by an internationally diverse crew. A need for money drove all the men to sea, and money along with hardship or suffering could make them monstrous in their passions. Captain Ahab, who commanded the *Pequod*, sought both profit and revenge against a great white whale, Moby Dick, which had maimed him in a previous voyage. He drove his ship and crew toward utter disaster—the destruction of his ship by an enraged whale, drowning the crew, leaving only the narrator Ishmael alive and floating in the open sea on an empty coffin. In part the difference in perspective between Crèvecœur's pastoral island and Melville's apocalyptic voyage reflects changes occurring in Nantucket society, as it became motivated by an insatiable economic hunger that demanded more from land and sea than either could yield. Whaling had begun as a way out of an environmental dead end, but eventually it worked its own demise.

If Nantucket and other whaling ports had remained small and local in their markets, or if they had accepted John Stuart Mill's way of thinking, they might have avoided the crash that lay ahead. But the prospect of oceans full of whales was impossible to resist. They drifted from the local to the global rather quickly, as capital accumulated and commerce expanded. By the heyday of the 1830s the average whaler sent into the Pacific represented a $50,000 investment (or about $1.5 million in today's purchasing power), and it could bring that much home in profit from a single voyage. Ten percent of the earnings went to the captain, while the crewmembers' shares could be as little as two hundred dollars each, and the bulk of money went to the ship's owner. Not everyone got rich; great disparities appeared, but everyone made some dollars, a process they hoped could go on forever.

Records from New Bedford, a larger port nearby, show that mean profit rates fluctuated widely from year to year, sometimes as high as 30 percent, sometimes 300 percent, but tellingly the highest rates came in the early years and the lowest rates came much later, after the industry had shifted primarily to the Pacific.[14] As voyages increased in length profit margins declined, ships had to grow bigger, the pay scale become more unequal, and the return on investment shrank. By scaling up, the industry hoped to continue making money, and they did for a while. In towns like Nantucket or New Bedford, the top capitalists used their wealth to build rows of luxurious mansions, substantial banks, and other onshore businesses. They constructed handsome gray houses trimmed in white along Nantucket's New Dollar Lane. One of the more successful Nantucket entrepreneurs, Joseph Starbuck, after his ships had brought back 80,000 barrels that earned him an estimated $2.5 million, hired a master mason to construct three Federalist-style brick mansions for his sons on Main Street. Those houses looked like they were built for eternity. But they were among last of their kind to be built.[15]

In Melville's novel, Captain Ahab goes down with his ship, a warning by the novelist that violence begets violence. Ahab's home port, however, remains out of sight for most of the novel and seemingly unscathed by the disaster, while the whale that did the damage, Moby Dick, escapes to live and breed another day. The novel focuses thus on the darkness that lies within a single man and what it can do to those under him.

But the novelist was by no means indifferent to the fate of the animals Ahab hunted and posed the question of their possible extinction: "Does the whale's magnitude diminish?—Will he perish?" The possibility of extinction had become one of growing concern, for Americans were beginning to ask themselves about the results of their exploitative ways. How can Leviathan, Melville asks, "endure so wide a chase, and so remorseless a havoc?" The answer he gives is optimistic: "We account the whale immortal in his species, however perishable in his individuality." Would this great beast go the way of the herds of bison on the western prairies? The bison once were plentiful in places like Illinois, but now were dead and their habitat taken over by towns and farms. The whales, he decided, were much safer because they had more refuges available. They could always retreat to the Polar Regions. The nature of the seas would protect them. Then there was the fact that whales are more intelligent than bison—more wary, more socially cohesive, more equipped to confront and elude their human predators.

Also aiding the whales was the fact that the whaler's technology was less impressive than the animals' maneuverability. The ships were made of wood and depended on wind filling their sails to get around. They were primitive and clumsy compared to the natural abilities of the whale, and thus they might seem too weak to have a lasting impact. Forty hunters in a single whale ship, Melville pointed out, would do well to kill forty animals in forty-eight months. The same number of bison hunters, in contrast, when armed with rifles could kill 40,000 animals in the same time. The whale was comparatively safe, the novelist reassured his reader. Leviathan cannot be defeated. He "swam the seas before the continents broke water; he once swam over the site of the Tuileries, and Windsor Castle, and the Kremlin. In Noah's flood he despised Noah's Ark, and if ever the world is to be again flooded, like the Netherlands, to kill off its rats, then, the eternal whale will still survive, and rearing upon the topmost crest of the equatorial flood, spout his frothed defiance to the skies."[16]

Other observers were not so confident that the whale could survive so relentless a hunt. If a sea as broad as the Atlantic could be decimated, what might be the future of the Pacific and even the polar seas? Primitive though it was, the whalers' technology had proved potent enough to put a large dent in several populations, had even exterminated at least one species. How many whales of all the many species were still alive? Which ones were in danger? What had been their numbers before extensive whaling began in the decades following Columbus? If those original numbers had been huge— infinite, profuse beyond counting, according to early attitudes— then it would seem that little Nantucket and its rivals could not do any lasting damage. The oil filling so many lamps must be a mere drop in the oceanic bucket and could be endlessly replenished. But if those original numbers turned out to have been much smaller than people assumed, if the hunters were taking a substantial toll, then the whales and the whalers alike had reason to worry.

Before the twentieth century people had developed no good methods of making reliable counts of historic or contemporary animal populations, especially those in the sea. A sailor might try to count the number of whales in a migrating pod, but getting a comprehensive global total was all but impossible. Later on science would develop new methods and make better estimates, but even then animal demographers would often disagree vehemently with each other, leaving the nonspecialist unsure which baseline to use for this or that species.[17]

In the 1920s the naturalist Ernest Thomas Seton made some of the first continental estimates of land-based wildlife, including the grizzly, wolf, elk, prairie dog, and pronghorn antelope. His method relied on gathering early travel reports but also trying to calculate the carrying capacity of the environment for each species and then, assuming that populations always breed up to capacity, make historical estimates. Seton's estimates were always high. For example, he came up with 75 million bison inhabiting the continent at their peak. Later scholars found that number inflated—more than double in fact what their methods suggested—leading them to question his assumptions and to argue that populations do not necessarily expand to the full maximum of carrying capacity.[18]

Seton did not ask how many whales or other marine animals had once inhabited the world's oceans. In 1972 Farley Mowatt tried to do so and came up with an original population of 4.4 million for all nine of the most popular species; of that number 1.2 million were sperm whales. By 1930, he went on, the numbers had fallen to 1.6 million for those nine species, and to 600,000 for sperm whales.

Those figures would seem to show that the old whaling technology of wooden boats and steel harpoons had been devastatingly effective, but they also showed that most of the species did survive the early onslaught and it was the twentieth century that was putting the whole Cetacean order into mortal danger. By the time Mowatt set about gathering his estimates, those whale numbers had crashed to an estimated 200,000–300,000, and to only 150,000–200,000 sperm whales. Mowatt identified four species that, at the time he wrote, were either extinct or hovering on the brink—the Atlantic grey, the Atlantic right whale, the bowhead, and the blue.[19]

The scientists who study whales have proved more difficult to pin down for estimates, but most agree with Mowatt's picture of an overall decline, occurring in two distinct stages: the nineteenth century and the post–World War II period. Thus, in recent years the scientists have generally supported international bans on whaling. They have created a detailed history of the hunt over the centuries. For example, the History of Marine Animal Populations (HMAP) project, which gathers data on all the separate seas and basins, has come up with careful numbers of the historic toll taken. Only negligible numbers of sperm whales, say Tim D. Smith and other scholars active in HMAP, were killed in the eighteenth century. But in the nineteenth 271,000 were killed, and in the twentieth an astonishing total of 721,000, by modern floating factory ships that swept the seas with sonar and harpoon bombs. The species reproduces very slowly, so those precipitous declines meant that recovery took many decades, perhaps more than a century.[20]

What then were the original numbers of this remarkable species that gave us *Moby Dick*? Perhaps the best estimate comes from biologist Hal Whitehead, and it is roughly the same as Mowatt's: one million sperm whales swam in all the world's oceans before whaling began in earnest. By 1880 their population had fallen to about 70 percent of that total, and by the end of the twentieth century to 32 percent. At neither point, it would seem, was the species vanishing from the seas—again, the pattern is radical diminution, not extinction. Whitehead points out that from 1830 to 1850 sighting rates in key parts of the Pacific were down by 60 percent, but cautions that those rates may not mean a similar decline in absolute numbers. Changes in whale behavior—learning to hide from their pursuers, or seeking other grounds where they could be free from the harpoon—could make their sighting harder. If so, the whale's strategies did not work for long, as new hunting technology eventually tracked them down, even in the deepest waters and in the farthest refuges of the sea.[21]

Melville was right that whales are comparatively more resilient than bison, although without a global ban on whaling the sperm whale might have gone the way of the bison, protected in a few reserves but otherwise finished as a vital part of the world's ecology. It was not for want of effort on the part of the whalers that cachalot survived.

By the 1840s a decline in the Nantucket enterprise was becoming apparent to all. Fewer ships were outfitted each year, meaning fewer jobs and lower income. The decline continued over the next twenty years. In 1844 a mere sixteen vessels went out and returned to Nantucket's harbor, all but one of them fishing the Pacific grounds. Each ship brought back anywhere from a thousand to nearly three thousand barrels of sperm oil, along with barrels of whale oil and tons of whalebone. By 1864 only one ship went out and returned, the *Rainbow*, owned by J. B. Macy, and it had fished exclusively in the Atlantic, bringing back a mere 120 barrels of sperm oil, 340 barrels of whale oil, and less than a ton of whalebone. There was no pot of gold at the end of its discouraging voyage.

Nantucket reached its peak before other American ports did and declined before they did, largely because its favorite prey, the sperm whale, could not be found in the old abundance. Other species were still being hunted, although the hunt took the remaining whalers into dangerous Arctic waters. Nantucket could not easily shift away from the sperm whale or compete in the race to exploit the next target of choice, the baleen whales. It watched as its former rivals, ports like New Bedford, went on for several more decades before they too ended the hunt.[22]

Inventors had been experimenting with kerosene as a substitute illuminating fluid, originally deriving it from coal. In 1859 a drilling crew struck a deep underground pool of petroleum in western Pennsylvania, and within a decade and a half refineries were turning out barrels and barrels of kerosene. Eventually the new fossil fuel replaced whale oil in the lamps of America and the rest of the world. But kerosene was always highly explosive, and its development as a safe, dependable fuel for city and household lighting took years to achieve. Other uses for the "oil that came from rock" emerged, including lubricants for industrial machinery. The new products, however, did not drive a successful whaling economy into bankruptcy. Nantucket's whaling had gone into decline well before it faced competition from kerosene or other fossil fuels. The prices that sperm oil fetched in the market remained high throughout the 1850s.[23] There was demand, but there was not enough supply. The new fuels did help remove pressure from the remaining populations of whales; they did not "save" the whales. Nor did capitalism or the supposedly benign and rational play of markets save them. Whales were saved only by the passage of laws and the exercise of moral restraint.[24]

Crèvecœur had called Nantucket "a barren sandbank, fertilized with whale oil only."[25] The problem was where to find a replacement for the whale oil to make the island fertile and prosperous again. Human fertility was also a matter of concern. At its peak Nantucket had counted 10,000 human residents, equal to the flocks of sheep grazing at the same time on the thin crust of soil and grass. The human population would not reach that level again until the twenty-first century. Its lowest level was reached in 1900 to 1910, when it bottomed at around 3,000 people.

Men had begun leaving in droves as the whaling economy declined, abandoning homes and businesses. Some noted that the island seemed more than ever predominately female. Young men had gone to California to mine gold, others had left for seafaring jobs in other ports, and still others had moved to New York City, among them one of the Macy boys, who founded the most famous department store in American history. Whaling had made them competitive capitalists, hard workers, and high risk-takers. But those were not the character traits needed to rebuild a stable community composed of men, women, and children.

The island's growing gender imbalance inspired the title of Edward Bellamy's first novel, *Six to One*, a light romance published in 1877 and far removed in theme from his later utopian socialist writing. Nantucket had become a good place to search for a wife, he argues, but was no place for a man of ambition. The novel opens with a big-city physician telling one of his patients, an overworked, neurasthenic newspaper editor, that the island could offer the rest cure he needs. "I was down there last summer," the physician says, "and I don't believe there is a more out-of-the-way, switched off sort of place in the United States." The sickly editor snorts in reply: "What! That ridiculous little dead-alive down-east sandbank, where there are six women to one man!" But desperate for a cure, he goes to that "reservoir of femininity" and finds, surprisingly, "the fountain of youth," a place that offers freedom from work and cares, an abundance of healthy outdoor recreation, and a bevy of smart, lovely women who clamor for his attention and a marriage proposal. In the end the editor finds his woman—and brings her back to the city.[26]

Bellamy's frothy story of male-and-female courtship has none of the imaginative power of Melville's novel about the sperm whale fishery. It shows that the island had fallen in popular esteem from its status as a legendary port out of which aggressive men departed to exploit the wide bounty of Second Earth and then became nothing more than a convalescent home for tired and impotent men, where only the women were numerous and strong and had color in their cheeks.

Some of the residents had fought the decline all along and had tried hard to transform the island into a thriving, if modest economy. Their dream was to recreate Nantucket as a place of intelligent farming mixed with light industry, where families could settle and sustain themselves far into the future. For two or three decades they pursued their vision of agrarian domesticity. As one of their leaders, the Reverend Edward Hatfield, put it, "We have made a slight mistake in supposing, because we are placed in the midst of the sea, that we are to obtain our subsistence from the water; but ... our business lies rather within the limits of the island, than abroad."[27] Accepting their environmental limits and making the most of them seemed to indicate a future of farming, which in the minds of its promoters was an idea that had never really been tried.

The founding of the Nantucket Agricultural Society in 1856 was meant to stop the decline and create a new, more stable ecological and social foundation. A few of the prominent remaining men, with their womenfolk supporting the cause, organized an agricultural fair and cattle show. Stock-raising was a key part of their alternative economy—producing well-bred stallions and mares, pure Devon and Durham cows, and pigs, ducks, chickens, and geese as well as a better assortment of rams and ewes. They did not propose to make Nantucket over into a nationally competitive farm, but only to recreate traditional agriculture along more modern lines, compatible with science and the mechanic arts, conserving of the soil and other natural resources, and producing a healthy product that would find a good market.[28]

Besides livestock, the agricultural visionaries called for planting more flowers and fruit trees on the island and experimental field crops of barley, corn, hay, oats, potatoes, rye, wheat, cranberries, turnips, beans, and carrots. Forest restoration was also needed. Improved soils were another essential item in the plan, and the means for their improvement, it was said, lay offshore in the form of kelp, a form of large algae growing in shallow waters that could be collected by hand and applied to the land as fertilizer. No stable community would ever emerge without fertilizer. The new kelp-based agriculture would solve that problem. Later generations would call this idea "sustainable agriculture," but whatever the name, the vision of a more permanent husbandry seemed for a while possible for a community desperate to rescue itself from oblivion.

Twenty years after the agricultural society's founding, the vision was still far from being realized. In fact Nantucket's residents had begun looking beyond farming for a solution. Despite elite support and urging, most islanders did not want to become farmers, progressive or traditional; they preferred either to emigrate or to try something besides husbandry. Apparently, the prospect of turning a sandy moraine swept by salt air into an abundance of food was too daunting and unrewarding. Cutting kelp and hauling mountains of it back to shore and getting it to their fields entailed too much hard labor for too small a reward. Perhaps it had worked for peasants elsewhere who were pushing against the limits of their land, but it did not seem like good family economics in the new world, at least not yet.

Ironically, writes historian James Alsop, the schemes of the agricultural society did bear some fruit, but not the fruit that was expected or wanted. Nantucket, through the reformers' efforts, became "a healthier, more beautiful, and more diversified island, but not one capable of sustaining its population." When growing numbers of tourists began to arrive during the 1870s, among them Edward Bellamy, "they found an island untouched by large-scale industry, with beautiful gardens, bountiful fruit, developing woodlots, and diverse, expertly created, small crafts."[29] They liked what they saw and decided to stay wherever they could find lodging. Observing that positive response from off-islanders, Nantucket decided that milking the tourists for their dollars was easier than milking a Jersey cow. By the early twentieth century tourism, with all its costs as well as rewards, had become a way of life on Nantucket.

The declining whaling industry had left behind rotting wharves, decrepit warehouses, and empty streets and family dwellings. Much of the island had become a ghost settlement. Ironically, tourists loved ghosts. They loved the gardens and woodlots, but they were even more entranced by old tales of going to sea, fighting with toothed whales, and bringing back millions of dollars worth of cargo. Thrilling rumors told of whale crews that out of desperation turned to eating each other. After fossicking around in that ghostly past, reliving the old whaling days, the tourist could stroll along an unpopulated beach, indulge in a few hours of "sea bathing," and refreshed by cooling breezes from the ocean, feel liberated from his dreary life at home.

Tourists began to visit the island from mainland Hyannis or Woods Hole by a steamship line, which in 1874 added the *River Queen* to transport the growing day-trippers. That same year, in August, the president of the United States, Ulysses Grant, came to Nantucket, generating invaluable publicity. To accommodate the increase in tourists, the islanders built their first hotels and boarding houses, sold their shabby old fishing cottages to the newcomers, fixed up their own residences, and invested in the Surfside Land Company, which began subdividing the island and promoting a real-estate development for seasonal use. They even built a short railroad line to move tourists about, avoiding the rutted, sandy tracks that had long connected the island's population. It would be many decades before the summer tourists outnumbered the local residents, but the day would come when in a single season as many as 50,000 visitors— a dozen times the number of year-round residents—came to pedal about on bicycles, eat clams and hot dogs, buy souvenirs, and take photos at the beach.[30]

The island could live by selling hot dogs and postcards to the tourist hordes, but it was another precarious strategy. Whaling had brought in profits on a scale that would never be duplicated in subsequent years. Not enough income came from tourism to maintain the artifacts of the past or meet the visitors' expectations in lodging and dining. By the 1950s the place still could not say that it had truly recovered from the heyday of a century earlier.

Then entered a wealthy businessman, Walter Beinecke Jr., heir to the S & H Green Stamp reward program for retail consumers, to try to save the islands one more time. He would work to undo the damage that popular tourism had caused, repair neglected historical treasures, take over local businesses, and attract only the wealthiest investors in local real estate.[31] Nantucket would perforce become a much more expensive place to live—a refuge for the rich and powerful trying to escape from the modern world that they had had a large hand in creating. But as a seasonal residence for the upper bourgeoisie, a vacation retreat for very wealthy urbanites, the Beinecke strategy seemed better than the vicissitudes of popular tourism alone.

In the old whaling days one of the most dreaded dangers of the chase was a "Nantucket sleigh ride," when a harpooned whale took off in frenzied fear and pain, pulling a whaleboat of hunters in its wake. Up and down the waves they bounced, like a winter sleigh racing over drifts of snow. If the pace became too rapid and the boat was near to capsizing, someone might have to cut the tethering rope. They would lose the whale but save their own lives. Now, after three and a half centuries of exploiting every possibility, intensely hunting whales and then tourists, Nantucket's wild rides of the past seemed to be over, and all was safe. But there was still a tethering rope, making the island dependent on outside money and resources.

This last Nantucket acquired a calm, permanent look. Few of the old families lived here, but the old windmill still stood near the once busy little jail, and streets of antique houses were now carefully preserved against decay. Nature once more covered much of the land with a stunted but green forest, and the birds found a secure place to nest. Through corporate intervention the place became carefully protected from the ravages of growth, with rigid enforcement of heritage and nature conservation standards. But to conclude that life in this no-longer new world had reached a point of equilibrium would be erroneous. Nantucket kept itself alive by importing virtually everything it consumed. Its food came from around the nation and the world, and so too did the energy needed to support its high standard of living. The island's latest mode of existence, as a well-endowed and well-maintained enclave for the affluent, might turn out to be the most vulnerable and unsustainable mode ever devised.

As a parable of Second Earth, the story of Nantucket illustrates how the opening of a hitherto unknown hemisphere awakened among Europeans a yearning for infinite riches. Millions felt that hunger; a few thousand of them found their way to this small, spare stretch of sand and saltwater. When they found more disappointment than fulfillment, they began looking beyond their immediate surroundings toward the farthest horizons. Always someplace else, out there in the blue, was the promise of more. No small island, nor even large continents or oceans, could long satisfy their dreams of plenty.

But what if the whole United States or even the whole Western Hemisphere came to be seen as nothing but a small island? What if the earth itself became a kind of island floating in cold, sterile space—overpopulated, shrinking in resources, vulnerable to limits? Would the experience of Nantucket serve as a helpful guide to inhabitants of that earth? The barren little sandbar could offer many insights into how a spirit of expansion and opportunism had worked, or at least worked for a while before failing. Call it whaleboat economics. But the island had not yet provided a model of how to live more permanently in a place, an example of John Stuart Mill's civilized stationary state. Perhaps it never would.

PART II

After the Frontier

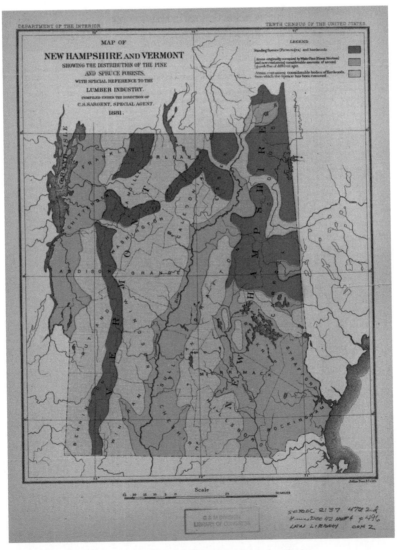

Watershed map of New Hampshire and Vermont (*see color plate*)

CHAPTER 4

The Watershed

A HORSE-DRAWN CARRIAGE STOPPED AT the summit of a low hill nestled among Vermont's Green Mountains, and while the horse rested the driver explained to his small son the view below. Charles Marsh, a prominent lawyer in the village of Woodstock, pointed out to four-year-old George that rain falling on the hills ran off in many directions, forming streams and rivers that ended in the sea. The summit where they sat was called a dividing point, or "watershed." Waters ran down one side to form a stream, while other waters ran down the opposite side to form another stream. Sometimes those streams came together, sometimes they flowed toward different seas, but in the end their common destiny was the Atlantic Ocean. Waters divided, and then they united. That was how all of nature worked: conflicts, divisions, and contraries existed, but always they were integral parts of a harmonious cycle of balance and renewal.

That concept of a harmoniously integrated watershed was etched in little George's mind for the rest of his life. Three-quarters of a century later, in 1881, he published an article on the subject in *Johnson's New Universal Cyclopedia*. A watershed, he declared, is "an imaginary line which runs along the ridge of separation between adjacent seas, lakes or river-valleys, and represents the limit from which the water of precipitation naturally flows in opposite directions into different basins." While most of his contemporaries thought hard about their sins, commodity markets, Manifest Destiny, and slavery, George Perkins Marsh grew up thinking about the intricate order of watersheds. So did a few other Americans, and together they created a national conservation movement. One of its guiding principles was that the nation's watersheds must be protected from ignorant assault. The watershed was a natural order or limit that must be respected.[1]

"Limit" can seem a dull word, old-fashioned in its tut-tut warnings, dampening fires in the human spirit. Vermont's frontiersmen wanted to see a green light on the horizon and dream exuberantly about nature and the future. To conserve the natural order was to stay home and take care of things, when what they most wanted was to find a bonanza over the next hill. When conservation became an organized political and intellectual movement in the United States during the nineteenth century, its mission of teaching sobriety and caution encountered resistance from many frontiersmen and entrepreneurs. They did not want to learn its lessons and fought back with fierce passion. But conservation came with a passion of its own— a new urgency to protect the fragile earth, to learn about nature's limits, and to savor the beauty of an unspoiled ridgeline clothed in heathy forests or a river edged by trees and alive with bird songs.

Forests, the conservationists began to insist to whoever would listen, protect watersheds and assure a continuous flow of water. Cut them down, and floods or droughts increase. Save the forests, and the nation can secure a permanent supply of essential natural resources: wood, water, biota, and soil, and not least of all a surpassing elegance that humans did not create. To understand the deep coherence of the earth as an integrated system requires the combined knowledge of many sciences, including geomorphology, hydrology, botany, and what some scientists in the late nineteenth century began calling "ecology," the study of the interdependence of all life in its environment. If humans failed to acquire that knowledge or chose not to see nature's coherence, they would suffer consequences. Eventually they would run out of resources, destroy their livelihoods, and feel insecure in their homes and settlements.

Thus, to conserve nature meant first and foremost protecting the watershed. This protection was practical and scientific, yet it was also ethical and aesthetic. It promised to sustain the nation and yet also satisfy the soul and teach reverence and respect for the earth. It was the beginnings of a new ethic for a postfrontier society.

For Americans the conservation movement began in New England among educated and yet non-metropolitan people like Charles Marsh and his son George. Their home village of Woodstock was located on the Queechee River, a tributary of the Connecticut.

Both father and son year by year witnessed a wholesale forest devastation going on around them to create pastures for sheep and fields for grain, and they asked whether there were better ways to live on the land. Because of increased danger of flooding, the family was forced to move from the banks of the Queechee to higher ground. Yet the clearing of hillside forests continued, increasing the run-off, and would go on doing so until the sheep industry collapsed. Conservation was born among those who may have experienced danger firsthand, but not among those frontiersmen who were sure nature would always bend to their will.[2]

Young Marsh was never cut out to be an axe-wielding frontiersman, nor for that matter was he well suited to law, business, the ministry, or other leading occupations available in the Vermont of his day. His parents had endowed him with a keen intelligence and a stern view of the world, derived from their Puritan-Congregationalist ancestors. But he grew up something of a misfit in his society. In the eyes of his wife, he was "a timid, gentle, solitary bookworm who preferred to be indoors," not tramping up and down the hills or following a plow or drawing up deeds and wills. After graduating from Dartmouth College, he entered legal practice in Burlington, Vermont. Eager to escape the backwardness of a frontier life, to experience a larger world with more cultural richness, he decided to run for national political office. At age 43 he became a candidate on the Whig ticket for a seat in the US House of Representatives, and he won. He was, however, no partisan and proved no more suited to politics than to other popular professions.[3]

For George Marsh, being useful to society meant thinking in broader terms than making money or solving his constituents' mundane problems. He wanted to probe into the depths and origins of things. He wanted to learn languages and understand the evolution of culture. He loved exploring theories of how the earth worked. No pedant or dilettante, he was a problem solver, but the problems he saw went deeper than those that daily faced a small-town Vermont farmer or lawyer. Ultimately, they came down to the great problem of how Americans should live sustainably on the land after the frontier had passed.

With a huge question like that buzzing in his head, Marsh should have become a scholar. But when offered a professorship at Harvard, he declined because it did not pay enough. Somewhere in his growing up he had acquired the tastes of an aristocrat, always hungry for the finer things in life, especially art and books. Lacking inherited wealth, he could not afford those on a professor's salary. Fortunately, he found a way to thrive both as a scholar and aristocrat, scientist and lover of the arts, by joining the American diplomatic corps.

In 1849, the year of the California gold rush, Marsh became foreign minister to Turkey, pushing him eastward into antiquity as his nation swept westward toward an uncertain future. President Abraham Lincoln later appointed him chief diplomat to Italy, where he served for twenty years, escaping not only the trauma of America's Civil War but also its Gilded Age of rapacious greed. As an expatriate, he was spared the problem of finding a place within American society. In his mind, however, he never left the Vermont frontier and its damaged watersheds completely behind. On the contrary, he was haunted by that place and its history. Wherever he went ravaged forests and flooding rivers were running through his mind. After his undemanding duties as ambassador were completed, he had enough time to read and think deeply about what should follow frontier expansion. What should be conserved? What should be, he asked himself, a nation's long-term relation to nature?

Marsh's most important intellectual achievement was his book *Man and Nature; or, Physical Geography as Modified by Human Action* (1864). Written in an old manor house in Italy's Po Valley, the book was an amalgamation of his life's observations, some of them gathered from a buggy seat in Vermont, others from the back of a camel in the Middle East, and still others from hikes into the ice-carved heights of the Alps. He also synthesized the writings of numerous European scientific thinkers who had begun to make the forested watershed their frame of analysis. German and Swiss writers led the list, including Alexander von Humboldt, Karl Ritter, and Arnold Henry Guyot, but there were many French, Italian, Dutch, and British authorities as well. Together, they taught him that the "earth is fast becoming an unfit home for its noblest inhabitant," and for reasons quite unflattering to human pride.[4] Noble in their own self-image, humans everywhere were behaving in stupid, brutal, and improvident ways, threatening self-extinction. *Man and Nature* was a doomsday warning, announcing that the species must learn to live within the limits of the earth or lose its civilization.

Marsh allowed that it was "rash and unphilosophical to attempt to set limits to the ultimate power of man over inorganic nature." Sharing his age's faith in human reason, he speculated than someday humans would discover how to tap directly the energy of the sun, which would expand the possibilities of wealth beyond imagining. But such technological optimism needed to be balanced by awareness of the damage that people were doing, and had long done, to the order of nature. "Man," he wrote, "is everywhere a disturbing agent. Wherever he plants his foot, the harmonies of nature are turned to discords."[5]

Looking back on the history of Europe and Asia, Marsh saw warnings for his own country. Given enough centuries to recover, all damaged lands would eventually restore themselves to fertility and stability. But could people wait that long? Where would they live in the interim? Three and a half centuries after Columbus, it was beginning to appear that there were no infinite frontiers where one could go and wait for that recovery to take place. "Man, who even now finds scarce breathing room on this vast globe, cannot retire from the Old World to some yet undiscovered continent, and wait for the slow action of such causes to replace, by a new creation, the Eden he has wasted."[6] There was no Third Earth coming into view; there was only a single planet that was united by a common, universal history of frontier expansion and frontier degradation.

Marsh's book represents an important intellectual moment in the transition from an age of plenty to an age of limits. Before his time the currents of thought flowed heavily toward celebrating the plentitude of the world and an unbounded future of progress. But with the rise of the conservation movement, in North America and elsewhere, a new set of attitudes emerged—a hopeful response to an environment that had been severely deforested, overfarmed, and ecologically disrupted, but could be restored to wholeness. As the destruction gathered force, so did the opposing current of conservation. Marsh was pivotal in shaping those new attitudes, within the United States but also in Europe and around the world.

Two chapters in his book, one on "The Woods" and the other on "The Waters," capture the two halves of the early conservation movement, one focused on forest conservation and the other on water and watershed protection. Other chapters discuss plant and animal species and drifting sand dunes, but those two central chapters, constituting nearly two-thirds of the book, were the keys to understanding land unity. The significance of forests began back as far as the Book of Genesis. If the earth had been all one Eden in the beginning, Marsh wrote, then the fall of Eden began with "the destruction of the woods, man's first physical conquest, his first violation of the harmonies of inanimate nature." Cutting down forests led to extreme oscillations in river flow, climate, temperature, wind, and humidity. "The majority of the foresters and physicists who have studied the question," Marsh concluded, "are of opinion that in many, if not in all cases, the destruction of the woods has been followed by a diminution in the annual quantity of rain and dew." Or, as he put it more pungently: "The face of the earth is no longer a sponge but a dust heap."[7] Soil loss followed forest clearing, lowering the capacity of the countryside to support farmers, livestock, and crops. Floods increased in the downstream valleys, wreaking damage to town and country alike.

Agriculture was not for Marsh, as it was for Moses in the book of Genesis, a punishment that followed disobedience to God—a hard way of life that was the consequence of expulsion from the Garden of Eden. Agriculture was the original sin, the force that had invaded Eden and destroyed it. The ancient invasion of the biblical garden was now continuing in North America, and again farmers were mainly to blame. "The needs of agriculture," Marsh pointed out, "are the most familiar cause of the destruction of the forest in new countries." Such criticisms would not have been taken easily by Vermont's farmers or foresters or by the peasants and woodsmen of France or Italy, all of whom saw themselves as virtuous improvers and their rural landscapes as aesthetically pleasing.[8] But statistical evidence supported Marsh's case that deforestation by agriculturists had acquired a dangerous momentum. In the hundred years that preceded his book France had lost more than half of its forests, while in the United States the cutting of trees had nearly doubled. Indeed, the whole planet was losing forests at an accelerating rate, and everywhere it was mainly due to expanding agriculture.[9]

Marsh demonstrated how massive changes to the flow of water followed the farmer's frontier—draining wetlands, constructing dikes, and diverting rivers into irrigation ditches. While all seemed well on the surface, and the increased production fed more people, he wondered what the unforeseen consequences would be and how long the rearranged landscapes would work. Floods were increasingly destructive across Europe, as though imposing order in one place made disorder break out someplace else. History taught that all conquests over nature lasted for only a limited time and then collapsed. New civilizations seldom flourished where old ones had self-destructed. "A question of vast importance" emerged out of this sweeping view of the past: "How far it is practicable to replace the garden we have wasted?"[10] Humans had learned how to take the world apart, but so far they had not learned how to put it back together again.

The New York publisher Charles Scribner published Marsh's book in May 1864, just as Ulysses S. Grant and Robert E. Lee were pitting their troops and armaments against each other to decide the fate of the Union and General William T. Sherman was launching a campaign to bring down Atlanta. Yet amazingly, above the din of battle, the book found eager readers. Thousands of copies sold in the first few months. A London edition appeared simultaneously, and an Italian one in 1869. Five years later Marsh published a second edition titled *The Earth as Modified by Human Action*, and in 1885 a posthumous third edition came out.

The change in title suggested that the author saw his most important contribution to be the idea that humans in general, not only farmers, exercised a growing and dangerous power to modify the earth. But that was not altogether a new thought. In the eighteenth century France's celebrated naturalist Comte de Buffon had heralded the arrival of an age in which humans had become dominant. "The state in which we see nature today," he wrote, "is as much our work as it is hers."[11] Buffon was enthusiastic about a new age of human domination, as were Karl Marx and Friedrich Engels, who in their *Communist Manifesto* of 1848 pointed to a drastic transformation of the earth:

> The bourgeoisie, during its rule of scarce one hundred years, has created more massive and more colossal productive forces than have all preceding generations together. Subjection of Nature's forces to man, machinery, application of chemistry to industry and agriculture, steam-navigation, railways, electric telegraphs, clearing of whole continents for cultivation, canalisation of rivers, whole populations conjured out of the ground—what earlier century had even a presentiment that such productive forces slumbered in the lap of social labour?[12]

Compared to those predecessors, Marsh went much further in describing scientifically the "subjection of Nature's forces." His most unique contribution, however, came from the fact that unlike Buffon or Marx, he saw the power of humans as destructive, not progressive.[13]

"Man has too long forgotten that the earth was given to him for usufruct alone, not for consumption," Marsh wrote. "Man is everywhere a disturbing agent. Wherever he plants his foot, the harmonies of nature are turned to discords." While others had trumpeted the great revolutions in economic production going on, Marsh took a darker view: "Man alone is to be regarded as essentially a destructive power." He did not call for a return to more primitive days, but he saw arrogance and folly, not happiness, in that vaunted human power to conquer the world. And therein lay his surprising impact on a war-ravaged nation, for Americans at that moment were feeling shaken in self-confidence by their capacity for violence.[14]

Unlike his predecessors, George Perkins Marsh was awed by the original forests that had once covered the world, and nowhere more so than in North America. Buffon, Marx and Engels, and the priests, aristocrats, and peasants among whom Marsh lived in Italy did not share that awe, for they had never seen such forests. No such wild green splendor remained anywhere in Western Europe, and had not since the medieval clearances. But it was spectacularly on display in New England and New York, around the Great Lakes, down the eastern mountain ranges from Maine to Georgia, and scattered across the mountainous West. Vast inroads had been made into that forest splendor by the mid-nineteenth century. Marsh's contemporary Henry David Thoreau had lamented in his journal that "the woods within my recollection have gradually withdrawn" from his home village of Concord, Massachusetts, just twenty miles west of Boston. "Thank God," he wrote, "men cannot as yet fly, and lay waste the sky as well as the earth! We are safe on that side for the present."[15] Forest laments like those, based on direct observation of losses, laid the foundation for American conservation.

Marsh, like other conservationists, accepted that Americans had a right to use forests to further their development. But his countrymen should learn, as the Europeans were learning, the arts of forest conservation, protecting what they could and planting new trees where old ones had been cut down. He called for a remnant of the original wild forest of the new world to be preserved for future generations.

> It is desirable that some large and easily accessible region of American soil should remain, as far as possible, in its primitive condition, at once a museum for the instruction of the student, a garden for the recreation of the lover of nature, and an asylum where indigenous tree, and humble plant that loves the shade, and fish and fowl and four-footed beast, may dwell and perpetuate their kind, in the enjoyment of such imperfect protection as the laws of a people jealous of restraint can afford them.[16]

A wiser and more restrained use of forests, then, and in places a restraint from all use, was what conservation meant to Marsh, as it did for others in the postfrontier era.

Although he lived abroad much of his life, Marsh taught his fellow Americans to see and accept the vulnerability of the country they had come to possess. During his lifetime the United States had expanded its borders from the Mississippi River to the West Coast, sweeping up much of what had been northern Mexico and taking possession of Russia's former colony, Alaska. It was an immense stretch of land, but it was quickly occupied and exploited. Within a few years after Marsh's death, citizens would learn from the Census Bureau that the once open frontier of settlement was closing. The historian Frederick Jackson Turner, speaking at the Chicago World's Fair of 1893, lamented the end of that frontier and its role in making the nation unique in the world. Now every part of the country was inhabited by at least a scattering of white Americans, while Indians were confined to reservations. Cities and factories were proliferating across the continent. America could go no farther in territorial expansion. After reading Marsh's book, James McCosh, president of Princeton, remarked about the nation: "We have been brought sharply to a realizing sense of our natural limitations."[17]

Introducing a new sense of limits, Marsh's book also pushed many to begin rethinking the role of government in the United States. The frontier period of infinite abundance had created a culture of personal freedom, individual enterprise, and hostility to government that now began to seem excessive and irresponsible. Marsh was not a critic of all private enterprise, but neither was he a defender of unlimited rights for people to do as they pleased with the forests. Commerce had gone too far toward anarchy. Freed of all protection, nature had been "unscrupulously plundered and wantonly laid waste" both by unregulated business corporations and by the common folk, who had neither the knowledge nor wisdom to exercise restraint.[18]

The notion that those who lived directly on the land were best equipped and motivated to conserve it was an idea that ran counter to what Marsh had observed on the frontier of Vermont and in the history of Europe. Local protection was always late in coming, too weakly enforced to be effective, too susceptible to business interests, too narrow in its understanding of nature's complexities. Conservation required a stronger government informed by science and awakened to its responsibilities to legislate, preserve, and regulate on behalf of all the people and indeed all forms of life.

No one felt that fear of local control more than Charles Sprague Sargent, professor of botany at Harvard College and director of Boston's Arnold Arboretum, established in 1872. He was Marsh's most important disciple in the nineteenth century. "I have long been a student of *Man and Nature*," he wrote to Marsh, "and have derived great pleasure and profit from your pages." So inspiring was the book that Sargent undertook, with government support, the first comprehensive inventory of America's remaining forests for the Tenth Annual Census. Published in 1884 as *Report on the Forests of North America (Exclusive of Mexico)*, the book was almost six hundred pages long and filled with graphs and charts that provided the best data base of its time for the forests. It also featured colored maps of forests and their watersheds, showing the connections that nature created through flowing water. (See Plate 3 for Marsh's home state of Vermont). Those maps were guides to the limits of the land—here is how nature has organized the landscape, they said, and here are the lines and limits that humans must respect. The information came from scientific investigation backed by government.

Above all, it was the mountain forests that worried Sargent, as they had Marsh. "Their destruction does not mean a loss of material alone, which sooner or later can be replaced from other parts of the country; it means the ruin of great rivers for navigation and irrigation, the destruction of cities located along their banks, and the spoliation of broad areas of the richest agriculture land." Individual trees could be replaced; they were a renewable resource that could be harvested and replanted. But complex, self-renewing, well-functioning forests could not be so easily replaced, and they were essential to the hydrological cycle, serving as reservoirs of precipitation and playing a stabilizing role in the economy of nature and of humankind. Only government could protect them.[19]

Another man who heard that call for a more vigorous governmental role in providing information and protection was Franklin B. Hough, a physician and naturalist living just west of the Adirondack Mountains. When the American Association for the Advancement of Science met in Portland, Maine, in August 1873, the members listened to Hough's address, "On the Duty of Governments in the Preservation of Forests." He argued that government's role should mainly be to educate rather than to force "the great masses of our rural population and land owners" to adopt more correct ideas about planting and protecting forests. But "there will still arise the need of laws to regulate, promote, and protect the growth of wood."

He called on New York legislators to establish a public park in the Adirondacks to preserve its densely forested mountains and the state's critical water supply. Hough's address was cited widely in the press and led to his appointment as the first special agent for forestry in the US Department of Agriculture.[20]

The backwoods doctor who became the government's forest expert was not the only voice for saving the Adirondacks as a vital watershed. Covering an area the size of Connecticut, its wild lands were increasingly seen as a last refuge where people could camp on the shores of pristine lakes and hear the wild call of the loon. But lumbering companies and railroad corporations were threatening to invade that remote country and reduce it to stumps and slash. Already water levels in the Hudson River and the Erie Canal were falling, and business interests downstate were becoming alarmed, demanding that politicians protect their state's most important watershed. In 1885 legislators set aside 715,000 acres in the Adirondacks as a permanent reserve of "wild forest lands." Nine years later they put into the state constitution an even more secure protection for the mountain watersheds, specifying that they be kept "forever wild."[21]

Legislators in the nation's capital were also beginning to accept that they had a duty to restrict the use of forests and protect their timber, beauty, and role in stabilizing the water supply. In 1891 Congress passed a bill to curb the liberality of western homesteading laws, making fraudulent entries more difficult, and they surprised many by including a clause that authorized the president to establish a series of forest reserves in the West. President Benjamin Harrison seized the power given him and designated western forest reserves covering 13 million acres, beginning with the area around Yellowstone National Park. Their purpose was not unlike that of the Adirondack state park: the reserves would protect natural forests both for their aesthetic and utilitarian function. Every reserve was drawn up as a watershed unit, based on extensive mapping that showed how woods and waters were united in the landscape.

Congress also began protecting large sections of the Sierra Nevada range in California for similar reasons of watershed protection, forest conservation, and outdoor recreation. Three national parks were created there in the single year of 1890: Yosemite, Kings Canyon, and Sequoia (Yellowstone had become the first national park in 1872). The California naturalist John Muir had drawn the boundaries of the largest of those new parks, Yosemite, covering 2 million acres—and he drew those boundaries to conform to the watersheds creating two rivers flowing from the Sierra highlands, the Tuolumne and the Merced.[22]

Muir, author of *The Mountains of California* (1894), was another forest activist influenced by Marsh. First seeing the Sierra Nevada in 1868, Muir read Marsh's book just a few years later. Under its influence he published a newspaper article on saving the Sierra's coniferous forests and warning that they were "the most destructible of the natural resources of California."[23] From Marsh he learned that European governments, especially in France, Germany, Italy, and Austria, had begun to promote conservation, but "whether our loose jointed Government is really able or willing to do anything in the matter remains to be seen." In fact the US government was beginning to do quite a lot and eventually would create a national forest and park system far grander than anything in Europe. Nothing said more clearly that a time of unlimited forest and water plenty was over, and that a new day of limits had dawned.

When in 1896 Congress set up a National Forest Commission to create that public land system, Charles Sprague Sargent became its chairman and recruited Muir as an unofficial member. The commission's secretary was a young man eager to join the conservation movement, Gifford Pinchot. On his twenty-fifth birthday his father, a rich New York merchant, had given him a copy of Marsh's book, hoping it would inspire him to become a forester and a conservationist. The book convinced Pinchot that he should spend a year at the French forestry school in Nancy, after which he returned with ambitions to create a public forestry program for the United States. In 1898 he became Hough's successor in the Division of Forestry, and from 1901 to 1910 he served as chief of the US Forest Service. In his autobiography, *Breaking New Ground*, Pinchot called Marsh's book "epoch-making." But by then he had come to see himself, not Marsh or anyone else, as the greatest pathfinder in the conservation movement.[24]

Pinchot had a point in his self-aggrandizement. Marsh's book was only one of many calls to action, and his call needed political leadership to have a lasting impact. The former congressman, however, had long ago abandoned politics for the library. A photograph taken late in his life shows a portly, bearded man, wearing thick eyeglasses, seated at a large, heavy reading table with a book propped up before him. Marsh is sitting in his library in Florence surrounded by the accoutrements of gentility: a large chandelier hangs overhead, marble busts are arrayed on dark tables around the spacious room, the walls are lined with books and decorated with classical

Italian friezes and antique landscapes. Nothing in the picture suggests the New England forest or stream. Nothing suggests a political activist. Such a scholar working in his study might change thousands of minds, but then those readers had to organize themselves and act. It was men like Muir and Pinchot who established parks and forests covering millions of acres, set limits to America's pursuit of happiness, and in doing so redefined the role of the state.

There was, however, an unsuspected weakness in the conservation movement's early program of action. They demanded reform of the old ways, while new ways of living on the land were gathering momentum. Marsh's call for preserving watersheds was a rational response to a problem created by frontier agriculture. He was right that farmers had been a disturbing force for a very long time, and that modern science was needed to check their wasteful ways. But what if the farmer was not the only threat? What if the disturbing force began coming from industry as well as agriculture? What if water, trees, and soil were no longer the only important resources in the economy, and other resources—minerals like oil, coal, and iron—took their place in a new, postfrontier society? What then would be the relevance of Marsh's idea of conservation?

Long after the frontier closed and agriculture was no longer expanding its empire, the United States would continue to press dangerously on the natural world and encounter new vulnerabilities. Even as Marsh was writing his epochal book, the nation was changing. Standing at its new economic center was not the farm or forest but the steel mill, spewing toxic waste, consuming the earth with great violence, and creating a new industrial order. Neither Marsh nor any of his readers and disciples were quite prepared to grapple with the destructive force that industrialization represented.

CHAPTER 5

Land of Coal and Steel

EXHAUST ONE RESOURCE IN THE land of plenty, and another will surely take its place. There can never be any shortage of nature's goods so long as some remnant of Second Earth is still out there waiting to be exploited and brought to market. So resource optimists, repudiating the limited-world ethic of the conservationists, began to teach Americans in the late nineteenth and early twentieth century.

A prominent spokesman for that view was Simon Patten, professor of political economy at the University of Pennsylvania's Wharton School of Finance. In *The New Basis of Civilization* (1907) he declared that scarcity belonged to the past, abundance for all lay within reach. "The final victory of man's machinery over nature's materials is the next logical process in evolution, as nature's control of human society was the transition from anarchic and puny individualism to the group, acting as a powerful, intelligent organism. Machinery, science, and intelligence moving on the face of the earth, may well affect it as the elements do, up building, obliterating, and creating; but they are man's forces and will be used to hasten his dominion over nature."[1] No nation, he was arguing, would ever run out of resources. Through developing its collective intelligence, no nation needed ever again to confront scarcity of any kind. Long live the age of abundance.

Resources, however, are not simply inventions of the human mind, conjured out of thin air. Some resources have been more basic and universal than others. Some have been indispensable requirements for all forms of life, not exempting humans, and have never lost their importance or become superfluous. For example, fresh water has always been a vital necessity. There has not been any substitute for water in the human body or in nature. Yet its overall supply is more or less a fixed quantity, barring a miracle that would make the oceans drinkable. Always replenished by the hydrological cycle, water is also limited by that cycle. It is a fixed resource—vital to our own nature and not merely socially defined. Its consumption might expand or contract, it might be polluted or wasted, but its necessity has not diminished.

No more water flowed in North America in Patten's day than during the time of Columbus, nor would there be any more water long after Patten was gone. In 1907, the year of his book's publication, 87 million people had come to depend on that fixed supply, and their demands for water had become greater than ever before. That resource would come under more and more pressure over the next hundred years. By 2005 the average American would use 80 to 100 gallons a day for personal consumption, bringing demand to dangerously high levels.[2] Water would become not increasingly abundant, but increasingly scarce. Only through more efficient reuse and recycling could the available supply continue to meet demand.

Wood was a somewhat more variable need. By 1870 it had been replaced as the primary source of the nation's energy supplies. But that did not mean the demand for wood declined; on the contrary, it continued to grow. Michael Williams has tracked the role of wood in the American economy from colonial times to the present and concludes that today "nearly as much wood is being used than was ever used before." While wood would cease to be needed for making tools, dinner plates, or wheeled vehicles, it would continue to supply fuel for stoves, lumber for housing, and pulp for paper, along with various chemicals for home and industry. There might be substitutes for specific wood uses, but there was no substitute for the forests.[3]

Patten was right in believing that a land so munificently blessed by abundance had not yet yielded all its treasures. There were still resources lying hidden under the surface and ignored by earlier Americans, and in his time they were beginning to come into heavy use. By the late nineteenth century the nation was recreating itself as an industrial economy, which meant digging up hitherto neglected resources from deep within the earth's crust. Most important were the fossil fuels, coal and oil, but iron and copper were important too.

The first European settlements, made in the early seventeenth century, had little knowledge of or use for the fossil fuels, but later they would become a necessity for economic growth, and by the twentieth century they would dominate America's energy supplies. Suddenly, over a span of mere decades, coal leaped to the forefront— neither human nor animal labor, wood or waterpower, could match the energy it provided. By 1850 the United States had become highly dependent on coal; nearly 10 million tons were mined in that year, with more than four times that amount in 1870. By 1900 the nation was annually mining 260 million tons.[4]

Throughout the nineteenth century Pennsylvania was by far the leading American producer of coal. So significant was the state that scientists attached its name to the geological period that ended 300 million years ago during which wood and other plants became fossilized on a gargantuan scale. In that period new species of bark-bearing trees had evolved, impervious to tree-eating bacteria, which could not decompose their thick outer fibers filled with lignin. Instead of turning into mold and dust, those trees had been preserved intact in swamps and bogs and transformed, under intense heat and pressure, into coal. Now those ancient forests lay folded and buried under Pennsylvania's long, narrow mountains. Their remains ran like dark stains through pages and pages of buried sediments.

Not only Pennsylvania but also parts of Ohio, Kentucky, West Virginia, Illinois, Missouri, Kansas, Colorado, and the northern Plains contained coal—hidden from view until Americans were ready to discover a need for it. Blessed with that mineral abundance, Americans would become the greatest industrial society in the world. Mining and burning fossil energy, however, would bring land, air, water, and human degradation as vicious as any in history. After the frontier came not only new resources but also new problems and new limits.[5]

Prior to mining, Pennsylvania was endowed with an estimated 23 billion tons of anthracite coal and 84 billion tons of bituminous.[6] Anthracite was coal that had been compressed in the earth so densely that it was nearly stone, brittle and shiny. Once ignited, it burned with a hot blue flame. A single pound could yield 15,000 Btu's of heat. Seams of this "stone coal" lay under the rugged eastern mountains of the state, in the counties of Schuylkill, Carbon, Luzerne, and Lackawanna. Those coal beds were close to eastern seaboard cities like Philadelphia and New York, but because of the torturous terrain they were for a long time hard to reach. When at last the coal could be dug up and brought to market via canals, it was expensive and used only for domestic heating and small industries. Despite those drawbacks, America's industrial revolution, which had begun with dams on New England rivers, began to catch fire with hard anthracite during the 1840s. The main future of that revolution, however, lay farther west in the state of Pennsylvania, where vast bituminous beds of coal and pools of oil lay beneath the forest roots.[7]

Quaintly, coal miners mapped their deposits as "fields," suggesting a traditional agricultural economy of corn or cotton, and they gave each field a name. In western Pennsylvania the prominent fields were Black Lick, Kittanning, Clarion, Pittsburgh, and, richest of all, Connellsville, each field named after a frontier settlement on the surface. All were steeply pitched mountainsides where miners "plowed" tunnels horizontally and "harvested" the black deposits under the surface. Bituminous coal is mainly carbon but mixed with bitumen, volatile matter (making it easier to ignite, and easier to explode), sulfur, moisture, and ash. After 1852 the western half of Pennsylvania became coal land as it also became steel land.[8]

Bituminous coal could be made into coke, and coke was the fuel needed to turn iron into its superior derivative, steel, by burning away the iron ore's impurities. But to produce coke, coal had to be "baked" in oxygen-free "ovens" at temperatures exceeding 1,000 degrees Centigrade. It took prodigious energy to produce energy. Large, looming coke ovens became a familiar feature of the Pennsylvania landscape. In 1885 a single company set up a mile-long stretch of them—475 in all—to produce coke from coal, and they yielded some 22,000 tons per month.

People could see and measure the number of ovens, but the average citizen found it more difficult to see or understand the full menace of the toxic gases and particulate matter they emitted each month. Some of that menace, to be sure, was highly visible: "The most conspicuous feature in coke oven surroundings," pointed out a state biologist, "is the general wretchedness of everything of the nature of shrub or tree, either individual or collective."[9] But much of the threat was invisible to the eye—colorless and poisonous vapors emitted by the ovens. With coal's growing use in city and factory, America began to experience serious air pollution, the contamination of the atmosphere (and water and soil) by harmful substances.

Pennsylvania was also the birthplace of the world's petroleum industry. Although Canadians had dug the first oil well in 1858, near Sarnia, Ontario, they did not tap a large reservoir like the one tapped by the first well drilled in the United States, at Titusville, Pennsylvania, one year later. Here in Pennsylvania oil lay under pressure until released by a drilling rig, and then it gushed its abundance

straight into the air. It fell like a shower of rain over farm and forest-
land and ran off into the rivers and streams. Decades would go by
while men experimented with capturing that flowing oil, refining it
into kerosene and gasoline, and turning it into a shower of money.
Not until the invention and proliferation of the automobile in the
twentieth century was the latent wealth in this resource fully realized. By the 1920s oil began to surpass coal as the most important
fossil fuel for the industrial world. By then, petroleum had stimulated what historian Brian Black has called a new American ethic
of "wasting a place for the common good, of extracting a needed
resource at the cost of all else in that locale."[10]

Before the ascendancy of oil, when coal was still king, the
United States began digging as much coal out of the ground as the
other two great industrial giants, Great Britain and Germany, combined. By that point the technology and social organization of coal
mining and coal burning had advanced considerably. When primitive "drifts" or lateral holes opened straight into mountainsides,
had exhausted the most accessible seams, miners began burrowing
downward, going deeper and deeper, creating labyrinths of tunnels
supported by pillars of coal and props of lumber harvested from
the forests. They abandoned their hand picks for electric cutting
machines and their coal wagons for steam locomotives and tracks.

They also went south into West Virginia and eastern Kentucky,
looking for more and more deposits. A major railroad, the
Chesapeake and Ohio, pushed into West Virginia in 1872, opening
the New River field for mining, and by 1910 it was producing 10 million tons of coal per year. Coal mining became a heavily mechanized and capitalized business, dominated by private corporations
seeking high profits. They needed armies of wage laborers, whom
they recruited from almost all the countries of Europe and from the
hitherto isolated rural communities of Appalachia.[11]

Was there ever a temperate forest more beautiful than the one
invaded by coal miners in West Virginia—forests at least as beautiful
as those of Vermont's Green Mountains or New York's Adirondacks?
Here were sugar maples turning golden in the fall. Here grew all the
"reds" (red maple, oak, pine); the "blacks" (black oak, birch, cherry,
walnut, locust); the "whites" (white oak, pine, ash); the "yellows" (yel-
low poplar, birch); the various hickories; along with sycamore, sweet
gum, elm, spruce, hemlock, cedar, and Virginia pine. They covered
the mountains thickly, and from their slopes ran clear, sparkling
water. West Virginia's mountains were densely clustered, and the valleys between them so pinched that rivers ran fast in narrow ravines

and roads were few. A beautiful country, it was not easy to penetrate, until the coal companies arrived.

The rural frontiersmen who had settled here found themselves living cut off from the rest of America. They enjoyed natural grandeur all around them, but they had little access to the outside world and little room for developing their own agriculture or towns. All they could manage to produce was a mere subsistence for their families. Before the coal men got there West Virginia's people were among the poorest in the nation, without education or religion, living on farms that became smaller and smaller as they were subdivided among the numerous offspring. From the beginning, the region was condemned by its environmental limitations to attract only those most lacking in enterprise or opportunities elsewhere.[12]

Desperate for a supply of cash that had been denied them by their isolation, the hill farmers of southern Appalachia were not reluctant to sell their mineral rights to the mining corporations and take jobs in the coal mines, while still trying to hold on to their traditional way of life. The coal and railroad companies, however, introduced a revolutionary new calculus into their lives; where they had long lived by barter, with no money passing from hand to hand, they were forced to learn the complexities of monetary exchange and to experience the social inequality that followed. The invasion grew powerful and ruthless, and the mountaineers' efforts to join with other workers to control their living conditions sputtered and failed for decades.[13]

The wages they earned by working in the mines were scanty by outside standards, but the effects of coal on their lives were not. Down in the tunnels they died from cave-ins, explosions, and dangerous air. Outside, the landscape they had known as farmers began to change too. Large expanses of forests were chopped down and hauled away to sawmills, while the mines left the denuded hillsides raw and prone to erosion, and the tailings leaked deadly acids into the streams. Those physiological and ecological effects showed up early, in the 1880s and 1890s, long before mechanization and thinning coal seams would lead mining companies to introduce, after World War II, the land-destroying practices of strip-mining and mountain-top removal.

Enormous quantities of coal underlay much of the Appalachian Mountains, though the richest deposits were soon depleted. But coke for burning in the big ovens was not enough to make an industrial revolution. The new postfrontier America required still another resource in order to be complete—an abundance of iron ore. It too had to be located and easily mined, and it had to be easily transport-able to wherever the coke was piled. Iron is one of the most common elements in the periodic chart. It comprises the earth's molten core and is widely distributed throughout the crust. But rich concentra-tions of iron lying near the surface are not distributed equally. They originated in the Precambrian, dating from 1.9 to 2.5 billion years ago, as rock eroded from the land, washed into the sea, and was pre-cipitated under high oxygen conditions, sinking to the bottom. Only a few places had the right conditions for that deposition to occur in concentrated magnitudes. Pennsylvania, New Jersey, and New York offered a few such deposits, although not enough to sustain indus-trialization. For that purpose, Americans needed another source.[14]

Once more Lady Fortune smiled on "the blessed nation," and Pennsylvanians happily discovered that they could find a wealth of ore within easy shipping distance of their coal supplies.[15] It was located near the shores of Lake Superior, the largest of the Great Lakes—and it was not merely a single deposit but four of them lying in "ranges" stretching across northeastern Minnesota, the largest of which was the Mesabi Range. Here the precipitates had accumulated in remarkable densities, protruding as outcroppings in a lumpy land-scape dotted by many lakes and covered by northern forests.

In 1866 a Minnesota state geologist declared the Mesabi to be an important potential source of minerals, particularly gold, silver, and copper, but it was iron that came to rule the day. The Mesabi belt of iron ore turned out to be 110 miles long, averaging one to three miles wide and as thick as five hundred feet. Much of it was easily reachable from the surface, requiring no tunneling. Presented with samples of its ore, capitalists, including the oil magnate John D. Rockefeller, were quick to invest in a railroad from the lakeshore to the open pits. In 1892 the Merritt brothers of Duluth began large-scale mining operations. Iron ore is heavy, of course, but reduced to little pellets it could be conveniently brought over long distances, by rail and barge, to wherever coal was abundant. That convergence of iron and coal took place in western Pennsylvania and in other states and provinces surrounding the Great Lakes.[16]

In the mining rush that followed, the Mesabi soon ranked as the nation's most important source of iron, supplying ten times as much ore as older sources in Pennsylvania, New Jersey, and New York com-bined. Mesabi joined with Appalachia to become the foundation for a new America built of steel.

That process of industrialization redefined the nation, but it also redefined the relation of humans to nature. While the forces of physical geology had put coal in one place, oil in another, and iron in still another place, the logic of industrial man was to bring them together as they had never been united before. Those immense bodies of fresh water—Lakes Superior, Michigan, Huron, Erie, and Ontario—left behind by the retreat of glacial ice sheets became highways for the transport of industrial raw materials. Canals supplemented them to create a new man-made system of unifying waterways. Most unnatural of all, railroads were constructed over terrain of every sort, obliterating time and space, carrying minerals and their products uphill and down, no matter where the waters ran. National railway maps of the late nineteenth century showed the continental extent of that technological dominion. Rail lines became so numerous and intertwined across the Midwest and across the northern tier of states, thrusting all the way to the Pacific, that they nearly obliterated the nation's political boundaries and obscured the natural features of its landscape with a tangle of artifact.[17]

The imposition of the new industrial order on the continent was like the coming of a new Ice Age, sweeping over the terrain with unstoppable force, grinding down the natural features, rearranging the flow of water, moving the earth from place to place, leveling whole forests, and driving off the wildlife. Those changes were easy to see in their particulars, although hard to encompass fully in the imagination.

Even harder to grasp were the changes that industrialization brought to the dynamics of the atmosphere. The Ice Age had changed North America's surface ecology in dramatic ways, just as it had changed the world's climate from a warm and wet to a colder, drier regime. But the Industrial Revolution was far more stealthy and difficult to understand, because it changed the invisible chemistry of the air. The change was gradual—localized at first but spreading over time to global proportions.

Even while George Perkins Marsh was worrying about the fate of the hydrological cycle and about frontier agriculture disturbing the "harmonies of nature" by deforestation, another vital cycle was being disturbed that he knew nothing about. This one was the carbon cycle. It too was essential to life on earth. All plants and animals are based on carbon compounds. Taken in the aggregate, their living tissues store about 500 gigatons of carbon, while another 1,500 gigatons lie buried in the soil. Some of that soil carbon makes the earth fertile and allows humans to produce food, but the rest is locked into fossil fuels or lies bonded in nonorganic forms like calcium carbonate. Additionally, huge amounts of carbon float in the atmosphere as carbon dioxide, averaging about 275 parts per million (ppm) of the air's volume in preindustrial times. Plants had evolved to draw down that CO_2 and send back oxygen, while other organisms, from beetles to buffalo, had evolved to breathe oxygen and exhale carbon dioxide. Overall, it had long been a remarkably stable cycle, with the amount of carbon dioxide remaining virtually unchanged over more than a billion years. Interrupt that cycle by even a small degree, and the quantity and distribution of life as a whole would change. Raise the level of carbon dioxide beyond 275 ppm and the ice sheets would begin to melt, the seas would rise, and the climate of the earth would shift toward warmer and wetter regimes in most places, drier in a few others.

The full complexity of the carbon cycle was not discovered until a Swedish chemist, Svante August Arrhenius, set out to find a theory to explain the Ice Age. In that search, he looked at changes in atmospheric chemistry as a possible cause. In 1896 he suggested that fluctuations in carbon dioxide might affect world temperatures, for CO_2 works like glass in a greenhouse, trapping solar radiation and keeping the earth's surface warm. The heat of the sun does not dissipate into space as fast as it would without the presence of carbon dioxide in the atmosphere. Raising the concentration of the gas, Arrhenius theorized, would be like adding more layers of glass. It would raise the temperature of the earth, which in turn would lead to a melting of glaciers in places such as Greenland and the Polar Regions. Lowering the concentration even slightly would have the opposite effect. Then ice would accumulate on the world's mountains and descend into the valleys, and large continental ice sheets would form in higher latitudes and creep south. Although the oceans along with living organisms acted as equilibrating forces, he wrote, "we yet recognize that the slight percentage of carbonic acid [CO_2] in the atmosphere may by the advances of industry be changed to a noticeable degree in the course of a few centuries."[18] Industrialization, in short, could change the world's climate. For Arrhenius, who feared a catastrophic return of the ice to countries like Sweden, this was a happy prospect. Industrialization was humanity's weapon of defense against future ice ages. Later generations would not be so complacent.

Had he followed those new scientific theories, George Perkins Marsh might have written *Man and Nature* from a different perspective. The impact of humans on the earth might have taken on new meaning and assumed a new scale. The industrialists, he might have noted, would threaten not merely the biota or the watershed but the invisible atmosphere, the carbon cycle, and the climate. Would Marsh, by the light of atmospheric science, have repeated his 1864 words: Man "is of more exalted parentage, and belongs in a higher order of existences than those born of [Nature's] womb and submissive to her dictates?" Or would he have seen new reason to repeat his darker views: "The ravages committed by man subvert the relations and destroy the balance which nature had established between her organized and her inorganic creations?"[19] Would he have begun to worry about the health effects of industry, or its impact on Pennsylvania and West Virginia miners and farmers, or about the air of cities or the catastrophic consequences of atmospheric warming?

Like Marsh, the conservationists who read and echoed his anti-frontier jeremiad about forests and waters could only act on the knowledge they had. On the whole it was not false knowledge, but it was partial and was framed in preindustrial terms. Meanwhile, industrialization was rapidly changing their world in ways they could not fully grasp.

After Marsh's death, industrialization would force scientists to ask new questions and find new kinds of data. They would begin to uncover environmental effects that were unprecedented in human experience and, in the process, gain a more comprehensive perspective on the planet and its limits. Whether nature's order would someday put limits on industrial development, or whether it should do so, was difficult to think about scientifically or ethically in the late nineteenth century. That would change with time. Meanwhile, those who were busy mining and smelting amassed great fortunes as they disturbed the earth and its atmosphere in profoundly new ways.

Among those industrialists no one was more important than Andrew Carnegie. It was he who led the way to large-scale production of steel, which in turn drastically remade the lives of people, from the structure of their cities to military hardware and transportation.[20] Carnegie, the world's greatest steel producer, helped redirect the flow of energy, transforming the American and world economy from one based on wood to one based on coal. He did so with a philanthropic spirit that lifted the hearts of his countrymen and made him the most beloved industrialist of his time. For this role as benevolent revolutionary he was well paid, becoming the richest man in America and the richest in the world.

"Nothing stranger ever came out of the *Arabian Nights*," wrote Carnegie's friend John C. Van Dyke, "than the story of this poor Scotch boy who came to America and step by step, through many trials and triumphs, became the great steel master, built up a colossal industry, amassed an enormous fortune, and then deliberately and systematically gave away the whole of it for the enlightenment and betterment of mankind." In 1901 Carnegie sold his steel company for $400 million and proceeded to give away most of that money to public libraries, universities, and the Peace Palace (home of the International Court of Justice) in The Hague. Carnegie sincerely believed that anyone who acquires great wealth should, before he dies, devote his abilities to disposing wisely of the surplus he has accumulated. Social inequality is the natural, inevitable result of capitalist enterprise, Carnegie lectured, but the man of wealth should then turn around and become "the mere trustee and agent for his poorer brethren, using his superior wisdom, experience, and ability for their welfare, doing for them far more than they would or could do for themselves."[21]

Born in 1836 in Dunfermline, Scotland, near Edinburgh, Carnegie immigrated with his family to western Pennsylvania at the age of twelve. In their new home, Andrew's mother, gentle but indomitable, took charge, pushing her men folk to succeed. Sacrificing her sons' formal education to family solvency, she sent Andy into the cold, hard world of child labor. Quickly he rose from a 72-hour workweek in a cotton mill to a promising career with the Pennsylvania Railroad. Older men adopted him as if he were a favorite son and helped set him on a path to success. Andy's lesson for the less fortunate was that they too must start from poverty, learn the value of humble beginnings, show an honest face, and practice temperance in all things, but he was not unaware of how heavily he had depended on the patronage of others.

Railroads were the greatest corporations of Andy's youth. Their powerful locomotives, the "iron horses," ran on iron rails but did not run very well. Every few months the rails wore out, particularly those that took the weight and stress of routes curving through the mountains. Steel, Carnegie realized, would make rails that lasted far longer and would save money for the companies. Steel would improve the old wooden bridges too. To make the switch he needed to find ways to make steel more cheaply. He was among the first to bring to the United States from England the new Bessemer process of mass-producing high-quality steel by blowing air through molten iron.[22] He invested shrewdly in this process, drawing on profits made in drilling oil. The result was steel produced at a cost of mere pennies a pound.

In the winter of 1873 Carnegie established a manufacturing plant to produce steel rails on the banks of the Monongahela River upstream from Pittsburgh. It began operations on the eve of one of the country's worst economic depressions, when company after company was spiraling downward into bankruptcy. Through careful management and powerful connections, Carnegie weathered the financial storm and grew even stronger. Later he expanded into a larger plant using a still newer innovation, the open-hearth system. His second plant was located near the center of Pittsburgh, on the riverbanks where it could take advantage of cheap water transportation down the Ohio and Mississippi Rivers to the Gulf of Mexico. He named that plant "Homestead," which suggested a little cabin on the prairie. In truth the plant was a dark, smoky behemoth that made Pittsburgh the world center of steel production and the keystone of industrial America.

Carnegie by his own lights was a generous boss, but he insisted that Homestead was his property alone, the fruit of his ideas and talent, and that the workers were mere employees and not partners. In 1892 he and plant manager Henry Clay Frick broke a workers' strike for better wages with the use of a private army, during which several men died and others retreated in sullen anger. Such an assertion of power was, in Carnegie's mind, exactly the way that the new industrial economy must function.[23]

Other decisions Carnegie made with similar assertiveness, free of any outside check. In a nation devoted to economic freedom he was unchecked by any public force when he went out to buy Mesabi iron ore, acquire a fleet of steel-hulled vessels to bring it to Pennsylvania, secure rights to Appalachian coal, and transport it to where the ore was being off-loaded at his mills. He was free to buy and sell land and resources on a scale that no farmer or woodsman had ever done before, and he was free to leave that land and the air as polluted as he chose.

There were unforeseen consequences in that unlimited economic freedom. The atmosphere in Pittsburgh, which had long been smoky and unhealthy, began to deteriorate badly. As early as the eighteenth century the city had suffered from a reputation for smoky air, and in the mid-nineteenth century, as conditions got worse, the county court ordered a local brick maker to stop burning bituminous coal because it injured the gardens, health, and comfort of his neighbors. But the steel industry convinced the courts and legislators that smoke was a sign of progress and prosperity, and it successfully defended its freedom from further regulation. Only after 1900 did that freedom begin to diminish, as public attitudes changed, until even the Chamber of Commerce began to call for the abatement of pollution. But by then Carnegie was gone.[24]

The only remedy for the dark, unhealthy pall of smoke hanging over the city that early industrialists would contemplate was to shift from burning coal to burning natural gas. Gas would generate less smoke, and since gas was abundant in the vicinity, an apparently happy remedy lay buried under their feet. "Instead of occupying the bad eminence ... of being by far the dirtiest city in the world, which it undoubtedly is today," wrote Carnegie in 1885, "it is probable that the other extreme may be reached, and that we may be able to claim for smoky Pittsburgh that it is the cleanest city." Once more the steelmaker found hope in the inexhaustibility of a new natural resource. "Pittsburgh," he declared, "is today, as far as subterranean resources [of gas] are concerned, the metropolis of the richest district in the known world."[25]

Later, however, Carnegie was forced to admit that natural gas might not be so plentiful or cheap as he had supposed. Burning natural gas would indeed improve air quality, but it would make steel production more, not less, expensive and hurt his company's profit margins. Faced with this disappointment, he wrote plaintively: "The man who abolishes the smoke nuisance in Pittsburgh is the foremost of us all ... Is there no Westinghouse [a pioneer in the generation of electricity] or Brashear [a famous Pittsburgh astronomer] among us to work the miracle of our salvation from this nuisance?"[26] Apparently there was no such wizard. Pittsburgh steel mills continued to burn coal, science did not find a cleaner or cheaper substitute, and the city's air quality continued to decline. It would improve substantially only when the steel mills and coke ovens closed, the last one in 1997, following the imposition of federal antipollution laws. Even then, the city would remain one of the most polluted in America.

The great steel master died in 1919, but he did not die from his own pollution, as so many others did, but instead from pneumonia brought on by influenza. Long before his end, he had fled Pittsburgh for better air. His desire to escape from the scene of his economic success followed a common pattern among Pittsburgh moguls, and indeed industrialists everywhere. For example, Carnegie's friend Thomas Mellon, son of a farming couple who had immigrated from Northern Ireland, first made a fortune in oil and then retired to the clear skies of Laurel Highlands, far above Pittsburgh's oil- and coke-polluted environs. Henry Frick, Carnegie's lieutenant at Homestead, retreated to the Upper East Side of New York, where he turned from manufacturing steel to collecting fine art. Some of those founders of industry had to move more than once to escape the pollution that followed them like a nemesis.

In 1898, as the United States was going to war against Spain, Carnegie discovered a retreat far away from America's industrial ecology and crowded cities, across the Atlantic Ocean in the Scottish Highlands. There he bought an ancient castle and estate named Skibo. Surrounding the castle were 20,000 acres of healthy moors and meadows, forests and trout streams. Carnegie paid $85,000 for the place, and then spent another $2 million to modernize it, installing massive steel beams in the castle to shore up its gray stone towers and battlements. With the renovations completed, he had a property fit for a new-age landed gentleman. The family began spending nearly half of each year at Skibo, as its laird sought to renew his Celtic roots. For months at a time he entertained powerful leaders from Great Britain and the United States, filling them with salmon and whisky, impressing them with his magnificent library and promoting the cause of world peace. Each morning bagpipers pierced the air with the tones of "Scotland the Brave" and "The Lone Piper."[27]

What Carnegie and his family discovered at Skibo was that they were hungry for unspoiled nature, a hunger that for a long while they had not understood or been able to satisfy. The castle's owner learned to fish, and he could swim in his own saltwater pool. A yacht stood ready for ocean outings. He could play golf on his private course or before bedtime take long walks as the sun was setting over heather-scented moors. "Heaven on Earth," he called this northern retreat. His wife Louise described it as a kind of paradise: "Sweet pastoral scenery ... perfect of its kind ... a beautiful undulating park with cattle grazing, a stately avenue of fine old beeches, glimpses of the Dornoch firth, about a mile away, all seen through the picturesque cluster of lime and beech trees."[28]

Carnegie always believed that the "good old times" were not really good at all. Industrialization had improved civilization for both master and servant. A relapse to preindustrial conditions "would be disastrous to both—not the least to him who serves—and would sweep civilization with it." Modern manufacturing had put "commodities of excellent quality" within reach of all. Admittedly, the costs of that manufactured plenty had been high, including a degradation of the environment, a widening gap between the classes, more friction between employer and employed, and a more fierce competitiveness in personal relations. But the costs were worth paying. After all, competition was the law of nature: "We cannot evade it; no substitutes for it have been found; and while the law may be sometimes hard for the individual, it is best for the race, because it insures the survival of the fittest in every department."[29] Carnegie was sure that the fittest of all was a man like himself, who could escape from polluted cities and poisonous mines into green, bucolic vistas where he could learn to relax and go fishing for his dinner.

Despite many gifts to charity, Carnegie did not give much money to protect the natural world that he disturbed. He did buy a small private forest and donate it to the people of Dunfermline, but he gave no money to save America's great forests, create national parks, or set aside wildlife refuges. He was no follower of George Perkins Marsh. What the steel master understood was not public ownership and protection of natural resources but rather an individual's right to conserve a piece of unspoiled natural beauty wherever he chose. That kind of privatized conservation was a common strategy of the day among the richest families. Their efforts to save and protect a few places under private ownership further segregated and fragmented the landscape—transformed nature's organic wholeness into a series of scattered pieces that lacked any ecological or social coherence.

Down in West Virginia a densely forested environment was turned into coal country, although the government would one day also establish a national forest in the state. In other places the land became broken into oil fields or iron ranges full of dust and stench— desolated places far away from the centers of wealth and far from private enclaves of peace and order like Skibo. In the new industrial ecology places of work and production became severed from places of leisure and consumption, and their vital connections became all but invisible to those who worked in the mills as well as those who made the largest fortunes.

The conservation movement was not to blame for that fragmented and polluted outcome. Its leaders did the best they could to save America's watersheds, where old harmonies could go on functioning and delighting the mind. Confronted by an economic power that they often did not fully comprehend or know how to contain, they found solutions that were practical and intelligent, but those solutions were also partial and confined in purpose. Conservationists did not quite know what to do with an America that was being made over into an industrial mosaic. Those who held economic power in the new economic epoch, on the other hand, commonly ignored the conservation movement and went looking for their own private heavens on earth.

CHAPTER 6

The Resourceful State

A SACRED WORD IN NINETEENTH-CENTURY America's vocabulary was "growth," meaning a change from a primitive to a more advanced state of society, from subsistence farming to industrialism and cities—meaning in simplest terms an increase in income and expenditure. For some people growth became more sacred than God or country, while for others it was God's plan for the nation. "Growth," or its synonym "development," moved the nation west and turned the sparsely populated continent into an economic giant, with many well-endowed institutions of culture and learning, imposing steel and coal-based industrial sites like Pittsburgh, and a consumer's paradise where mass-produced abundance flowed like the Mississippi River.

The rise of the conservation movement, in contrast, suggested that a substantial number of Americans were beginning to question that linear progression and to look for more than a future of endless and assured wealth. They may not have addressed fully the specific idea of industrial growth, but they wanted to protect their great land from runaway exploitation and development. They sought not an end to all growth but an end to uncontrolled and unlimited growth, which spoiled the earth for their children or themselves. Growth, they began to acknowledge, cannot forever ignore nature's limits.

So the nation was, by the turn of the twentieth century, in an increasingly ambivalent mood. The man who set out to reconcile the ambivalence was the twenty-sixth president, Theodore Roosevelt. A protean figure of enormous popularity, he was everything to almost everybody. Emphatically and permanently, he made conservation part of mainstream politics, but he did so by redefining conservation as a copartner with industrialization. By the end of his presidency conservation had less to do with observing the limits of the land than with promoting America as an economic superpower and imperial state.

No president before Roosevelt had taken so seriously the idea that the nation was threatened with resource exhaustion brought on by the unfettered play of the market and the chaotic forces of greed. He did not think the threat could be overcome by the likes of Carnegie or Rockefeller. Over time he grew more and more suspicious of the barons of finance and industry, the business class and its view of the world, and turned instead to disinterested experts devoted to public service. For this he was widely admired and praised by right-thinking people. But what they did not scrutinize carefully was his effort to reconcile conservation with Andrew Carnegie's industrial society and its insatiable need for resources, especially minerals and energy. Government, at the national as well as state level, Roosevelt promised, could assure a permanent abundance of resources where the private sector could not, and thus it could push national development to new heights.[1]

A popular image has President Roosevelt standing on a high platform, giving a speech without microphones to a sea of upturned faces. He is a stocky man with a broad chest. His ears lie flat against his blunt, round head. Unlike Abraham Lincoln, his face shows no ungainly angles or shades of melancholy. He looks completely transparent, all cheerful force and manly decision. Clipped to his nose is a pair of rimless eyeglasses, and behind them his small eyes squint hard, while his teeth seem to snap together as he speaks. A fist pounds into an open palm, beating a harsh rhythm like a boxer delivering blows.

> We have become great in a material sense [Roosevelt shouts] because of the lavish use of our resources, and we have just reason to be proud of our growth. But the time has come to inquire seriously what will happen when our forests are gone, when the coal, the iron, the oil, and the gas are exhausted, when the soils shall have been still further impoverished and washed into the streams, polluting the rivers, denuding the fields, and obstructing navigation. The time has come for a change.[2]

Those words President Roosevelt spoke to a historic gathering of governors at the White House in 1908, an event that more than any other made conservation part of everyday political discourse while at the same time it downplayed the theme of natural limits that Marsh had expressed so eloquently.

How did Teddy Roosevelt find his way to such a tangle of views? When he was born in 1858 to a wealthy merchant family in New York City, conservation was not a common household word, although it was on the verge of becoming so. But the word had a long history, and its meaning had been fairly consistent over the centuries: always it had meant to protect and preserve. That definitive record of the English language, the *Oxford English Dictionary*, traces "conservation" back to the early fifteenth century and lists the following meanings in order of first appearance and established usage:

- The action or process of conserving; preservation of life, health, perfection.
- Preservation of existing conditions, institutions, rights, peace, order.
- The preservation, protection, or restoration of the natural environment and of wildlife; the practice of seeking to prevent the wasteful use of a resource in order to ensure its continued availability.
- Official charge and care of rivers, forests, etc.[3]

Nowhere in the historic definition did conservation mean "development," but that is the meaning that Roosevelt and his presidential administration added to the dictionary. It was like Orwellian newspeak—political propaganda that made old words say the opposite of what they had always meant.

Roosevelt began by embracing traditional conservation, combining a boyhood love of hunting in the wild with a family understanding that with great wealth comes great responsibility. He grew up wanting to conserve the things that he and others shot. Biographers tell of his boyhood zeal for animals and natural history—little Teddy was an avid collector of skins and feathers. When he was fourteen and the family was on vacation in Egypt, he got his first gun. In a diary he recorded his triumphs as a naturalist armed with deadly force: "Blew a chat to pieces in a walk of a hundred yards. . . . the first bird I had ever shot and I was proportionately delighted. . . . In the afternoon I went out with the gun and shot a wagtail."[4] That gun and shooting fervor drove him into the outdoors, but they did not make him a conservationist. With maturity he came to understand, as the Roosevelts had long ago decided, that the pleasures of life require an ethic of protective restraint or they will not last forever.

When he was twenty-nine years old, a graduate of Harvard College, a gentleman of leisure, and a veteran of ranching and hunting in North Dakota and Montana, Roosevelt became president of the Boone and Crockett Club. Founded in 1887, it was one of the first conservation organizations in the United States, with a membership limited to one hundred of the nation's elite males who had killed, "in fair chase," the biggest game mammals, including bear, moose, elk, and cougar. Promoting "manly sport with the rifle" was the main purpose of the club, but it also worked "for the preservation of the large game of this country." To that end Roosevelt led the Boone and Crockett Club into battle against, among others, the renegade poachers in Yellowstone National Park who were killing off the last bison and elk herds.[5]

Without shame or embarrassment, club members loved to watch a big animal crumple to its knees, shot through the spine or heart— no weepy sentimentalism for them. But they also preached patrician responsibility, self-discipline, and sportsmanship. The club played a critical role in saving wild animals from extinction by market hunters and, some have charged, from the poor backwoodsmen who hunted for subsistence.[6] Saving game was what conservation meant to young Teddy: a struggle within himself and within society to balance a desire to shoot and possess nature while seeking to protect the hunted from a hunger and violence that knew no bounds.

When Roosevelt was elevated to the presidency in 1901, he set out to do far more than save game animals from the ruffian class of hunters. He aimed to preserve some of the last undeveloped places in the American landscape—vestiges of the mythic wilderness of the frontier era. Surprising many of his party's Old Guard, he was determined to create a legacy of public lands unlike any in the world for size and purpose—to create a permanent legacy of the frontier open to all people, protective of all species, with rules to govern their use and assure their availability to future generations.

With the support of Gifford Pinchot, his fellow Boone and Crockett Club member and the government's chief forester, Roosevelt, in his first message to Congress, declared that the existing forest reserves, established by Presidents Harrison and Cleveland, should be substantially enlarged and "set apart forever, for the use and benefit of our people as a whole and not sacrificed to the shortsighted greed of a few."[7] During his administration Roosevelt added 150 national forests, stretching from Maine to Alaska, and in all protected some 230 million acres. He did so by acting independently but legally, through issuing executive orders, bravely ignoring the bitter resentment in many western states and in parts of Congress where his actions were seen as "locking up" the country and preventing its exploitation.[8]

Roosevelt did more—much more—for conservation. Beginning in 1903 he created a system of wildlife refuges, the first of them located off the Florida coast, on Pelican Island, to protect the beautifully plumed birds that were being slaughtered for their feathers to adorn women's hats. Altogether Roosevelt decreed fifty-one wildlife sanctuaries, laying the foundations for a system of federal refuges that eventually would cover nearly a hundred million acres, where wild creatures could find at least some safety from unregulated guns and habitat destruction. Congress stopped him from creating all the national parks he wanted, but he managed to get five new ones established. Then the same legislators, in 1906, gave him the authority to set aside historic landmarks, so-called national monuments, and with that power he preserved the Grand Canyon and seventeen other sites, many of which later became national parks.

No president, before or after, did more than Roosevelt to protect and preserve land in the United States. No one did more to conserve wild nature for its own sake. For all the abuse and misuse they endured over time, Roosevelt gave his country the greatest expanse of protected public spaces on the planet, a model that other nations admired and often emulated. All of this was conservation as it had always been defined and established, but on a grander scale than Marsh or Muir could ever have imagined or achieved.

Roosevelt, however, never believed that conservation should merely mean preserving the natural environment. He also sought to exploit nature in new ways and places. Shortly after taking office, he put the federal government into the business of developing the nation's last undeveloped spaces by building dams and irrigation canals. He did this by supporting the National Reclamation Act of 1902, which used money from the sale of western lands to fund federal irrigation projects. The first major construction under this act was named Roosevelt Dam, a massive structure of concrete that created an artificial lake on the Salt River northeast of Phoenix, Arizona. Here again the president started something that would grow beyond anything he could have imagined. Eventually nearly every river in the West would be dammed, and dammed many times over, and the United States would create the largest hydraulic society in world history, in which the flow of water was controlled by technology to create a man-made agricultural system. Government reclamation would cost taxpayers a huge amount and would do enormous damage to the environment. All of it was done in the name of conservation.[9]

In the case of water it was not humans but nature that was declared guilty of wasting a valuable natural resource. An undammed river delivered all its water to the sea and thus, it was said, wasted a precious resource needed for economic development and future population growth. As the president promised in his first annual message to Congress, "the western half of the United States would sustain a population greater than that of our whole country today if the waters that now run to waste were saved and used for irrigation."[10] Roosevelt was speaking at a time when the United States counted fewer than 100 million inhabitants. Through federal irrigation, he promised, the arid West alone would someday support at least a hundred million all on its own. Excited by that prospect and by the promise of government support to "build the West," chambers of commerce in Los Angeles, San Francisco, Phoenix, and Denver modified their traditional opposition to the conservation movement. Roosevelt's dam-building program established an "infrastructure drive" to support economic development. Among its achievements, it thrust the federal government into a long-lasting alliance with private interests in the pursuit of development, establishing a model of "cooperation" that was later applied to the whole nation and its industrial underpinnings. Second, reclamation, through its many feats of conquest, exemplified a government-sponsored determination to overcome natural limits. Now, the president insisted, conservation should mean not merely protecting nature from feather hunters or loggers but also establishing a more rational, thoroughgoing exploitation of resources. Conservation should aim to turn "waste" into profit. Roosevelt described his overall purpose in plain, memorable words: "Conservation means development as much as it does protection."[11]

The president did not find his way to this new understanding unaided and untutored. Pushing him along were several shrewd advisors who understood politics as well as he, and were persuaded that conservation might become more popular if it were reimagined in term of expanding plenty and progress. Gifford Pinchot was one of those advisors. But behind him stood a former Iowa farm boy, a lover of grandiose words and visions, William John ("WJ") McGee, whom Pinchot identified as "the scientific brains" of the conservation movement. It was McGee who gave Roosevelt and Pinchot a memorable mission statement: Conservation means achieving "the greatest good for the greatest number of people for the longest time."[12]

McGee first entered government service as a protégé of John Wesley Powell, chief of the US Geological Survey, then headed the Bureau of American Ethnology, was elected president of the American Anthropological Association and the National Geographical Society, before Roosevelt appointed him in 1907 to the Inland Waterways Association, where he was charged with developing a grand plan to manage the nation's rivers as a single coordinated system of transportation, hydroelectric power, and water supply. Behind this man of many enthusiasms stood an even more shadowy figure, the American sociologist Lester Ward, a professor at Brown University who likewise came from a midwestern farm and aspired to reorganize nature and society along rational, scientific lines. Ward was mentor to McGee, McGee to Pinchot, and Pinchot to Roosevelt.[13]

Professor Ward was an implacable foe of laissez-faire economics, which he saw as wasteful, inefficient, and all too "natural" in its primitive competiveness. Nature, he argued in terms that the progressive economist and prophet of man-made abundance Simon Patten would have applauded, is irrationally organized and pathetically wasteful; an oyster, for example, might lay thousands of eggs where only one was needed for its reproduction. Ward sought to teach the oyster as well as the businessman how to lead more efficient lives. He would put trained experts in charge of remaking the planet's order.[14] Ward persuaded McGee to think like a scientific expert, and through him, influenced Pinchot and Roosevelt in turning conservation on its head to become a state-sponsored mission to transcend environmental limits.

In a 1911 article, McGee applied Lester Ward's hyper-rationality to conservation. With sonorous sweep, he portrayed conservation as evolving from the reorganization of rivers and streams toward comprehensive government regulation and management of all natural resources. It was to be a progressive evolution that supposedly would conquer the irrational beast within humans and lead to moral enlightenment as well as unimaginable affluence.

> On its face the Conservation Movement is material—ultra material. At first blush the moral and social [*sic*] in which cults arise and from which doctrines draw inspiration may

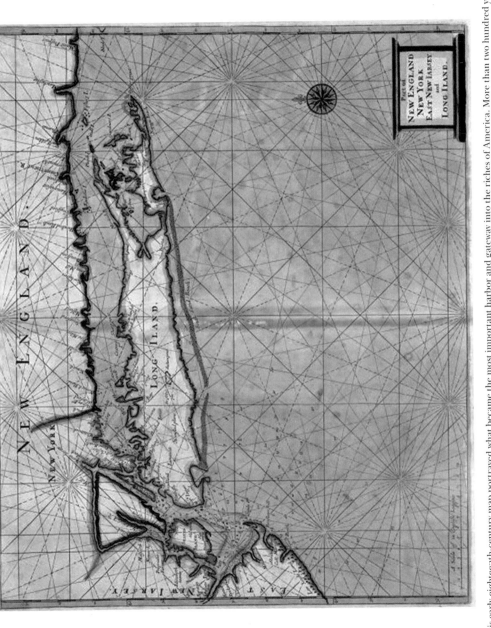

Plate 1. This early eighteenth-century map portrayed what became the most important harbor and gateway into the riches of America. More than two hundred years later it was where F. Scott Fitzgerald's fictional character Jay Gatsby built a grandiose mansion and pursued his futile dream of wealth. Lionel Pincus and Princess Firyal Map Division, The New York Public Library. "Part of New England, New York, east New Jarsey and Long Iland." New York Public Library Digital Collections.

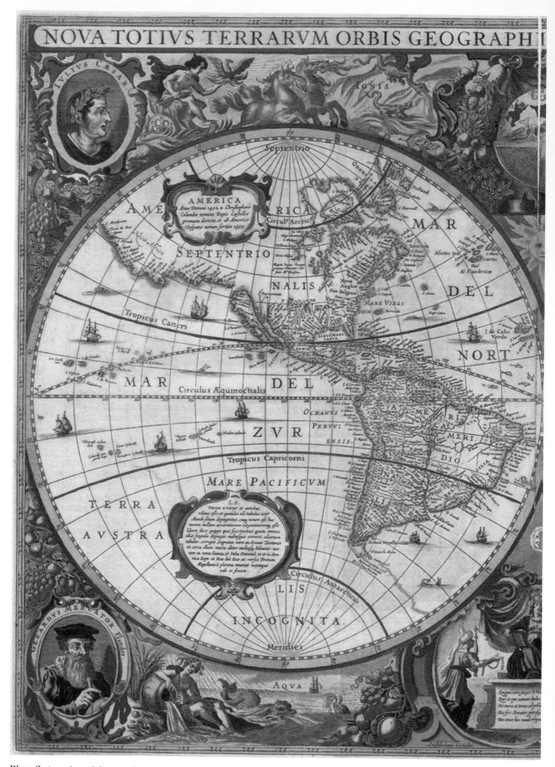

Plate 2. A version of the popular Second Earth map that appeared in the wake of Christopher Columbus and others who revealed that the planet has a Western Hemisphere. Now the increasingly populous, hard-pressed people of Europe had available a vast new bounteous world to exploit. "Nova Totius Terrarum orbis Geographica ac Hydrographica Tabula," Henricus Hondius, cartographer, Amsterdam, 1641. Derived from Rumold Mercator's 1587 map and published in *Weltkarte im Novus Atlas Absolutissimus des Johannes Janssonius*, 1647–50. National Library of Norway.

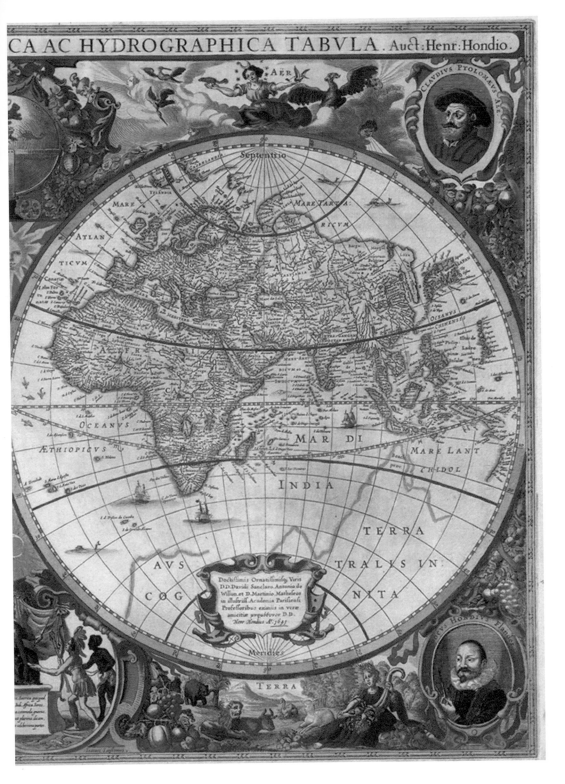

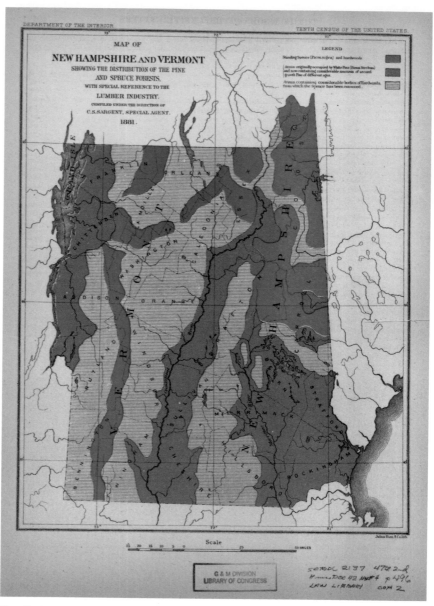

Plate 3. New images of the American landscape, from a watershed perspective, appeared in the late nineteenth century, based on scientific mapping and showing the interdependent but vulnerable relationship of forests and rivers. Following waves of frontier settlement and clearance, such watershed images helped inspire a national conservation ethic. "Map of New Hampshire and Vermont, showing the distribution of the pine and spruce forests," C. S. Sargent, *Report on the Forests of North America* (Washington, DC: Government Printing Office, 1884).

The headline-making report on the imminent global disaster facing humanity—and what we can do about it before time runs out. "One of the most important documents of our age!" —Anthony Lewis, *The New York Times*

DONELLA H. MEADOWS/DENNIS L. MEADOWS
JØRGEN RANDERS/WILLIAM W. BEHRENS III
A POTOMAC ASSOCIATES BOOK

Plate 4. The author's worn and tattered personal copy of a book that challenged the way Americans and others look at the planet: Donella H. Meadows, Dennis L. Meadows, Jorgen Randers, and William W. Behrens III, *The Limits to Growth: A Report for the Club of Rome's Project on the Predicament of Mankind* (New York: Signet Book/New American Library, a Potomac Associates Book, 1972). Photo courtesy of author.

Plate 5. A photograph of the Earth, popularly known as "The Pale Blue Dot," taken from the edge of the solar system. Our home planet appears as a tiny speck in the middle of the orange streak on the right side of the picture—almost lost in the darkness of space. US National Aeronautic and Space Administration, February 14, 1990.

role was decidedly marginal.[18] Mainly the invitees were governors, whether Republican or Democrat, and almost all of them showed up. McGee sought to inspire them with a new sense of their responsibility: a dedication at all levels of government to the scientific management of natural resources.

In orchestrating that message McGee succeeded remarkably well. Never before had so many prominent figures pledged their support for conservation. In the dawning decade of the twentieth century, they joined arms and began to dream on a utopian scale. The old raw capitalism of cutthroat competition would be tamed just as nature was being tamed for the good of humankind. Prices would stabilize, profits would increase at a steady rate, citizens would be able to consume more, and nature would come under firm control. The result would be a new America, master of its environment.

Conspicuously absent from the governors' conference was the most widely recognized and charismatic conservationist in the United States, John Muir, president of the Sierra Club. Although a personal friend of President Roosevelt's, with whom he had camped in the outdoors and shared a love of wildness, Muir was not invited. The reason for that omission was that he disagreed with the brand of conservation that the president and his advisors were selling. That resources should be used wisely as well as protected carefully and that government should take the lead in that protection was not an issue, but Muir disagreed that conservation should be redefined as a wholesale reengineering of nature with the primary objective to expand the nation's productivity, wealth, and power.[19]

A few days before the governors arrived in Washington, President Roosevelt, after much dithering, had given the city of San Francisco a permit to construct a dam in the pristine Hetch Hetchy Valley of Yosemite National Park. He had dithered because he had been torn between his preserving and modernizing impulses. The proposed dam would clearly satisfy the latter by securing a low-cost, publicly owned water supply for the city and promote its expansion, but his atavistic love of hunting and recreation made him regret the sacrifice. Roosevelt decided to turn Hetch Hetchy over to those who imagined a vast commercial metropolis around San Francisco Bay. Muir could not see any difference between the old frontier exploiters and the new urban ones. He had publicly opposed their effort to acquire and flood the valley, and therefore he was not wanted in Washington.[20]

In the place of Muir as a keynote speaker stood the little cherubic industrialist Andrew Carnegie. He was invited because he would raise no objection to a dam in some far-off western wilderness, although he would have fought hard if anyone had tried to flood his beloved Skibo estate. A man with no past record as a conservationist, he nonetheless was put in the highly visible position of speaking right after Roosevelt's opening address. Conservation, he proposed, should become an essential partner of business in the modern industrial society.

Tellingly, it was not watersheds or forests that Carnegie talked about most; it was the supply of resources needed by industry, especially "our mineral supplies, chiefly iron and coal." Those commodities formed the foundation of "industrial prosperity," he argued, and they were being mined and consumed in wasteful ways that threatened America's future. The national endowment of two and a half trillion tons of coal would be completely burned up within two hundred years, at current rates of consumption, while not more than 5 to 10 percent of that energy would be actually captured and used efficiently. Most of it would be wasted. He warned too that the Lake Superior iron supplies would be completely exhausted by 1940; in fact "all the ore now deemed workable will be used long before the end" of the twentieth century. Meanwhile, the coal and steel industry was befouling the cities, poisoning human lungs, and endangering the nation's greatest resource, its people. "It was not resources alone that gave this country its prosperity," Carnegie declared, "but inventive skill and industrial enterprise applied to its resources." In effect, he was admitting that his successors in industry had become a threat and needed restraint.[21]

The one-time devourer of coal advocated a program of developing energy alternatives to the fossil fuels. "The sun-motor," he pointed out, "still runs; its rays render the globe habitable, and may yet be made to produce power through solar engines." All the rivers and all the ocean tides could be harnessed for power. Each acre of the earth's surface could yield, on a clear day, the continuous equivalent of 7,500 horsepower in solar energy: "Thus, there is abundance of power lying around us, if we only knew how to harness it.... I urge research into and mastery over Nature, in order that two blades may be made to grow where one grew before, that the golden grain may be made to replace woody grass, that crude rocks may be made to yield fine metals." His advice to the political leaders seated before him was that they support "practical research" into making the earth yield its bounty. His ultimate goal was not radically different from what it had always been, but now late in life he wanted to see the nation's "career of prosperity" made more secure. Conservation offered a "completer [*sic*] control of material and power than we have thus far exercised."[22]

Although Carnegie's aim was to refocus conservation on the needs of industry, thrusting the long-term supply of minerals and energy front and center, he did not forget the importance of forest and water management, "for no forests, no long navigable rivers, nor rivers, no cheap transportation."[23] But conserving forests and water, like conserving the fundamentals of industrial production, required government-led research and action. He would put Roosevelt's Reclamation Service in charge not only of damming the West, but also of organizing all the nation's rivers into a cheap and secure method of public transportation. A well-developed and publicly controlled system of inland waterways would offer an alternative to the railroads. Like Ward and McGee, Carnegie's embrace of conservation was heavily dependent on the state, for the state alone could make a better transportation network out of all the rivers of a continent.

After hearing all the speeches, the governors went away in high spirits. But then unexpectedly the conservation movement seemed to fall apart. The new conservation lost its funding and positions of power for a while. Congress refused to fund a National Conservation Commission that would have made permanent the dream of a more coordinated, long-term, and systematic program of river management and resource exploitation. Then Theodore Roosevelt's second term as president ended, and he left Washington. His first impulse after retiring from the presidency was not to continue lobbying the rich and powerful on behalf of comprehensive resource management but to take his son on a hunting expedition to Africa, where they collected over five hundred carcasses for the American Museum of Natural History. With his friend Roosevelt off on a hunt and silent about the great cause, Pinchot continued as chief spokesman during the presidential administration of William Howard Taft, but then he was fired for insubordination and lost his public platform.[24] McGee likewise faded from view and by 1912 was dead of a heart attack.[25]

Pinchot did not leave the halls of power quietly but issued a parting blast from his warrior's trumpet. He prepared a series of magazine articles and book under the title *The Fight for Conservation* (1910). They were a rehash of familiar themes: the urgent need to reform business and yet apply business-efficiency standards to government, the need to avoid private monopoly and instill a public spirit, a call for a new patriotism that would put long-term sustainability ahead of short-term personal gain. "We have passed the inevitable stage of pioneer pillage of natural resources," Pinchot wrote, and now must come a new era of "government by men for human welfare and human progress." The old frontier must give way to the rule of disinterested intelligence and the "planned and orderly development and conservation of our natural resources." Once again Pinchot put conservation at the heart of America's future, and once again he insisted, "The first great fact about conservation is that it stands for development."[26]

Despite temporary setbacks, the technocratic redefinition of conservation did not end at that point, silenced and futile. On the contrary, it recovered influence and would inform the role of government for decades to come. Through the rest of the twentieth century the state would take the lead in securing abundance through planning for development. Washington would become the powerful center for a planned economy, just as the Rooseveltians envisioned, and their conservation would continue to serve the imperatives of growth.[27]

The Harvard economist John Kenneth Galbraith has called the modern American economy an "industrial state," an alliance of government and business in which both work as partners toward a common end. The business side of the alliance has become more and more concentrated, until by the beginning of the twenty-first century a mere hundred corporations control almost all the nation's production of goods and services, while the government has steadily enlarged its role as the economy's chief planning office. The project of that alliance is to make all things bigger and growth more secure. In the new industrial state "no other social goal," Galbraith writes, "is more strongly avowed than economic growth." He calls that alliance "the technostructure," comprised of those who "bring specialized knowledge, talent or experience to group decision-making."[28] Another name might be "the alliance of industrial capital and the nation-state."

Conservationists who joined McGee's cult, particularly experts in economics, forestry, reclamation, and energy, long ago formed part of the technostructure. They worked alongside their counterparts in industry to abolish the old laissez-faire capitalism that dominated the nineteenth century and to make America's growth more sustainable. As environmental historian Theodore Steinberg writes, "If conservation broke the pattern of unrestrained economic development of the natural world, it substituted in its place a subtler political agenda shot through with irony."[29]

John Muir saw and protested such an alliance in the name of conservation. Nature's sublime beauty and ecological integrity were under attack, he cried, "by despoiling gain seekers and mischief-makers of every degree from Satan to Senators, eagerly trying to make everything immediately and selfishly commercial, with schemes disguised in smug-smiling philanthropy, industriously, sham-piously crying, 'Conservation, conservation, panutilization,' that man and beast may be fed and the dear Nation made great."[30] What Muir hoped to see was what Marsh had in mind—a conservation ethic that regarded nature as beautiful as it was useful, that aimed to protect other forms of life and the ecological order. In Muir's mind humans had inherited an earth made glorious through eons of evolution—one that should evoke respect, even reverence. That, however, would not become the direction of government conservation in the new industrial state.

To be fair, the new conservationists who wanted so badly to be part of the industrial future, sitting at the table of power and influence, saw themselves driven by moral purpose as much as Muir. They would not agree that they were a sham or that their goals were phony. Nor did they see themselves through Galbraith's cynical eyes as part of a new ruling class interested above all else in their own self-perpetuation. In their self-image they represented the interests not of the few, but of the many, and not only the present but future generations. Above all, they saw nothing wrong with striving to make "the dear Nation great." Nature, they believed, should be made to serve that higher good.

Technocratic conservation, however, was never strong on self-understanding, inward-looking criticism, or clarity of purpose. What, the skeptic might ask, should that official slogan of the "greatest good" mean, beyond putting more money into people's pockets? Who after all constituted the "greatest number," and how could the expert know what all those people really wanted? How long was "the longest period of time"—a matter of years or centuries? Those development-minded conservationists were eager to exploit the country's natural resources in a more rational, efficient way, but what should be the ends of exploitation, and why should growing the nation be so important? None of those questions was ever fully considered by Pinchot, McGee, their president, or government agencies to come. Was it possible that they might be actually serving, not the greatest good of the people, but only an empty abstraction they called "growth?"[31]

The philosophers Pinchot and McGee never sorted out what government does well and what it does poorly. Like the man they

served, they did not consider deeply the possibility that their beloved
state might be ill equipped to serve as developer rather than pro-
tector. Consequently, they would invest public monies in building
water projects throughout the American West that made little economic sense, that were little more than extravagant wastes of money.
Later economists and environmentalists would decry the unsustainable development that reclamation represented—where costs outran benefits, where development was pushed beyond any established
need, and where damage to the natural world and human communities was ignored in the name of progress.

Any state finds it difficult to decide which resources it should
try to save for future use and which it should exploit in the present. Likewise, it is not well suited to figuring out which technologies
should be promoted and which should not. With so much power in
their hands and yet so little self-examination, government conservationists were likely to be more, not less, wasteful than businessmen,
pursuing grand designs that could not meet the test of practicality,
let alone the test of a higher ethic.

Protecting nature, on the other hand, was a role that government was equipped to perform very well, exercising a countervailing
power against the business community. But this balancing function
of the state became obscured in the rush to forge an alliance with
industry. Government could not both protect *and* develop the country's dwindling bounty of soils, forests, wildlife, and watersheds.
Conservation defined as development would make exploitation of
resources the dominant principle on the public lands, as it had long
been on private lands, by insisting that every "resource" perform its
duty of enhancing the power of the state and nation. And thereby
protection would suffer.

The founding fathers of the United States feared above all
else the concentration of power in a few hands. In particular James
Madison, the nation's fourth president, worried that the country
would not last for long without a careful balancing of power among
competing interests. "Ambition," he wrote in the *Federalist Papers*,
"must be made to counteract ambition."[32] Thus he advocated a system
of checks and balances everywhere he looked in politics: between
the three branches of the federal government (the executive, legis-
lative, and judicial), between the big and little states, between far-
flung regions, between the various classes of citizenry.

For Madison, writing in the eighteenth century, the principle
of checks and balances was mainly needed within the structure of
government, but as the nation developed a more complex economy,

the principle had an economic application as well. The rising power of corporations made a counterbalancing power of government necessary. As business proved more and more relentless in exploiting the country's natural resources, whether in the arid West or in Appalachia or along the rivers and streams, government was the only force capable of protecting those resources from depletion and abuse. So Marsh, Sargent, and Muir had understood.

Roosevelt and his advisors lost sight of this Madisonian wisdom in their enthusiasm for redesigning conservation to serve development and win support. They could not see any danger because they were confident that they knew what was right and that they could persuade businessmen to travel with them down a shining path of sustainable development. But what if conservationists began to think the same way as industrialists? Then they would lose their independence. They would cease to be a checking and balancing power. And then they would have in their hands the means and motive to do environmental and social damage under the guise of conservation.

That day would come, and then, as eager collaborators within the industrial state, conservation would stand accused of implementing not the protection but the planned destruction of the earth.[33]

Imperial Valley

THE GOLD MINES OF CALIFORNIA have been a potent symbol of American bounty, but there was no easy way to reach those mines over land or sea. During the fabulous gold rush of the 1840s and '50s the most difficult route required an aspiring miner to get himself first to Fort Yuma, located on the lower Colorado River near the Mexican border, and then to cross the vast aridity of the Colorado Desert before turning north toward the gold fields. Here was the other side of bounty—scarcity, privation, even death.

If anyone thought about lingering in that desert, he had a warning right there in Yuma. Food and building materials for the soldiers had to be imported all the way around Baja California and up the river. There was little that was local to support American troops. To be sure, the great river flowing by the fort, its currents darkened by soil eroded from the Grand Canyon, was teeming with life, at least within a narrow fringe of reeds and willows. But away from the river loomed a scarcity of food and wood, water and wildlife. There was only an abundance of fierce sunshine.[1]

Beyond Fort Yuma, the gold seeker confronted an imposing barrier of sand dunes, a classic symbol of sterility. It was like leaving the River Nile and wandering into the great Sahara. Here, however, there were no imposing pyramids or high civilization. For good reason then, not many wealth seekers chose this southwestern route. Most preferred to cross father north, through the Great Basin to the green slopes of the Sierra Nevada, and then descend to mining camps in the foothills. Down here along the border, they faced hardship behind and worse hardship ahead.

The sand dunes, which could reach a height of three hundred feet, stood like a blockade to American dreams. They were a legacy from the geological past, formed by sand blowing out of the dried-up bed of ancient Lake Cahuilla. Over millions of years the Colorado River had repeatedly shifted course, emptying itself into a low basin to the west, forming a wide inland sea, and then shifting away again toward the Gulf of California. As successive seas appeared and then evaporated, a low, harsh, flat, and severely dry land remained, receiving less than three inches of rain a year, and from it rose dense clouds of dust drifting against the foothills, forming dunes that rippled like waves on the sea.[2]

In the 1850s the geologist William P. Blake, traveling with the Army Corps of Topographical Engineers in search of a transcontinental railroad route, investigated the bleakness of the Colorado Desert and described its massive extent, stretching for a hundred miles northwestward toward Los Angeles and southward below the border. But in the spirit of manifest destiny that refused to be discouraged, Blake declared, "the alluvial soil of the Desert is capable of sustaining a vigorous vegetation. The only apparent reason for its sterility is the absence of water, for wherever it is kept moist vegetation springs up. If a supply of water could be obtained for irrigation, it is probable that the greater part of this Desert could be made to yield crops of almost any kind." Other scientists would be more restrained or disparaging. But Blake's plan of creating abundance by bringing in water was one that many Americans who had failed to succeed elsewhere were eager to hear.[3]

Prominent among them was one of the disappointed gold seekers, Oliver Wozencraft. He had followed the Fort Yuma route and survived, but after failing in the mining business, he began thinking back on the desert, so desperate was he to make his fortune. He became notorious for sporting a huge set of mutton-chop whiskers, for working to divest the California Indians of their lands, for lobbying to keep African Americans out of the state, and for repeatedly demanding that Congress give him no less than 3 million acres of desert. He promised that he would make those acres produce a bonanza of crops by digging "a series of canals traversing through all the practicable portions of this sterile waste." He would bring water from the Colorado River and force "the desert to yield to the wants of man her latent, reserved, and hidden stores."[4] Somehow he persuaded the California state legislature to support the scheme. When Wozencraft died in 1887, however, the US Congress was still refusing to give him the land. It was just too unbelievable a scheme— an old man's folly or an outrageous fraud.

The ancient bed of Lake Cahuilla did not meet the expectations of natural wealth to which Americans were accustomed. Most obviously it lacked the vital resource of water, but a shortage of water was not the only limiting factor. The soils lacked much organic matter, some of them were poisonous, the climate was like a furnace, and for all those reasons humans had always been scarce on the ground. Elsewhere in California the native population had increased substantially over the millennia, supported by a richness of natural resources, but not here. American pioneers, nonetheless, refused to accept those glaring facts. They were sure that a more far-sighted, aggressive race of settlers like themselves could turn this moonscape into a permanent home, supporting a luxuriant life for many deserving people and becoming a lasting asset for the nation. They would be proved wrong, but not before it began to seem they might be right.

As land seekers began running out of possibilities elsewhere, more began to show up here and to venture a positive reassessment of the desert. Among them was Charles Rockwood, who with his associates formed the California Development Company in the 1890s. That enterprise was always short on capital and knowledge, but never on faith. If the Colorado River had shifted course in the past, they were confident that it could be induced to do so again and, simply through gravity, flood the desert with water. Thus began an effort to raise capital in order to pay for making cuts into the riverbank and drawing off some of the flow, through long-defunct natural channels flanking the sand dunes and running across Mexican territory into the United States. That was the plan, but for years it too met with no success. Rockwood's biggest coup was getting a self-trained Canadian engineer with experience in Australia, George Chaffey, to join the company, raise bundles of money, and build a head gate to tap and regulate the water. In May 1901, Chaffey telegraphed his banker son in Los Angeles: "Water turned through gate at eleven a.m. Everything all right." So it seemed for the next several years, as water was successfully diverted from the Colorado River into the desert and settlers began the tough process of reclaiming the barren land.[5]

Chaffey's most lasting contribution was changing the region's name from the "Colorado Desert" to the "Imperial Valley." The word "desert," explained his biographer, "was the worst possible advertisement for the district, calculated to frighten off rather than lure home seekers." Calling it "imperial," on the other hand, promised that its inhabitants would add something green to the expanding nation, after the Indians and Mexicans were conquered and the land homesteaded by whites. But the "valley" part of the name was pure hyperbole. Such a flat, sandy, sun-baked plain could never become a peaceful, sheltering valley with a genuine river or stream singing along the bottomlands. Words, nonetheless, can work their magic where there is a will to believe, and by 1905 some 14,000 people had arrived, organizing themselves into two towns and plowing up 120,000 acres, which they watered by nearly eight hundred miles of unlined canals and ditches.[6]

Then the Colorado River interfered with the scheme. A heavy load of suspended silt came downstream, clogged the head gate, and diminished the diversion. To save his investment, Rockwood impetuously went below the international border and made a new cut into the Colorado's banks, this one without any proper head gate. Then the river, swollen with spring snowmelt, rushed through the open cut and flooded the so-called valley and its new farms. Throughout 1905 and 1906 the river emptied itself into the old seabed, running toward the deepest declivity and forming what became known as the Salton Sea. The Colorado drains nearly 250,000 square miles of the West, from Wyoming to New Mexico and Arizona (it gets nothing from California). Data at the time showed it carried enough water each year to flood over 12 million acres one foot deep. All of that runoff was surging across the reclaimed desert, wiping out fields and washing away houses and roads.[7]

This time the river changed course Theodore Roosevelt was serving as president of the United States, and as president he liked to control rivers. Surprisingly, however, neither he nor Congress felt the flood disaster was their responsibility. Roosevelt was not altogether indifferent, denouncing the irrigation entrepreneurs for their carelessness and short-term profit seeking. How much better would it have been, he blustered, if his new Reclamation Service had been put in charge of carrying out a broad comprehensive scheme of development for all the irrigable land upon Colorado River with needed storage at the headwaters, so that none of the water of the great river which can be put to beneficial use will be allowed to go to waste. He demanded nothing less than a complete turnover of the valley to his administration. That was his best offer—give all of it to me or ask for nothing.[8]

Valley residents were determined, however, to keep the government out of their lives. So it had to be left to a private inves-
tor, Edward H. Harriman, one of the richest men in the country
and president of the Union Pacific and Southern Pacific Railroads,
to take charge of the crisis and, by bringing in 300,000 carloads
of gravel, clay, and rock, to close the breach in the Colorado River
bank. At great expense, Harriman saved the valley. His only com-
pensation was that his railroad, which ran through the new settlements, was saved from ruin. The man-made Salton Sea also survived,
becoming the largest lake in California, attracting migratory birds
and happy fishermen, although its waters turned more and more
saline as the irrigation project recovered and began washing various
salts from the soil into its depths.[9]

Thanks to Harriman, Imperial Valley came roaring back from
its disastrous beginning—breathing a renewed spirit of conquest
that seemingly could not be stopped even by the unruly Colorado.
Farmers and other residents were determined to remain independent of all outside power and hold on to their farms. In self-defense
they formed the Imperial Irrigation District (IID) to stabilize their
water supply. They brought in farm machinery to make production
more efficient, collected mesquite and greasewood for their cooking
stoves, built a plank road over the sand dunes to Yuma, and pushed
another road westward over the mountains to San Diego. The IID
claimed enough water from the river, near 3 million acre-feet a year,
to grow an incredible array of crops.

By 1910 the crop value stood at 2 million dollars annually (out of
California's total of $153 million). A decade later there were almost
3,000 farms, averaging 122 acres each (a few of them were gigantic)
and supporting 43,000 dairy cattle. The cattle were introduced by
an intrepid band of Swiss immigrants who sought to produce milk
and cheese under the fierce sun. In 1920, about a decade after their
disastrous beginning, Valley farms were harvesting over 500,000
bushels of wheat, 123,000 tons of hay, and boxcar loads of apples,
peaches, and nuts. By the end of World War II the Valley was shipping over 50 million heads of lettuce each year, along with more
railroad cars filled with carrots, tomatoes, and cantaloupes. Above
all, the farmers produced mountains of hay—stacked high along the
edges of their fields, the most prominent markers in this featureless
landscape. About half of the farm acres would always be devoted to
growing alfalfa for hay.[10]

Growth in farm production required not only growth in water
consumption, but also growth in the labor pool. By the boom years of

the 1950s, Imperial Valley was employing thousands of farm workers. Most of them were impoverished migrants who came for the harvest period and then moved on. They included white Okies from the Dust Bowl disaster, black Southerners from the cotton belt, Asian immigrants who had previously known only rice paddies, and a horde of peasant workers streaming across the border from Mexico before the days of more stringent border control. As the farms increased in capital investment, and the pool of workers increased in number and ethnic variety, Imperial became one of the most diverse and most stratified rural communities in America with a steep hierarchy based on race, wealth, and power. The local historical society, however, saw this development as completely positive: "One of the largest irrigated districts in the world," it boasted, "a land of mechanized farming on colossal scale and of utmost intensity, a wonderland of [food] factories running 24 hours a day, 365 days a year." Best of all, the local boosters declared, "it is a community of happy, prosperous people," where once all had been "barren, sandy, burning wastes of the desert."[11]

How long could that community sustain itself? From the beginning Imperial Valley was teetering again and again toward a crash, as its resource base proved erratic, pinching, and expensive to maintain. Always a sinister hand of fate was ready to push this way or that, threatening the agricultural fields. Above all, changes in the Colorado River could quickly destabilize the valley, and there was only a limited amount that the valley's farmers could do on their own to prevent that from happening. Consequently, theirs was forever a vulnerable conquest.

The amount of water running down the Colorado continued to vary dramatically from year to year, from season to season. Making matters worse, other entrepreneurs in other places, above and below the international boundary, began demanding their share of the water supply. In the early 1920s, inspired in part by Roosevelt and Pinchot's conservation-as-development ideology, the Imperial farmers went to Congress to get help with protecting themselves against the river's volatility and their competitors' persistence. They did not want to lose control, and they did want to make the Colorado conform to their production schedules. For both purposes they needed help. First, they asked for a dam bigger than any other in human history to be constructed far upstream in Nevada's Boulder Canyon (near the tiny oasis of Las Vegas) and for a storage reservoir behind the dam to prevent downstream floods and stabilize and improve the water supply. The biggest single destiny of that stored water should be Imperial Valley, for it owned senior water rights from having been the first to file claims. Some of the remaining water, they allowed, might go to Los Angeles to promote urban growth along the southern California coast. The dam would generate hydroelectricity that could be sold to cities and thereby pay for almost all the construction costs. Second, the government should build a new waterway on the US side of the border, the All-American Canal, bringing water across the sand dunes, providing an irrigation supply that would not have to be shared with anybody in Mexico. The Valley's leaders in making their case played a racial and patriotic card: if such a dam were built without an All-American Canal, the river's flow might be stolen by alien investors sneaking into Mexico. "Japanese, Chinese and other foreigners would enjoy the waters which rightfully belong to the Americans, particularly to the Ex-service men and women." Valley leaders were suggesting that veterans of the recent World War might want to settle in Imperial, although few ever did, and that the government should want to keep the limited water safely in white American hands.[12]

The costs for this grandiose project of government-planned abundance were steep. In 1928 Congress, with backing by President Calvin Coolidge, authorized $165 million for both the dam (later named Hoover Dam) and the All-American Canal—an exorbitant expense, although it would not cost the Valley much as almost all the bills would be paid by the nation's taxpayers and urban residents. There was only one hitch in the scheme. Under federal reclamation law dating back to 1902, irrigating farmers relying on government help must divest themselves of all landholdings over 160 acres per farmer. The Valley's largest landowners would have to conform to federal rules designed to encourage a more egalitarian landownership and rural democracy.[13]

Few in the Valley wanted to risk losing the federal money or the construction projects, but instead of challenging the acreage limitation head on, the IID decided to acquiesce until the dam and canal were safely authorized, and then to claim exemption from the law on the grounds that they had started irrigating before the reclamation law was passed. It was a clever strategy, and it worked. The Bureau of Reclamation, so keen to dam the Colorado River and take control, quickly agreed to save Imperial Valley. The massive dam was finished in 1935 and the canal five years later. In the end the US Department of the Interior exempted the valley from federal reclamation law. Crops flourished, profits accumulated, and land redistribution never happened. But in that triumph lurked an unsuspected vulnerability that would become visible in the years ahead.[14]

As cities along with farms began to grow to extravagant proportions, fed on Colorado River water and irrigated food, the whole Southwest region began to press on the valley's claims to precedence. Why, many wondered, should a group of rich farmers raising mainly hay for livestock (along with quite a lot of vegetables) monopolize so much of the Colorado River? Why should they do so at public expense? All the way up and down and across the river basin the cry became loud and clear by the end of the twentieth century: Give the rest of us more water! The cry came from Salt Lake City, Las Vegas (eventually swelling to 2 million residents), Phoenix (over 3 million), Tucson, and all the cities and towns along the Southern California coast, from Los Angeles to San Diego. Voices were heard from the Mexican side of the border too, from towns like Mexicali (700,000) and Tijuana (1.3 million). By 2000, 40 million people depended on the Colorado River for water, but it was agricultural users in places such as Imperial Valley that were by far the highest per capita users. The farmers owned much of the water and therefore held considerable power. Those 40 million other people, however, began to contest that long entrenched power.[15]

Imperial Valley suddenly found itself the target of demands that its irrigators conserve the water and turn over any surplus to thirsty people elsewhere. The unlined canals were losing much of their water, raising groundwater levels, and feeding the Salton Sea. The sprawling Metropolitan Water District (MWD), centered in Los Angeles but stretching far down the coast, incorporating some three hundred communities, including all of Orange County and the most populous part of San Diego County, offered to buy Imperial's surplus water. The surplus, they suggested, could come from lining the old canals with concrete. That offer, however, would require a radical—and for valley farmers a highly risky—change in thinking about their most vital resource. Always it been regarded as the free gift of nature, but now some wanted the water put on the market for sale to the highest bidder. Those who had always enjoyed the right to use water freely were leery of where that idea might lead. Begin to think that way, they worried, and the change might put an end to valley autonomy, allowing outsiders to buy into and control their future.[16]

Farmers were among the most vocal opponents of water marketing to the cities. They were willing to sell lettuce and milk, but not their water. Yet during the presidency of Ronald Reagan the notion of setting up markets for water became an exuberant panacea. Supposedly markets would encourage efficiency and distribute water more fairly, while conserving and protecting the environment. Markets, above all, would let water flow where it could make the most money. Markets offered a free and democratic way to overcome nature's limits. This at least was what the farmers continued to hear.[17]

The free-market philosophy offered a simple solution based on simplified economics. Powerful figures in the valley, nonetheless, began edging toward that philosophy and concluding that they might make more money by selling their water than by using it to raise crops. Apply a market price of $300 per acre-foot to the IID's total water claims of 3 million acre-feet, and just how much that water might be worth now and far into the future begins to come into focus.

In 1998 the IID, after much debate, agreed to sell its unused, surplus water to the San Diego County Water Authority, part of the MWD. They took the step that could ultimately lead to diverting water from their lands altogether, leaving them without a farm economy and leaving the desert where it had been in the days of Wozencraft and Rockwood. A few recalcitrant farmers dissented, insisting that they could find lucrative overseas markets for all their irrigated products, including all the alfalfa. China and the United Arab Emirates were ready to buy as many bales of Imperial hay as they could ship to feed their own dairy and beef herds. But unmistakably, the water was already slipping away from local control. There was too much money to be made in selling water rather than in selling hay or lettuce. As the old western saying goes, water always flows uphill to money—to the Chinese renminbi if not to the US dollar.

Adding to those mounting tensions among California water consumers was a harsh and embarrassing fact: the state had long been diverting more than its legal share of the Colorado River and had to cut back and conserve somehow. In October 2003 Secretary of Interior Gale Norton, with the support of President George W. Bush, forced the state to undertake a substantial cut in its overall river consumption.[18] Because Imperial Valley was lapping up so much of California's share of the river, it was the obvious target for constraint. Line those canals with concrete, the critics kept demanding, to prevent seepage. Use the saved water only on the highest-dollar crops. Put water to its best economic use. Above all, pump more of it over the mountains and into the cities. Californians, living in what had long been the golden state, the new Eden, the Promised Land, were facing serious limits.

Water reallocation through marketing was bound to put parts, or all, of Imperial Valley agriculture out of business. But now an even more ominous force threatened not merely to redistribute water from one user to another but to shrink the overall supply, and shrink it not merely in California but across the entire West, and indeed across many parts of the planet. The world was facing global climate change. Imperial Valley and the American Southwest in particular were facing an increasingly arid climate. The free-market philosophy was useless in stopping this new trend, which might be disastrous for everyone bidding for water.

One hundred years after Svante Arrhenius had predicted climate change from the burning of fossil fuels, the effects were at last being felt. Some places were becoming wetter than ever, others much drier. One of its outcomes likely would be the decline of irrigation throughout the entire American West and the return of the Colorado Desert.

Sprawling from the Great Plains all the way to the Pacific Coast and northward to Alaska, the American West is mostly dry, despite including some of the wettest places on the North American continent. It has been dry for a long time—but now and then in the distant past it had been much drier than Americans have ever experienced during their short occupancy. The most comprehensive scientific report on the future of the West's changing climate can be found in the federally funded *Global Climate Change Impacts in the United States*, put together by thirty scientists from the National Oceanic and Atmospheric Administration, the National Marine Laboratory, Environment Canada, and various universities. "The global average temperature since 1900," they write, "has risen by about 1.5 degrees Fahrenheit. By 2100, it is projected to rise another 2 to 11.5 degrees Fahrenheit." Those are world averages. Temperatures across the United States will exceed those numbers, and the western states will exceed both world and American averages.[19]

Imagine what the western half of the continent may feel like in the year 2100 A.D. Follow the old trails of commerce and migration, jumping off from Kansas City or Council Bluffs, and crossing the Great Plains. On the Plains, according to the scientific report, the annual temperature mean may be as much as 13 degrees higher on the Fahrenheit scale than during the 1960 to 1979 period (the size of increase will be determined by the amount of carbon dioxide emitted into the atmosphere through the rest of the twenty-first century). A future Nebraska may experience average summer temperatures not of 72 degrees, as it does today, but 85 degrees. The hottest days of summer will soar to 120 to 130 degrees. Nebraska will still freeze in the winter, but it will never fall far below zero as it once did.

Move on to the states of New Mexico, Colorado, Utah, Nevada, Arizona, and California, following the trails of the forty-niners. Those parts of the West will experience an annual temperature rise of 4 to 10 degrees Fahrenheit. In tomorrow's Las Vegas the midsummer daytime temperatures will average 115 degrees and in Salt Lake City 100. Farther south and lower down in elevation, Imperial Valley will exceed both those places in setting new heat records.

Because of global warming the western mountains will get less snow; their forests will become more susceptible to insect population explosions; fierce fires will erupt more and more often, turning the forests into blackened stumps; and household utility bills will soar with rising demands for air-conditioning.

The biggest problem that climate change will bring to the American West is not heat, however, but drought—and not periodic drought lasting a mere two or five or ten years, but long-term drought that will seem in human terms permanent. The most optimistic scenarios suggest that the West will become more desert-like than it has ever been before: a harder, more desiccated land that could stay that way for hundreds of years.

Over the past century or so the United States has moved more than half of its food-growing capacity west of the Mississippi River, thanks largely to irrigation from rivers or underground aquifers. That achievement is one of the most acclaimed, but also one of the most fragile, in American history. Western aquifers are rapidly depleting, and western rivers are failing because the mountain snow packs are diminishing. The biggest state in terms of agricultural value is California, and almost all of its production depends on snow falling in the Sierra Nevada or in the Rocky Mountains. In recent years the state has been suffering the most severe drought in half a millennium, and the Sierra snowpack has fallen to less than 20 percent of normal in some areas, 30 percent in others. It may stay at that level or it may decline even further; either way the state might experience a drop of 70 to 80 percent in its current water supply.[20]

Many eyes are watching the Colorado River, on which all those cities and Imperial Valley's farm economy depend. Increased heat and drought are already decreasing the flow in the river and lowering levels behind Hoover Dam and other big water control structures built during an overly optimistic period. Lake Mead, the enormous upstream reservoir that stores water for Imperial's farmers, has fallen to half-empty, and statistical models indicate that it will never recover. Conservative scientific projections indicate that those who depend on this river might have to cut their water consumption by at least 20 percent within four decades. Such a cut might seem modest, but the cut may in fact not be so slight. If the Rocky Mountains follow the pattern of the Sierra Nevada and their snowpack declines to less than 20 percent of what it has been over the past century or so, the cut will have to be much larger—as much as 70 or 80 percent of the water supply. How can 40 million producers and consumers adapt to such a desiccation?[21]

The future of Imperial Valley certainly will not get easier than it has been—and the place may even become impossible to inhabit. None of the options look attractive. One is to stop American population growth, whether from foreign immigration or natural increase—and even reverse it substantially. Yet in the valley as elsewhere in the West, people continue coming from all directions, seeking better lives for themselves and their children, and it is not clear how that migration can be slowed or redirected. The federal government has constructed tall, somber steel fencing along Imperial's border with Mexico, resembling nothing so much as a prison barrier, to stop people entering illegally. All along the fence the US Border Patrol sits in conspicuous white SUVs, their officers looking for anyone trying to climb the fence and drop into the United States. Meanwhile, millions more continue coming into the country legally, many arriving at Los Angeles International Airport, and all of them come expecting flush toilets and water flowing from a tap. There is little political will to slow legal foreign immigration nor to slow internal migration from America's snow belt to sun belt.

Another option is to transfer water, as Imperial Valley has begun to do, from raising crops to slaking the thirst of cities and industry. Yet people want both food and water in abundance, and want them both to be as cheap and secure as possible. Reducing the scale of agricultural production in places like Imperial Valley would require shifting farm production back east or moving it overseas. Either way, the valley loses.

Still another option, and by far the most popular, is to bring water in from someplace else—from outside the West. People dream of finding a substitute supply in the East or in the North, transporting it by canal or pipeline, although that water may be claimed by others who want to keep it close to home. Another popular idea is to extract fresh water from the ocean, disregarding the fact that the energy required to do so would be scarce, expensive, or possibly dangerous. Desalination would need a long chain of nuclear power plants constructed along the California shore to provide energy, and then some means of rendering harmless the immense quantities of brine and radioactivity that would result.[22] Even if those drawbacks could be solved, no source of cheap water for agriculture will likely appear and save the valley from decline.

Highway 111 makes a wide corridor connecting the valley towns of Calexico and Brawley. The highway passes the Pioneers Museum, established and managed by the Imperial County Historical Society, where tourists can learn how the valley's prosperity has been achieved. Its low beige-colored main building tells an astonishing story of environmental transformation, going back to Juan Bautista de Anza's exploring expedition of 1776, to Oliver Wozencraft's dream of reclaiming the desert, to the founding of the most powerful irrigation district in the country. One large gallery celebrates, in a show of ethnic tolerance, the diversity of people who have come here to live. There was Karl Wilhelm Brandenberg, who arrived from Basel in 1887; George Canaris, a Greek immigrant whose first home here was a tent; Gene Quon Mah, who immigrated from China's Pearl River district, escaping a crowded village, a diminishing supply of farmland, and increasingly depleted soils; and many others in a cavalcade of restless aspiration and fleeting success. Another exhibit features the career of bestselling author Harold Bell Wright, whose novel *The Winning of Barbara Worth* (1911) told the tale of a runaway Colorado River and its heroic conquest; his book sold nearly 3 million copies and inspired a silent-film classic.[23] The museum exhibits, however, make clear that agriculture is the top commodity here, not novels or films. The visitor learns that beef cattle are the number one product; annually as many as 350,000 head are raised and fed with hay on local feedlots. The museum does not add the outrageous fact that each pound of beef raised in California requires nearly 2,500 gallons of water.[24]

The most dramatic exhibit, however, is a map representing the entire Colorado River and its watersheds. The map covers most of a large wall, and with a panel of electric switches connected to tiny bulbs, the museum visitor can illuminate on that wall the many dams and canals, lighting up like stars in the desert sky. The map demonstrates the high level of control that humans have achieved over the river, this mighty force of nature, now so skillfully managed that water seems to flow as reliably as man-made electricity through ingenious circuits. Water like power has become a stable, dependable utility. Or so it seems.

George Perkins Marsh, standing on a Vermont mountain in the early nineteenth century, learned a very different view of watersheds. For him they were integrated natural systems, where vegetation and waters influence one another in highly complex ways, systems that must be protected in their ecological integrity. But the Colorado River map reflects a very different kind of watershed thinking. The federal government's Bureau of Reclamation and its engineers, following thinkers like William John McGee, have imagined the flow of water made over into a mechanical system of plumbing under total human control. The museum map is meant to reassure us that the Colorado is now under secure management; it can never break free from its concrete straitjacket or fail to provide a steady stream of profit and commodities. The map's creators, however, have not asked what global climate change might do to disrupt their impressive contrivance.

Coming out of the museum into the bright desert sun, the visitor passes through what at first glance looks like a junkyard. Really it is an outdoor exhibit of vintage tractors and farm implements, old railroad locomotives, and outdated irrigation equipment. Rusting and derelict, they sit there to remind us of the old days and the tough lives of those who came before. They are meant also to demonstrate the progress the valley has made since settlers appeared a little more than a century ago. But the dozens and dozens of broken-down machines, the peeling paint of antique buildings, the kapok stuffing erupting out of old truck seats, can tell a different story than the unstoppable forward march of progress.

This graveyard, like those where human corpses end up, speaks emphatically of death, change, and replacement. Death happens to places as well as people. Mortality, we learn, is not only the fate of individual human beings—sad but inevitable—but also the fate of towns, farms, and whole civilizations that fail to foresee or prevent their collapse. The last impression then is not one of triumph but of defeat and decline. The thoughtful visitor goes away asking, how much of Imperial Valley will some day look like the Pioneers Museum's graveyard of rust? Will this place turn out to be one of the West's biggest ghost towns ever?

PART III

Planet of Limits

THE
LIMITS
TO
GROWTH

The headline-making report on the imminent global disaster facing
humanity—and what we can do about it before time runs out. "One
of the most important documents of our age!"   —Anthony Lewis,
The New York Times

DONELLA H. MEADOWS/DENNIS L. MEADOWS
JÖRGEN RANDERS/WILLIAM W. BEHRENS III
A POTOMAC ASSOCIATES BOOK

Paperback cover of *The Limits to Growth* (*see color plate*)

CHAPTER 7

Plunder and Plenty

I N THE LAST DEADLY DAYS of World War II, the president of
the New York Zoological Society, Fairfield Osborn Jr., sat thinking about another major conflict that had been all but forgotten
in the deadly din of bombers, tanks, and torpedoes. That other war
was "man's conflict with nature." The enemy was nothing less than
the earth and its intricate web of life from which humans sought
escape and over which they sought domination.

Neither the United States nor its allies had played a noble role
in fighting the war on nature. Blithely intent on plundering the planet's natural resources, they had become ruthless aggressors, not in
this case battling against manifestly evil forces like Germany's Nazis
and Japan's warlords but instead attacking the very sources of life
and civilization. By waging that one-sided war on nature, they could
never arrive at any true victory and must become unwitting victims
of their own violence. "Parts of the earth, once living and productive,
have ... died at the hands of man," Osborn wrote, while "others are
now dying." And every nation or tribe would suffer from that dying.

This "most cruel and deadly world-wide war" had begun far
back in time, with humanity's evolution as hungry predators seeking
to extend their territory to every continent, but in the modern age
it had become nothing less than an endless technological assault
that knew no limits. Osborn turned those chilling thoughts into *Our
Plundered Planet*, published in 1948, a time when the official mood
in the United States was one of high expectations for the postwar

future. Amid triumphal cheers and expressions of relief throughout the allied world, he was a prophet of environmental apocalypse.[1]

Osborn was the son of a wealthy and much admired paleontologist, but after studying at Princeton and Cambridge universities he chose a business career instead of science. Then the day he retired, he devoted the rest of his life to the cause of conservation. The work he took up was different from that of his father's generation, which had been led by such stars as Theodore Roosevelt and John Muir. In contrast to them, Osborn Jr.'s concern was for nothing less than the great round whole of Planet Earth. He did not write as an *American* conservationist, expressing a protective pride in his nation's beauty and resources, but rather as a citizen of the world. Two global wars had opened his eyes beyond America's natural legacy and its domestic efforts of reform.

The first part of Osborn's book described the planet's development over deep geological time, while the second part surveyed the accumulated damage that had been done by humans on every continent. Soil erosion was the most common form of destruction everywhere, but behind erosion was the compulsion to feed a growing population that daily was adding 175,000 new mouths to the human population. Osborn was not blind to the fact that babies were not all equal in ecological impact, but every one of them added to the demands the species made on the soil and ecosystems of the earth. Both rich and poor nations, the old world and the new world, were facing a common set of material limits. Both needed to see the human species as "part of one great biological scheme" and to learn to care for the greater good of nature and of humans as part of that whole.[2]

The year 1948 also saw the publication of *Road to Ruin*, written by another American author, William Vogt, an ecologist and head of the conservation office of the Pan-American Union. Like Osborn, he was an internationalist who feared that humans everywhere were disturbing the natural order. "Few of our leaders," Vogt charged, "have begun to understand that we live in one world in an ecological—an environmental—sense." Once upon a time the newly discovered Western Hemisphere had offered a fabulous outlet for overcrowded countries, but nearly five centuries later the Americas were becoming as crowded as the old lands, and there was no new hemisphere appearing to absorb the surplus. Taken together, humans had come to resemble the great serpent Ouroboros, which in Egyptian mythology swallowed its own tail, symbolizing a hunger that led to self-destruction. Vogt was one of the first to use the word "environment" in its modern sense, referring to the sum total of soil, water, plants, and animals on which all humans depend. Like Osborn, he warned that the limits of the earth were fast approaching and that the constantly expanding rate of reproduction and consumption must come to an end.[3]

Both books sold well, despite their dark, unwelcome themes, and reached millions of readers, including most likely that historian of American scarcity, Walter Prescott Webb, whose book *The Great Frontier* appeared just four years after the Osborn and Vogt books. Besides encouraging a more critical-minded view of history and progress, Osborn and Vogt initiated a long-lasting debate among natural scientists, engineers, foreign aid advocates, economists, policymakers, and the public over the limits of the earth. Like a prairie tornado, their specter of impending material limits advanced relentlessly, frightening many and leaving in its wake a trail of shattered complacency.

The postwar turn toward a sense of nature's limits, similar to the sensibility widespread in traditional societies but more ethically sophisticated, scientific, and global, was full of paradox. It began at a time when, ostensibly, Americans were interested only in getting back to enjoying their land of good fortune while other nations, temporarily free of war and invasion, were eager to advance their economic development. From October 1929, the year of the stock market crash, until the surrender of Japan in August 1945, Americans in general had been forced to postpone material gratifications and buy fewer consumer goods. During the war they learned to live on ration books and to use recycled rags, paper, and metal. Stopping the horrible loss of fathers and sons to the enemy more than justified that pinching thrift. The end of international conflict was supposed to bring an end to self-denial and self-imposed scarcity and a beginning of happier times. When factories started producing consumer products once again, Americans rushed to buy, and throughout the 1950s and after they kept on buying—baby clothes, suburban houses filled with shiny white appliances, and that mesmerizing new invention of entertainment and communication, the television set. The American economy was by far the strongest in the world, and compared to other peoples American citizens had a lot of money in their pockets, money saved from good jobs they held during the war, money they were eager to spend. But underlying that mood of expansion was a new worry about how long it could last.[4]

In 1945 automobile manufacturers, after years of concentrating on making tanks and aircraft for battle, began once again turning out a flood of passenger cars on Detroit's assembly lines. Factory sales soared to over 2 million automobiles in 1946. Within four years manufacturers were selling over 5 million a year, then in 1973, 9.7 million, the peak year for the nation's car industry. Eventually the United States would accumulate 250 million cars on its streets and roads, while consumers elsewhere in the world would catch the same mobility mania and come to possess three or four times that number. (Astonishingly, by the twenty-first century most of those cars would be made in China, Japan, Germany, and South Korea.) Similarly, US housing production exploded in the aftermath of the war—from over three hundred thousand new residential units started in 1945 to nearly 2 million in 1950, the peak year, and 1.4 million in 1970. The rest of the world soon learned to follow the American lead, throwing up apartments and offices, until the construction crane became the most common "bird" seen in the skies of cities everywhere.[5]

Those nearly two hundred thousand babies added every day around the world meant a dramatic postwar upsurge in population, unprecedented in size and impact. By 1950 the human population had climbed to 2.5 billion, with half that number living in Asia. During the ensuing decade another 500 million would crowd the earth, and in the 1960s another 700 million. In the United States the population would grow from 151 million in 1950 to 179 million a decade later, then to 200 million—and would keep on growing, though at a declining rate, into the next century.[6]

That postwar explosion in human beings and their consumption of goods drove a radical intervention into the environment. The Swiss historian Christian Pfister has referred to this impact as "the '50s syndrome." In Europe as well as North America, he writes, "the consumption of energy, the GNP [gross national product], the surface area of settlements, the volume of garbage, and the pollution of air, water and soil were undergoing the crucial growth spurt" that has defined the contemporary world. The important driving factor, he argues, was not only population but also a huge expansion in oil production, especially in the Middle East, where American entrepreneurs and others discovered vast deposits of petroleum. Oil reserves in that single region increased from 28 billion barrels in 1948 to 367 billion barrels in 1972. With that expansion of supply the price of oil dropped dramatically, encouraging a wholesale shift in energy consumption from coal to oil and a more profligate use of resources.

People began going places, moving things, and rearranging the earth with such ease that they quickly took that power for granted.

Both an exploding population and exploding energy consumption were potent forces. Working synergistically, both were devastating. Even a poor peasant family in India might buy a gallon of gasoline to work their fields, adding to air and water pollution, while their American suburban counterpart was buying ten or twenty gallons a week to cruise the nation's expanding network of highways. Every baby, wherever it lived, meant a lifetime of bigger and broader demands on energy, water, air, soil, and every nonhuman form of life.

Pfister argues persuasively that the postwar shift to oil from coal far overshadowed the dramatic transition to coal from wood that had occurred in the early stages of industrialization. Suddenly, with such an easily mined and transportable source of energy as oil, a source ridiculously cheap and widely available, material life changed everywhere. Not only did automobiles with gasoline engines proliferate in city and countryside, but cities also sprawled outward into their suburban margins and turned the countryside more than ever into an appendage of the city. Plastics made from oil became ubiquitous in the home and factory. New, more energy-intensive farm machines and chemical fertilizers revolutionized food production, and with cheap transportation linking all the continents more of the world's population began enjoying a greater nutritional abundance and variety. The transition to oil and the overall boom in US fossil fuel production and consumption lasted for more than two decades, the longest in postwar history, before they hit a wall.[7]

Did cheap oil in the postwar era reopen a wholly new world of abundance to replace the one discovered by Christopher Columbus? Was it a Third Earth? Not at all. The Columbian discoveries had opened a far more diverse and revolutionary set of resources and opportunities, with greater social and economic consequences. The long boom it brought added more than a copious source of energy; it provided the people of Europe, Africa, and Asia with a much fuller and more complex bounty that included soil, minerals, plants and animals, fresh water, and vast spaces for aspiring common folk to inhabit. Cheap oil could never substitute for all of that. But for a while its abundance could and did work a miraculous change.

As long as it flowed smoothly and steadily to refineries and customers, the postwar energy abundance obscured for many a startling truth: the growing dependence of the once-blessed United States on hitherto unexploited parts of the world. At least in terms of energy and a few key industrial minerals, parts of Asia and Africa became its suppliers. Not only did they supply the American metropolises, from Boston to Los Angeles, but also they supplied those of Europe and much of the Third World. What had long been regarded as America's bounty was vanishing, threatening the end of the hemisphere's remarkable rise to global economic and political success. The day was coming when it would be forced to import even more resources from someplace else, if there was anywhere they could be found.

America's future, therefore, would be radically unlike its past five hundred years. All nations, in whichever hemisphere they were found, would become more vulnerable than they had been for centuries to resource demands and environmental degradation.

Among the prophets of global limits was a Shell Oil company geologist, Marion King Hubbert, who during the early postwar period repeatedly warned that the oil boom would not last forever. The United States, he pointed out, had invented the oil industry in the first place and had enjoyed a huge domestic supply, but even this favored country would reach a peak of conventional oil production somewhere around 1970, after which it would have to rely increasingly on imports to sustain its economy. More than that, every oil field on earth, including those of the Middle East, would follow a similar bell-shaped curve: first production would rise, then it would peak, and then it would decline toward exhaustion. In 1970 Hubbert was fully vindicated when the United States did in fact reach that domestic peak, one that may prove to have marked the high point of United States oil production, conventional or nonconventional, for all time. Hubbert put the *global* peak farther off into the future, but that sobering moment would come just as surely and just as permanently.

The short, explosive history of oil and its consumption suggested to Hubbert a larger lesson than America's growing dependency on foreign suppliers. The earth was finite and getting smaller in relation to human demands, and the species must ultimately adopt a more sustainable economy for this shrinking planet. To do so would require mustering the best scientific knowledge available as well as learning habits of personal and collective restraint.

We may continue our unbridled expansion, as we have in the past, until crises result from overpopulation and exhaustion of non-replaceable resources, and thereafter

decline almost as rapidly as we have risen; or we may manage to level off our population at some comfortable figure and make an orderly transition over to new sources of
energy and inexhaustible low-grade material deposits—a
state capable of being maintained more or less indefinitely.
Whether we shall make the former or the latter choice is
one of the great problems confronting modern civilization,
and appears to rest largely upon whether we can overcome
the cultural lag between the comparatively simple physical, chemical and biological requirements of a high-energy
social order, and our behavior based on an agrarian and
prescientific past.[8]

Even as the dream of endless growth in human numbers and consumer delights seemed to be taking hold in America and elsewhere,
scientists like Hubbert were looking beyond such popular fantasies
toward a more sober reality. But did any of the nation's policymakers
understand that reality?

President Harry Truman became worried enough about
impending resource scarcity to appoint in his last year in office a
Material Policy Commission to make recommendations. As its chair
he named William S. Paley, head of the Columbia Broadcasting
System's radio and television empire—obviously a man with no particular credentials for the job other than high public visibility. From
the beginning the Paley Commission was a sham, favoring select
economic and business voices more than the natural sciences, a fact
that became obvious in 1952 when it published its report under the
revealing and highly ideological title *Resources for Freedom*. The Cold
War between the West and the expanding Soviet regime was raging,
rapidly replacing the just completed war against Fascism and overshadowing once more the war on nature. "Freedom" was becoming
a rallying cry for Western nations lining up under American capitalist leadership in opposition to Communist nations. Paley and his
commission, like President Truman, seemed more worried about
defeating the new enemy than about relieving an overstressed environment. Yet for all their blinders, they saw and admitted some
uncomfortable truths about America's prospects.

"A hundred years ago," the report pointed out, "resources seemed
limitless and the struggle upward from meager conditions of life was
the struggle to create the means and methods of getting those materials into use." The success of that struggle had led Americans to
adopt an overconfident attitude about natural resources. "We think

about materials last, not first." But in the future American demands on the land might not be so easily satisfied as in the past: "The plain fact seems to be that we have skimmed the cream of our resources as we now understand them." Most ominously, this once well-endowed nation was now the world's largest importer of copper, lead, zinc, and even lumber, while domestic demand for those commodities was continuing to rise.

In the end, the commission skirted the environmental issues and failed to call for radical new thinking. They reassured the country that its traditional belief in "the principle of Growth" through "free enterprise" was still worth preserving. Although they could find no "absolute reason for this belief," it seemed "preferable to any opposite, which to us implies stagnation and decay."[9] Growth was an engrained part of their thinking, and indeed of all the capitalist economies of the West. Admitting that they had no firm, objective reason to believe in the value or feasibility of infinite growth, the commission took refuge in optimism. American policy and institutions, they were saying, had been and should continue to be based on assumptions for which they could find no irrefutable support. The commissioners wished that growth could continue merely because they feared "stagnation." Their only concern was how to find enough resources to make that happen.

At least one domestic economist was not convinced by the president's Material Policy Commission or its call for renewed faith in old verities. John Kenneth Galbraith of Harvard University scoffed at what he saw as the illogic and overconfidence of Paley Commission resource policy. "If our levels of consumption are dangerously high in relation to the resource base, or are becoming so," he wrote, "it would obviously be better to risk stagnation now than to use up our reserves and have not stagnation but absolute contraction later on." What the commission had avoided asking, he put bluntly: "How much should a country consume?" Americans, he argued, had too vast an appetite for resources of all kinds. Technology might make more efficient use of those resources, but Galbraith could not find "resource salvation" in technology. The postwar dream of infinite numbers of people enjoying an infinite flow of goods must be examined more critically. While Galbraith could not contemplate abruptly abandoning "the principle of Growth" any more than the Paley Commission, he could see that restraint and conservation might be better strategies than plunging on toward collapse.[10]

Galbraith, for all his acerbic critiques of his fellow economists, refused to embrace the traditional conservationists with their narrow concerns about public lands, watersheds, forests, and wildlife. He charged that they were too timid to take on the bigger problem of the nation's material appetites and try to direct them away from private ends and toward the greater public good. That was a bit unfair and misinformed: conservationists were in fact becoming increasingly critical not merely of how American wealth was pursued and spent but also of the common assumption that wealth could grow indefinitely on a finite planet. Unlike Galbraith, moreover, some of them were already contemplating "a theory of the limit of growth."

That phrase belonged to Samuel H. Ordway Jr., a New York lawyer and businessman, and briefly in the 1960s the president of the Conservation Foundation. Although affluent himself, he questioned endless affluence as an unrealistic obsession. Why do we seek such growth, he asked, and what should "growth" mean beyond accumulating more stuff? What are or what should be the limits to expanding the American economy? Ordway was as disparaging of the Paley Commission as Galbraith, but he went further in questioning the cultural forces behind "our current fantastic consumption of raw materials."[11]

Growth, Ordway fearfully concluded, had acquired the power and scope of a new religion, with a potential for suicidal fervor. Older religions were losing their hold and giving way to a worldly faith in mass-produced goods. Thoroughly secular and materialistic, the religion of growth promised salvation through increasing the gross national product rather than spiritual improvement through prayer and good deeds. We have become, he wrote, "a race working, struggling, inventing, fighting, living *to create an ever higher level of living for all mankind. This is our great inspiration, our almost universal goal, and it may turn out to be our great illusion."[12] For Ordway the growth religion seemed new to the postwar era, but he might have tracked it back to the origins of capitalism, to Adam Smith's *Wealth of Nations*, and to the discovery of Second Earth. What was indisputably new was that someone as prominent and influential as he had become a nonbeliever in that religion. He represented a new agnosticism toward the economic gods of growth mania. The growth concept of salvation was doing great damage to the natural world. And worst of all, salvation through consumption might not be even possible to sustain. Growth had become in his eyes a false gospel.

Ordway dubbed the most devoted advocates of the new religion the "Cornucopians," meaning those prophets "who say that earth and sea and atmosphere can deliver to the ingenuity of man, as he becomes more skilled, an unending, inexhaustible supply of raw materials." Opposed to them were the "New Conservationists" like himself—skeptics and nonbelievers raising more radical questions about wealth and its uses than ever before. For Ordway, the obvious ally for the growth agnostic was natural science. Just as science had undermined older supernatural beliefs, it was beginning to question the religion of growth. The New Conservationists acknowledged that human ingenuity might continue for some time to expand wealth, but they were persuaded by science that "the limit of expansion will be reached within a foreseeable time despite new technological discovery and application." Ordway's theory of limits held that "basic resources" would eventually come to be in short supply and become every more costly. As that happened, "industrial expansion will cease, and we shall have reached the limit of growth."[13]

The religion of growth was not based on any faith in other-worldly deities who could suspend natural law and perform unnatural miracles. Instead, it was founded on faith in nature's endless abundance and, above all, in human ingenuity. Ordway was skeptical about both assumptions. The soil, he admitted, was still able to produce more food, although global food production would increasingly have to come from chemical fertilizers, with diminishing returns. The world's supply of soil was not increasing; on the contrary, it was becoming smaller. In a single decade the United States lost some 16 million acres of tillable land to urban and industrial use. How long could such losses continue? How many times could the US population double and redouble and still be fed? At what point would Americans be forced to import food, as they were already importing a long list of industrial resources? Those were hard questions that the nation had never had to ask before, and rosy assurances from the Cornucopians were becoming harder to believe.

Among the Cornucopians that Ordway might have had in mind were two resource economists, Harold Barnett and Chandler Morse, whose classic work *Scarcity and Growth: The Economics of Natural Resource Availability*, became almost a sacred text among their professional colleagues in ensuing decades. Published in 1963 for the organization Resources for the Future, a newly formed group inspired by the Paley Commission, *Scarcity and Growth* spoke for a more mainstream elite than either Ordway or Galbraith did. Barnett boasted close connections to the Department of the Interior and the Rand Corporation as well as outstanding academic credentials. Morse taught economics at Cornell University and was a highly regarded authority on African economic development. Both were high priests of the economic establishment where growth had become received wisdom, and both adhered closely to that way of thinking. For the two authors, labor and capital had become the only important determinants of prosperity. Nature mattered little. Given enough labor and capital, the role of natural resources in generating wealth could more or less be disregarded. Against all the alarming data about population increase, soil erosion, a diminished land base, and declining domestic production of vital resources, Barnett and Morse focused on only one issue: the international cost of natural resources over time. That cost, they declared, was actually falling, not rising. Resources therefore must still be abundant. They will always be abundant so long as labor and capital are abundant.

Tracking the cost of natural resources over time is a difficult process because cost itself is an ambiguous concept: What does it include, and what does it leave out? Then, deciding which resources are scarce and which are abundant at any point depends on where one looks and how one measures. Barnett and Morse chose to focus on only one method of computing: isolate the unit cost of a specific resource in the United States (copper, fish, etc.) in terms of the cost of labor or capital invested in it. They made long charts tracking those costs in resource extraction. From 1870 to 1957 they discovered for agricultural and mineral resources that costs had declined, but not for forestry or fisheries. Mineral demand over that period had increased many times, but the costs per unit of minerals mined and refined had fallen to only a fifth of their original levels. This was because American mining companies had developed new machinery and learned how to save on labor. Coal, for example, had become less expensive to extract as the coal miner with the pick going down deep into the earth had given way to the driver of a bulldozer stripping away the overburden of soil and exposing coal seams to the light of day. Setting aside what it did to the soil, water, air, or biota, strip mining was a cheaper way of digging coal. That kind of cost reduction, the economists argued, could go on forever, so that minerals need never become scarce. If they ever did become so, then buyers would shift to cheaper substitutes. Conservationists, therefore, were foolish to worry about natural resource shortages that might endanger growth or industrial stability. The record of the past assured a glorious future.[14]

A few years later Barnett had become giddier than ever about the growth economy. The word "resource," he maintained, has no fixed meaning but shifts with society's level of knowledge. As new extractive methods are devised, resources in new forms are created. Extraction is becoming no longer simply a matter of digging a conventional ore out of the ground. It has become a process of changing the very form and structure of nature. "Atoms and molecules and their energies," he wrote, "not fields and trees and fossils, are the building blocks of our time." He was emphatically and proudly a Cornucopian, but it was "the cornucopia of scientific advance and technological change," not the abundance of nature, that he celebrated. Humans could burn down all the forests, wash all the soil into the sea, pave over the green fields, and strip mine the mountains for coal—and yet always there would be atoms and molecules waiting to be fashioned into whatever the consumer desired.

Ironically, Barnett soon began sounding more like a conservationist or environmentalist as he thought about not merely the quantity of resources but the quality of life. Shortly after his book appeared, he admitted that he had overlooked some important costs ("externalities" in economic language). Those were costs that had not been part of the record of market transactions, costs that sellers and buyers had disregarded—social and environmental costs. Now he began to acknowledge them. "Preservation of natural beauty, urban agglomeration, waste disposal and pollution, changes in income distribution, water supply, land use—these are a few of the social problems related to natural resources and the quality of life." Some might call that list the true costs of resource extraction, which eluded the economist's narrow methods of calculation. But even while acknowledging that growth generated such "problems," Barnett's ingrained habit was to try to assign a price to those externalities—a price for human health and welfare. Such costs, accumulating beyond those of mere production, he began arguing, should be paid by the government through programs to clean up the water and air. Then they would not become a drag on doing business or slow down the engines of growth.[15]

Barnett and other economists of his day were never more utopian than when they decided Americans could both pursue infinite growth in the industrial economy and still protect vigorously the earth's beauty and health for future generations. No hard choices had to be made. But by the later 1950s and into the 1960s the New Conservationists challenged that utopianism. To move beyond narrow, outmoded questions of natural resource "costs," they began also calling themselves "environmentalists." Forests, they pointed out, and not only trees or wood, might become scarce. Good soils might become scarce and depleted, as well as coal, oil, or industrial metals. Birds might become scarce, along with clean rivers and clean skies—and those scarcities might be as vital to human survival and welfare as the scarcity of ore in a mine tunnel.

The emergence of modern environmentalism occurred most dramatically with the writings of Rachel Carson, author of *Silent Spring* (1962), which prophesied a world in which no birds sang after massive pesticide contamination. It found other powerful voices in Paul Ehrlich, a Stanford University population biologist and author of *The Population Bomb* (1968), in Barry Commoner, antinuclear activist and author of *Science and Survival* (1967) and *The Closing Circle* (1971), and in David Brower, executive director of the Sierra Club from 1952 to 1969 and founder of Friends of the Earth. Like the New Conservationists, environmentalists of the postwar period reacted to a time of intensified plundering in the pursuit of plenty. The costs of that plundering, they saw, were economic in the broadest sense—costs to human welfare and to ecological integrity, but the costs lay beyond the scope of market transactions and were impossible to measure in terms of Gross National Product. No superficial program of "cleaning things up" could ever pay those costs in full.[16]

Was there a limit to American or world growth? *Should* there be a limit, a self-imposed restraint on using the earth in the long-term interest of both humans and other living things? Environmentalists answered yes to both questions and declared that the earth must be seen as a finite place, far smaller than it had appeared over previous centuries. They perceived that its limited and more complexly understood resources had to support more people than ever and support their rising expectations. Future generations, they believed, must have a chance to enjoy the world's natural resources, not least the resource of a healthy, stable earth. It was too risky to nature's health to expect that technology could always extract more resources from the sea or land without consequences. The miracle of technology was in fact making the earth a more dangerous place to live. Nuclear fallout was one example of that danger. So too was strip mining for coal, digging deeper into the earth while turning it into a wasteland. Turning the planet into one vast strip mine or toxic wasteland was the full and true price of making coal or iron or uranium abundant and attractive to manufacturing.

Americans in the early postwar decades went on a global consumer binge, but they also began reading more books and magazines warning that the promises of mass production could be tragically oversold and prove unsustainable and destructive. Along with glittering shopping centers came a rising postwar angst about the future. The simple picture of a nation, or world, overpopulated by heedless consumers, stampeding to buy whatever was offered for sale, does not explain why writers like Osborn and Vogt, Ordway and Galbraith, Carson and Commoner found a large audience, or why that audience continued to grow as the twentieth century rolled on toward a day of reckoning.

Postscript: David Potter's America

For a certain poor family living on the edge of a windblown Great Plains town in the years immediately following World War II, still remembering the Dust Bowl tragedy and the Great Depression and profiting little from the subsequent war economy, the fabled consumer society was a distant prospect. They lived in a small, shabby house on a dirt street, and their sole wage earner took the bus to work. They had enough electricity for household lighting, but no electric refrigerator or vacuum cleaner. The kitchen tap gave running water but there was no indoor bathroom—so they used, as their ancestors did, an outdoor privy through winter and summer alike and took baths on Saturday night in a galvanized tub. Millions of Americans lived that way just a few decades ago. Almost nobody does so today, even in impoverished ghettoes, where cable television is ubiquitous, along with cell phones and hot showers.

Back then it would have sounded strange but hopeful to hear the six lectures on American abundance given by the acclaimed Yale historian David Potter in the summer of 1950, lectures that became the basis of the book *People of Plenty*. Born in Augusta, Georgia, forty years earlier, growing up politically conservative and well educated, Potter managed to become perhaps the greatest historian of his generation. His scholarly work on the South and the Civil War would hold up extraordinarily well over time, and his reading of American society and politics in *People of Plenty* would have remarkable staying power as one of the best analyses of the so-called American character. Though not devoid of a critical attitude, the book promised the poor of the world that they too could enjoy a plenitude of wealth if they imitated the more successful habits of the United States.[17]

On a theoretical level the book attempted to reassert the value of history to the social sciences. Potter argued that scholars in psychology, sociology, and anthropology had identified common traits that made Americans unique, but none of them could explain how that uniqueness originated. They needed the historian to demonstrate how Americans had become different from other peoples.

The proximate cause was simple: Americans had acquired to a high degree "the competitive spirit." As he elaborated in the opening chapters, that spirit had been associated with a strong inclination toward self-reliance, hard work, private initiative, and a fierce hunger for personal success. Competitiveness led Americans to an unprecedented geographical and social mobility—moving here or there in space, up or down the social ladder, always ready and willing to leave behind their place in society. Competitiveness made Americans more egalitarian than other peoples, at least equal in aspirations and opportunism if not in rank or income. Those linked traits ultimately came, he argued, from an extraordinary abundance of material wealth. Abundance made a democracy, not the other way around. Abundance came out of America's past and explained the national character.[18]

Though never bumptiously so, Potter belonged to a generation of academics who celebrated America's exceptionalism and its rise to global power. He wrote to understand but also to extol the competitive spirit and to offer it to a world recovering from war, colonialism, and poverty. In his book Potter included a 1949 chart showing a huge gap between US per capita income and that of other nations—the United States standing twice as high as Britain, three times higher than Norway or France.[19] To overcome that gap other nations, he implied, must learn competitiveness too.

In later years that international gap in affluence would narrow considerably, as Western Europe and Japan began to produce more goods and as once desperately poor nations like China also made significant gains. In fact, six decades after Potter wrote, the United States would fall from first place to nineteenth in per capita income, although those higher on the list would all be smaller and more homogeneous nations rich in oil or trade, like Qatar, Norway, Luxembourg, and Singapore. Despite those shifts in rankings, the world would continue to look on America as the avatar of modern affluence. In 2014 its GDP per capita stood at a whopping $54,800.[20]

For all that impressive American success in accumulating wealth, however, a few historians have criticized Potter's book and its analysis. Robert Collins, for example, has called it a "dazzling but fundamentally flawed classic." He objects to the basic idea of an "American" character, which suggests a conformity that does not exist and a prosperity that has not been widely shared. "The concept of a national character," he writes, "has been shattered by ... historical pluralism" so much so that a single, unified character is a fiction. Potter may describe the white middle class more or less accurately, but he fails to give sufficient weight to the persistence of poverty in America, whether among black, Latino, or white communities.[21] In his defense Potter acknowledged that blacks had not been allowed to compete as vigorously as whites, and he never claimed that all Americans had ever agreed on everything. He merely claimed that certain "adaptive traits" had developed, competitiveness most importantly, and that most Americans had enjoyed a higher standard of living than other peoples.

Another critic, Jackson Lears, has argued that Potter presents too flat and narrow a notion of abundance, ignoring the culturally rich meanings that the concept has carried throughout American and Western European history. Potter's notion of abundance is exactly what the Chamber of Commerce wants us to think about— all the stuff found at the shopping mall, "a surfeit of mass-produced, disposable commodities"—and to regard that simple definition as sufficient. For Potter abundance was defined in terms of "usable goods," including automobiles, whiskey, television sets, white bread, and sulfa drugs. It's the stuff once purchased from the Sears, Roebuck catalogue and today procured from Wal-Mart or Safeway. But abundance, Lears is right to say, has meant far more than such processed and manufactured things. It has meant a chance for a new life, a promise of economic sufficiency and creative opportunity; it has meant a place to pursue dreams with enough resources to realize them; it has meant a richness of experience and relationships. One could add, it has meant too a richness of health and ecological well-being. Because Potter does not acknowledge that fuller meaning or take a more critical stance toward factory-made abundance, he seems indifferent to the fact that people might feel "a nagging sense of want even amid a superabundance of things."[22]

But the most questionable of Potter's assumptions was his definition of abundance not as a gift of nature but as almost purely a product of labor and capital competing freely. Abundance, he emphasized repeatedly, was created by culture, not furnished by the natural environment. This reasoning led him into a confusing argument. He made the competitive spirit both the consequence of material abundance and its root cause. Setting out to explain historically where the competitive spirit and democracy had come from, he ended by arguing that abundance was in turn created by the competitive spirit.

In that circular reasoning he broke with an alternative way of thinking embodied in the writings of the historian Frederick Jackson Turner and his protégé Walter Prescott Webb. The Wisconsin-born

Turner had believed that the uniquely favorable environmental conditions of the Americas and particularly of the United States had been powerful influences giving rise to new cultural traits. Potter rejected Turner's emphasis on America as the *land* of plenty mainly because he did not like where it led: to a bleak future of rising inequality and class rigidity as the original natural abundance disappeared. Both Turner and Webb had warned that an abundance of free arable land was vanishing. Potter felt that was too pessimistic. The factory, he insisted, had replaced nature as the creator of American abundance.[23]

Potter rejected what he saw as rigid environmental determinism. But where the earlier historians may have assigned too much power to the natural world, Potter assigned too little. Good soils may not produce good crops without a good farmer. The good farmer may need a plow and a spirit of enterprise. But the quality and quantity of his soils has always been a powerful factor in his success. Had Potter grown up, as Turner did, in the Midwest, where good soils had played such a vital role in economic development, he might not have been so quick to toss nature aside. He might have understood that nature has been and will always be a powerful force in cultural evolution. Nature has provided, and nature has denied. Explaining history by a simple cultural determinism is no better than explaining it by a simple environmental determinism.

Potter offered the phrase "competitive spirit" as an alternative to earlier historians' emphasis on the economic culture of capitalism, and on its divisive, conflict-ridden, and destructive ways. In fact he refused even to say the word "capitalism." It was tainted with bad memories of the stock market crash of 1929 and robber barons from the Gilded Age. It was an epithet spat out by a rabble from the South and West, the populists, by leftist voices during the Depression, and by those enemies of the "free world," communist revolutionaries. So Potter preferred to speak more positively of "the competitive spirit," "access to market," "American libertarian principles," and "free-enterprise democracy." But surely all those phrases were inextricably linked to the history of capitalism and were mere euphemisms for that institution and its powerful ethos. It was in fact the *"capitalist* spirit" that Potter was talking about, the spirit that had been so widely celebrated among Americans and that was supposed to generate their remarkable abundance.[24]

Whatever words Potter used, the distinguished historian was trapped in a strangely ahistorical way of thinking. His competitive or capitalist spirit had no earthly origin, no moment of conception or gestation, no life span and no change over time. It was a disembodied spirit that had no real past and no endpoint. It could survive forever. He was quite sure that Americans, if they kept the competitive (or capitalist) spirit alive, could go on creating mass abundance indefinitely into the future. There could be no limit to human resourcefulness so long as it was animated by that transcendent spirit.

Potter thus appeared to offer a materialist explanation for American exceptionalism—an economic abundance that appeared early in the nation's history—but in fact his explanation was in the end more ethereal and timeless, a cultural force that owed nothing to time or place, and nothing to nature. If that spirit is put back into a real American and European history, with the acknowledgment that it came from somewhere at some point in time and out of some relationship to nature, a more complicated history emerges. The United States became large, rich, and successful, first, because of its natural resource abundance and, second, because of the capitalist revolution that followed the discovery of Second Earth.

At the same it is clear that not all of America, or all of the Americas, was equally blessed, or became equally rich. Ecological inequality—the unevenness of nature's bounty—has been as real as social inequality. The modern world has told a story of people "creating" plenty. But it has also told stories of people facing failure and deprivation, in place after place, because of environmental limitations that could not be easily overcome by any amount of competitive enterprise. And that history shows the vital role of nature in making men and women wealthy and healthy—a truth that should humble us and dampen our nationalist pride.

Abundance has a more complex history than Professor Potter understood. It has been a historical condition based on material discoveries as well as cultural traits, full of change and reversals as well as advances. From a scientific rather than an exclusively cultural perspective abundance is a measure of the planet's ability to support life, to provide food and fiber, to recycle wastes, to provide clean, fresh water, to be resilient in the face of change. By this more complicated perspective, what would that poor Kansas family have said about their state of abundance in 1950? Were they poor, or were they rich? More than a half century later what can we say about our own state of abundance? Potter would say that we are getting rich on the strength of our ideals and traits. But is it true? Might it be that we becoming poorer in many ways? Natural scientists, along with environmentalists, would make that more complicated analysis of plenty and poverty in the decades that followed.

CHAPTER 8

The Wolf at the Door

IN THE SUMMER OF 1969 two young scientists left Cambridge, Massachusetts, bound for India, their new PhD diplomas in hand. They went seeking holiday escape, but a year later they returned to the United States, chastened and shocked by what they had seen, ready to take on a research agenda that would change their lives and challenge boldly the established doctrine of infinite economic growth. It would lead to the biggest selling and most controversial environmental book of the postwar era, *The Limits to Growth* (1972). No single work could claim to be decisive in shifting popular and scientific opinion from an age of abundance to one of vulnerability, but *Limits* expressed better than any of its predecessors a deep cultural transformation going on that would become unstoppable over the decades to follow. It was the book that cried wolf. The wolf was the planet's environmental decline, and that wolf was real.

The main authors of *Limits to Growth*, Dennis and Donella Meadows, were both born during World War II and grew up in sheltered, middle-class Minnesota and Illinois families representative of David Potter's people of plenty. They first met in an undergraduate science course at Carleton College, a lab encounter that led to marriage and migration eastward, Donella to a doctoral program in biochemistry at Harvard University, Dennis to Massachusetts Institute of Technology's Sloan School of Management. Her dissertation was on the subject of bovine pancreatic ribonuclease, while he wrote just as densely on hog market cycles. So far they were simply two supremely talented minds focused on barnyard research. Those were worthy subjects but a far cry from where the two scientists would end up.

Neither had been active in conservation or environmental causes, beyond Donella's youthful enthusiasm for saving prairie wildflowers, nor had they read Henry Fairfield Osborn, Rachel Carson, or Paul Ehrlich. They were self-absorbed, technically astute nerds who would stumble almost accidentally into the dangers facing the world—earnest innocents who on their return to America would manage to put into simple but dramatic words and graphs what earlier, more famous, and charismatic critics had been trying to say for some time.

Investing everything they had in a new Land Rover, the Meadows pair set out in the summer of 1969 on an adventure-seeking trek that would take them across Turkey, Iran, Afghanistan, and Pakistan before reaching their destination, the Asian subcontinent. They did not travel, as many from their generation were doing, to look for drugs or ashrams or to drop out of modern life. Their original purpose was to climb rugged mountains and raft down white-water rivers. Along the way they camped in deserts, jungles, mountains, and villages. But as they left their bourgeois lives farther and farther behind, they became more observant of how ordinary Asians raised food, built dwellings, and managed (or mismanaged) the land. Through the dust and sweat of travel, they discovered a world of intense poverty, overpopulation, and environmental degradation they had not anticipated, a set of conditions they came to fear as portents of America's future.

Donella later recalled that she began her trip through Asia as "a child of the Sputnik age, a technological optimist" who believed science could solve all problems. Insulated from the persistent poverty in America, she encountered for the first time in her life "malnourished children and kids with the open sores of smallpox. We saw beggars, and houses collapsed by earthquakes, and sewage running in open drains alongside streets." In the Indus Valley they witnessed severely eroding soils, in Sri Lanka the flooding of farmlands and jungles by a massive hydroelectric project. Yet they also discovered "dancing and singing, beautiful handicrafts, simple but ingenious native technologies, and ceremonies of deep spirituality." Their travels made them wonder about the causes and persistence of poverty in a world that supposedly was on the road to universal happiness.[1]

Naïve they may have been, but undoubtedly they had left the United States already harboring some disillusionment in their hearts. Their lives of relative comfort and first-rate education had not been completely satisfactory, or they would have headed to a vacation spot in the Colorado Rockies or on the coast of Maine. Returning home in the summer of 1970, their awakening to a harsher global reality continued. In Donella's recollections, they were "appalled at the violence and the corrupt and divisive politics" they encountered in their own country. The Vietnam War was still going on, for almost a decade already, and President Richard Nixon, despite campaign promises to end the war, was bombing Cambodia. On campuses antiwar students were protesting that war. In May 1970 at Kent State University, the Ohio National Guard shot down four protestors and wounded nine others. Neither Donella or Dennis felt welcomed by that America, nor could they understand "why the people in our home towns needed so much stuff" or why, despite such apparent material satisfactions, they seemed so dissatisfied with their lives. "Vastly wealthy by Asian standards," Donella wrote, "they were not noticeably happier than the villagers with whom we had spent the last year."[2]

Perhaps the young scientists would have been more cheerful had they arrived in time to witness the first Earth Day, which was celebrated on April 22, 1970, and marked the full-blown emergence of the modern environmental movement. Old and new issues, ranging from nature conservation to industrial pollution, had flowed together on that day to create a moment of planetary optimism as well as calls for radical action. Before and after that event, Nixon and Congress, although bitterly divided over the politics of race and war, managed to cooperate again and again to pass many landmark pieces of environmental legislation, culminating in the establishment of the Environmental Protection Agency. Because of the environmental movement and its early political successes millions of citizens had already begun making permanent changes in their habits, careers, and personal values. They were putting photographs of an endangered Planet Earth on their walls and taking about how to heal and restore its health.[3]

Outside the United States, much had been happening too, some of it at high levels, some of it at the grassroots. A visionary Italian industrialist (formerly a socialist and antifascist), Aurelio Peccei, while expressing sympathies with Third World desires for economic development, was worrying about the social and environmental consequences of those desires. In 1968 he met a Scot named Alexander King, the top science adviser to the Europe-based Organization of Economic Cooperation and Development (OECD). The OECD was dedicated to promoting industrial capitalism, but

King had become increasingly critical of that organization and its devotion to endless growth. Like Peccei, he was worried about a long list of problems, including environmental pollution, inequalities of wealth and power, loss of faith in institutions, rejection of traditional values, and the growing potential for conflict over resources. The long and complicated list of problems added up to a bad dream for all nations, contradicting their plans for universal progress. Peccei and King perceived those problems as interrelated parts of a single whole they called the "world problematique." Piecemeal solutions, they felt, would never work. Nor would more growth by itself, nor technology or the accumulation of more money.

Intent on addressing that problematique more comprehensively, Peccei and King established the Club of Rome, named after the site of its founding, whose purpose was to promote the view that "we cannot expect technological solutions alone to get us out us of this vicious circle."[4] They were not technocrats seeking to rule that world in industry's own terms. On the contrary, they sought a more comprehensive moral and philosophical understanding of the world's failures than narrowly focused businessmen, economists, engineers, and short-term-thinking politicians had offered. Thirty individuals from ten countries composed the original club, coming together like professors in an invisible college to pursue a deeper knowledge and intellectual coherence. Other club leaders included Eduard Pestel of the Technical University of Hannover, Germany; Saburo Okita, head of the Japan Economic Research Center in Tokyo; and Carroll Wilson of the Massachusetts Institute of Technology.

After searching vainly for someone who could help analyze the world problematique, they turned to Wilson's MIT colleague Jay Forrester. He was an inventor, a brilliant academic maverick, a statistician seeking truth. Early on a professor of electrical engineering, he became one of the nation's first computer experts, then tried to apply his mathematical expertise to social analysis through a method he called "system dynamics." Originally developed in the 1950s to help corporate managers understand complex industrial processes, system dynamics used gargantuan computing machines, filling whole rooms with their bulky electronics, to create abstract models of dynamic processes. Those processes were at some level remarkably alike; they could be found in any system, network, or organization, ranging in size from a single business to a whole city. The computer model was supposed to identify the key variables in any system, visualize how they might interact with each other, and experiment with possible improvements in their functioning.

Societies are like machines, Forrester argued, in that they comprise many interrelated parts, though vastly more complicated than, say, the parts of an airplane. Systems dynamics promised to clarify a society's inner workings and ask how they might work more efficiently.[5]

In July 1970, several members of the Club of Rome assembled on the MIT campus for a seminar with Forrester to learn his methods of analysis. On a white bed sheet draped across the seminar room wall he drew a sketch of what he called the "world system." Sprawling across the sheet was a complicated set of arrows, circles, and loops featuring six key variables: human population, capital investment, geographical space, natural resources, industrial pollution, and food production. Each was connected intricately to all the others. Changes in one of those six variables could affect changes in the others—through "feedback loops" that could be tracked and predicted. For the first time, club members felt they could discern some rational order in the wild chaos of the modern world.[6]

The Meadows pair, who had seen real-world versions of those abstractions in their holiday travels, arrived back in Cambridge just in time to sit in on the seminar. Forrester had been Dennis's teacher. But this time Forrester did more than provide a technical lesson in generating lines and arrows, systemic flows and feedback loops. He provided broad, compelling ideas. His model was based on an assumption he made perfectly explicit: each of those variables faced limits, and the world must adjust to those limits or it would crash. In contrast to the prevailing Cornucopian ethos of world leaders, Forrester had concluded that the world was finite and vulnerable. That conclusion may have derived in part from his exposure to the environmental movement, but it also came, he believed, from lessons learned from his ancestors' struggle to survive on a drought-plagued cattle ranch in Nebraska's Sand Hills. There he had learned lessons in practical ethics and economics. "Mankind throughout history," he wrote, "has focused on growth—growth in population, standard of living, and geographical boundaries." Now, he was convinced, it was necessary to begin "the transition from growth to equilibrium." The "world problematique," he argued to club members, was caused by trying to force infinite material growth on a finite planet.[7]

Peccei and the others were so impressed by Forrester's clarity and logic, and by the philosophical outlook behind his bed sheet graph, that they asked him to gather supporting data and assemble a written report. They offered to fund such a document with a $250,000 grant from the Volkswagen Foundation. Forrester,

however, declined, having other projects in hand. On his recommendation the club hired Dennis instead. Dennis accepted and quickly
recruited his wife Donella. Although she had planned to take up
a postdoctoral fellowship at Harvard, over the next year she would
provide unpaid assistance and do most of the writing, while Dennis
provided the computer skills and directed the data gathering. They
were assisted by Jørgen Randers, a doctoral student in physics at MIT
and the son of the head of Norway's nuclear energy program, and
by William Behrens, an undergraduate student in electrical engineering. Thirteen others, drawn from such diverse countries as the
United States, Germany, Iran, Turkey, and India, joined the team.
What drove them all was the challenge of furnishing lots of data for
Forrester's computer model (renamed "World3") and demonstrating his core assumption that human societies had forgotten that
there are natural limits and thus were facing collapse.

Donella summed up what she learned from Forrester's tutor-
ing: "The limits to physical expansion of the human economy are
flexible, dynamic, and interconnected. Some are being pushed
upward by technology, some are been eroded downward by overload
and mismanagement and waste. We don't know where they are, but
we do know that on a finite planet limits are inevitable. If we evade
one and continue growing, we will run into another. We don't have
the option to grow forever ... We shouldn't even want to, because
growth against limits is itself a problem. Our option is to choose our
own limits, or let nature chose them for us."[8]

Some Club of Rome members were made uneasy by such thinking, but not Peccei, nor another businessman in the group, Robert
Lattes of SEMA International in Paris, a global marketing association. Lattes passed on a French riddle that illustrated the dangers of
growth as seen from a traditional peasant's perspective. Suppose you
own a pond on which a water lily is growing—doubling in size each
day. If unchecked, it will completely cover the pond in thirty days,
choking off all the other forms of life in the water. For a long time
the growing plant seems small and manageable, so you decide not to
worry about cutting it back until it covers half the pond. On which
day will that be? On the twenty-ninth day! You have one day to save
your pond. It was a simple illustration of the dangers in "exponential
growth"—that is, growth that occurs at a constant rate, like interest
on a bank account. Exponential growth was in fact occurring in all
the variables the MIT team set out to track. No one could say exactly
when the twenty-ninth day would arrive for the planet as a whole,
but it would surely come and most likely would come stealthily in the

night. Before nations had time to react, a most daunting crisis would be upon them.

That there are limits to exponential growth was not a completely new or astonishing idea, but apparently it was not easy for many moderns to grasp. Over the next year the team's effort to prepare an exhaustive technical report kept getting interrupted by questions from club members who did not understand the basic ideas, forcing the team to stop and write a kind of glossary of terms and concepts. That scattershot manual proved so helpful and impressive that Peccei decided it should be turned into a book for distribution to a mass audience. Such a synopsis would not try to present all the data and modeling, which would take much longer to assemble, but only lay out the main ideas in simplified form. Potomac Associates, a nonpartisan and nonprofit organization in Washington, DC, agreed to publish the book, and in March 1972 it was finished and rushed into print.

Titled *The Limits to Growth*, the book was a mere two hundred pages long—dynamite in a small package. Donella's text amounted to an extended essay, while the remaining pages consisted of more than fifty figures and tables, some of them covering whole pages with boxes, circles, dotted lines, and parabolic curves, but carefully omitting long mathematical equations that might discourage readers. Over the next few years the little book surprised everyone by selling over 12 million copies (none of the MIT team received a nickel from the royalties) and getting translated into more than thirty foreign languages. No one expected such an excited response. Just as unexpectedly, the Meadows couple found themselves propelled into the ranks of international environmental gurus. Randers, meanwhile, left the country to assume a prominent academic position back home in Norway, while Behrens chose to retire quietly to private life in rural Maine.

The book's paperback edition appeared with a cover portrait of a shrinking earth, a visual clue to the argument inside (see Plate 4). From the outset the book claimed to be only a preliminary effort to create a formal, written model of the world. As a progress report it was admittedly "imperfect, oversimplified, and unfinished." The team went on to acknowledge that they were not the first to look at the world with "a global, long-term perspective" or to reach what might be unfashionable conclusions. Then they got bolder. Present growth trends, they warned, must eventually bump up against natural limits—not one limit, but many limits—and would likely do so "sometime within the next one hundred years." Given humanity's tendency to procrastinate and resist change, they warned, "the most probable result will be a rather sudden and uncontrollable decline in both population and industrial capacity." If nations took those limits seriously, however, they could create "a condition of ecological and economic stability that is sustainable far into the future," one that would satisfy the basic material needs of every person alive. But making the transition from growth to equilibrium would take a lot of time, and the sooner nations began working to attain it, the "greater will be their chances of success."[9]

The book did not offer a set of hard predictions about what would happen, but rather a series of scenarios about where the world might be headed if it did not change course. The first two chapters, comprising more than half of the book, were titled "The Nature of Exponential Growth" and "The Limits of Exponential Growth." Much of their content was cribbed from Forrester, but the team reduced his key variables going through exponential increase to a slightly shorter list—"accelerating industrialization, rapid population growth, widespread malnutrition, depletion of nonrenewable resources, and a deteriorating environment." Again, these were not separate, independent variables but complexly intertwined in their relations and nonlinear in their outcomes. They were also simple colloquialisms for complex phenomena, none of them easy to measure. What numbers, for example, could one assign to "a deteriorating environment?" The data describing changes going on in those variables was unrefined and sketchy, but the book drew on sources that were careful and not inclined to exaggeration—including the US Agency for International Development, the US Bureau of Mines, President Nixon's new Council on Environmental Quality, and articles published in such journals as *Scientific American*.[10]

The biggest scare the team aroused was one that echoed the work of the Paley Commission—depletion of nonrenewable sources needed for further industrial growth. But now they could draw on somewhat better data. Not merely the United States but the whole world was facing a decline in the raw materials needed for industrialization. The MIT team calculated that virtually all the resources on which modern economies relied might disappear within less than a hundred years—that is, before the year 2072. One table listed nineteen critical resources, ranging from aluminum and copper to lead, tungsten, tin, mercury, natural gas, petroleum, and zinc. All of them could well be exhausted, some within a single lifetime or two.

Chromium, for example, a gray lustrous metal that resists corrosion and is a main ingredient in stainless steel, was in short supply.

At current rates of consumption the world's known supplies would last for 420 years. But chromium was being consumed at an exponentially increasing rate of 2 to 3 percent a year, so current rates were meaningless. Exponentially viewed, current stocks might be gone in only ninety-five years. What then would take chromium's place? What other element or substance could do the job? Even iron, which had come into use around 1200 B.C. in the Ancient Near East and around 600 B.C. in China, and had been so indispensable to the Industrial Revolution, might last no longer than chromium—only ninety-three years, *Limits to Growth* calculated—for here too consumption was increasing exponentially. The silvery-white element of mercury, useful in a multitude of ways, might last a mere thirteen years, copper twenty-one years, natural gas and conventional petroleum for only two more decades.[11]

Mining companies and oil explorers were assiduously looking for more of everything, and they would find it, putting those depletion dates off for a while. So the computer programmers obligingly increased the size of potential reserves by 500 percent! Enormous bonanzas lay in the future, they agreed—yet, and this was the sobering reality of exponential growth, ever-increasing consumption would soon exhaust those future supplies too. Chromium, even if granted five times its current reserves, would last only a century and a half. Quintupling the supply of copper would put off its date of depletion by only twenty-seven years, petroleum by thirty years, zinc by fifty years. What then? After every last ton or gallon of those essential materials had been found and consumed, what resources would take their place?

None of those resources would ever actually disappear from the chemical composition of the planet. "In one sense," admitted the report, "they are never lost." But after mining and consuming they would become so dispersed in the air, soil, and water that it would be nearly impossible to recover or reuse them. Not only would they become more and more highly dispersed but also often they would become more harmful to life. Those used supplies of mercury, for instance, were already ending up as a toxic residue in the bodies of fish, while lead from automotive fuel was poisoning the city air, and oil was washing up on polluted beaches or migrating into the atmosphere in the form of CO_2. Thus vital resources, whether abundant or scarce, would first produce consumer goods and then would produce poisonous wastes.[12]

Perhaps it was unwise for the MIT team to provide overly precise dates for when specific resource depletions might occur. Again and again those dates would draw attention and controversy. They would be attacked as inaccurate or too pessimistic, and the broader argument they pointed to—the vulnerability of the global economy and ecology—would be obscured. The main point was that no economy, including the industrial species, could last forever. When cheap and plentiful resources disappeared, when they were "gone," it was anybody's guess how industrialization could continue. But an even more important theme in the book, which became obscured by all the disputing over dates, was the fact that using up resources not only threatened the stability and health of the economy but also the stability and health of the earth's ecological processes.

Forrester called his view of natural limits "Malthusianism," but it bore only a loose resemblance to the worldview of Thomas Malthus. Malthus's *On the Principles of Population* had posited an inherent tendency for all species to reproduce faster than their food supply. He was concerned only with whether soil productivity could keep up with growing numbers of mouths and bellies, ignoring broader environmental problems. The history of food production, he argued, showed that people always tend to overshoot their supply, leading inevitably, in the absence of prudential restraint, to a bitter struggle for survival and starvation among the less fortunate. Remember that according to Reverend Malthus, it was God who had made this world so in order to spur the human species to greater effort in the conquest of the earth. Forrester and the Meadows team were not making the same argument. They were not insisting that poverty is inevitable or productive of a greater good, nor did they blame poor people for environmental degradation. Rather, they were saying that growth in all factors could not continue forever on a finite planet. Far from being orthodox Malthusianism, they were sharply at odds with some of its core beliefs.

Above all their view of nature was radically different from Malthus's. "It is not known," the MIT team pointed out, "how much we can perturb the natural ecological balance of the earth. It is not known how much CO_2 or thermal pollution can be released without causing irreversible damage in the earth's climate, or how much radioactivity, lead, mercury, or pesticide can be absorbed by plants, fish, or human beings before the vital processes are severely interrupted."[13] Malthus never worried about disturbing the ecological balance. He never imagined that atmospheric carbon might change the climate or man-made radioactivity or pesticides proliferate across the planet. On the contrary, he thought that improving the environment was part of God's plan. Something new had entered the conversation since the late eighteenth century: a concern for an overstressed planetary ecosystem that was highly susceptible to dangerous technologies, to disruption and disequilibrium.

That post-Malthusian view of natural limits, whatever it owed to Forrester's memories of cattle ranching on the Great Plains or the Meadows's encounter with Asian poverty from the windows of a Land Rover, received strong support from the science of ecology. Although it had been around for decades, only in the postwar era did ecology begin to alter popular perceptions.[14] In writing their report the Meadows turned to America's two most prominent ecologists, the University of Georgia's Eugene Odum and Yale University's G. Evelyn Hutchinson. Both saw nature as a series of interrelated, interactive wholes adding up to a single complex "biosphere." Nature's systems, they argued, were under assault by human numbers and activity. As Hutchinson put it, there is "reasonably objective evidence that the length of life of the biosphere as an inhabitable region for organisms is to be measured in decades rather than in hundreds of millions of years. This is entirely the fault of our own species."[15]

Understandably, then, it was ecologists and other natural scientists, and their lay disciples, the environmentalists, who responded to the publication of *The Limits to Growth* with the greatest enthusiasm and who found the perspective of the MIT team perfectly rational and convincing. Obviously, they echoed, the world cannot go on adding more and more to its population, agricultural production, and industrial output without increasing pollution and threatening the natural cycles that sustain all life.[16]

But scientists and environmentalists took a while to get their reviews and supporting data into print, while the news media rushed to publicize, dramatize, and occasionally trivialize the MIT team's ideas. *Time* was first out of the gate, running a kind of advanced review two months before *Limits* appeared in print, a review that was based more on hearsay than printed text. The magazine alluded to the Massachusetts work in progress while highlighting the sensational contents of another book that appeared in Great Britain in the early weeks of 1972, *Blueprint for Survival*, published by *The Ecologist*, a book that anticipated much of the MIT team's thinking. *Time* noted that thirty-three distinguished scientists, including Julian Huxley and C. H. Waddington, had endorsed *Blueprint*. Unrestricted industrial and population expansion, those scientists warned, must lead to "the breakdown of society and of the life support systems on this planet—possibly by the end of this century and certainly within the lifetime of our children." For all its apparent concurrence, however, the British book and its endorsers were in fact forecasting a far more immediate and catastrophic fate than the MIT team ever imagined. One group heard a wolf chewing on the cabin's door, while the other heard it approaching from over the hill.[17]

The Club of Rome–sponsored book was launched with an open forum at the staid, old Smithsonian Institution in Washington, and it was well attended by journalists and a few prominent government officials. Hardly anyone attending the forum had had a chance to read the book, admitted a skeptical journalist in the audience, and it was not clear that he had done so either.[18] After the television crews left the Smithsonian's Great Hall, a hype- and counterhype circus began. Dennis felt obliged to continue giving interviews to the media to satisfy the club's desire for publicity. One March morning, for instance, he found himself appearing for a full three minutes on the National Broadcasting System's "Today Show," sandwiched between a dog food commercial and a story about a dart-throwing champion.[19] What understanding television viewers could gain from that mix of the trivial and serious, the comic and catastrophic, was hard to say. Peccei's well-intentioned launch ran the risk of generating a backfire, turning serious readers off even while selling lots of books.

Extravagant blurbs on the book's cover were so breathless that they too could discourage serious, thoughtful discussion. "Mark this book," declared a sensational appraisal from *The National Observer;* "it may be as important to mankind as the Council of Nicaea and Martin Luther's 95 Theses. It is a revolutionary new way of looking at man and society." Another blurb read, "It looks like any other book you might pick up. It's not. It's a bomb. It could make the noise that wakes up the world." Anthony Lewis of the *New York Times* gravely called the book "one of the most important documents of our age!" And on the back cover the president of the Avis car rental company was even more melodramatic: "If this book doesn't blow everybody's mind who can read without moving his lips, then earth is kaput."[20]

Professional economists could certainly read without moving their lips, but often they did not read the book carefully or treat it with the respect they might have given to one of their own. They were quick to push reviews into print and dismiss what they perceived as an amateur challenge to their expertise. Carl Kaysen, for example, an influential economist and advisor to President John Kennedy, wrote in *Foreign Affairs,* "The problems they call us to attend are real and pressing. But none are of the degree of immediacy that can rightly command the urgency they feel." That was one of the milder dismissals; others were less generous, even vitriolic. In the *New York Times Book Review*, three economists, Peter Passell, Marc Roberts, and Leonard Ross, in a joint review, did not even try to probe the book's complex arguments but simply tossed it aside as "an empty and misleading work, ... Garbage In, Garbage Out." The conservative economist Henry C. Wallich, who wrote a regular editorial column for *Newsweek*, denounced *The Limits to Growth* as "a piece of irresponsible nonsense," while his Yale colleague William Nordhaus sneered at the book for predicting "an end to the economic progress that the West has experienced since the Industrial Revolution." Those reactions, though none were careful appraisals of the MIT team's data or conclusions, came from top leaders in the economics profession.[21]

"We could not understand," wrote Donella, "the intensity of the reaction our book provoked. It seemed to us far out of proportion to our simple statement that the earth is finite and cannot support exponential physical growth for very long. We couldn't have guessed that the idea could generate so much surprise, emotion, complication, and denial." Twenty years later, Jay Forrester was still shaking his head in disbelief over the negative reactions to both his own and his students' books: "Particularly surprising were the bitter and emotional attacks ... by many economists. We would have thought the books lay outside their area of interest until we realized that the books threatened the underlying theology supporting the belief that growth can continue forever. Even though largely unjustified, such published criticisms have left their impact, especially on people who have not read the books."[22]

No economist or other scholar could dispute that all five variables identified in the book were like locomotives hurtling down different tracks at faster and faster speeds, or that they were bound to converge at some point. Few denied that at least some of those locomotives must be stopped or slowed—pollution, for example, or world population growth. Even the most unsympathetic reviewers tended to acknowledge that the earth is indeed finite and that some day all societies must deal with that fact and learn restraint. But a common refrain was that the limits were a long way off and exponential growth could continue as far into the future as anyone could see. Especially what critics hated was the authors' recommendation to stop dead in its tracks one locomotive in particular—the one marked "industrialization," for it was pulling boxcars full of money and consumer goods.

Not all economists were upset or enraged. John Kenneth Galbraith, for example, was far less confrontational and more willing at least to question the holy grail of economic growth. Since the 1950s he had been questioning the moral fiber of the "affluent society" and asking whether America's great appetite for material goods, "if it continues its geometric course, will ... not one day have to be restrained." This, he complained, "is the forbidden question. Over it hangs a nearly total silence." Even more supportive was the British-born and Oxford-educated Kenneth Boulding, who earlier had called for an end to the freewheeling, wasteful "cowboy economy" of the past and the beginning of a new "spaceship economy" in which resources and the environment would be more carefully protected. Boulding turned sarcastically on his fellow experts. "Anyone who believes exponential growth can go on forever in a finite world," he quipped, "is either a madman or an economist."[23]

Then there was the most widely read writer on economics in the English language, Robert Heilbroner of the New School for Social Research in New York. More than any other leader in his profession, he accepted the seriousness of the ecological crisis and would write his own jeremiad, *An Inquiry into the Human Prospect* (1975). To extend to everyone in the world an American standard of living, he pointed out, would require staggering amounts of raw materials and energy—amounting to some seventy-five to one hundred times the level of present consumption. As the population continued to increase, those requirements would soar to stratospheric levels. Could civilization meet that demand and continue on its present course? In a review of *Limits to Growth*, Heilbroner called for a changed attitude toward life itself—for a new awareness of the fragility of the planet. That, however, was a most uncommon reaction among his colleagues.[24]

Why was there so much hostility among so many thoughtful people, in economics, business, engineering, and politics, as well as enraged segments of the general public? Part of it came from scholarly resistance to Peccei's hype. Part came from deficiencies in data that a preliminary report could not avoid. But Forrester was undoubtedly right that it also came from "theological" attitudes lodged deep in the minds of many moderns, but far less commonly found among natural scientists, for whom "growth" was a biological phenomenon that had fixed trajectories of increase and decline. The economists had borrowed their growth language from biology, but they had turned it into a policy loaded with moral values not grounded in physical reality.

One of the most careful and respectful readings of the book came from a small group of social scientists at Sussex University in Great Britain, and clearly it was conflicting moral principles that were the basis of their disagreement. They did not try to assemble counterdata of their own or write a new computer model. Rather, they complained that *Limits* was lacking the right ethical outlook, by which they meant its ethics were not theirs. "Since we believe that brute poverty is still a major problem for most people in the world," wrote one of the group, the economist Christopher Freeman, "and since in general we do not believe that the physical constraints are quite so pressing as the MIT team suggest, we do not accept their enthusiastic endorsement of zero growth as the ideal for the world." Never mind that the MIT team did not "enthusiastically endorse" but only stressed the inescapability of zero growth, and tried to make that outcome as humane and fair as possible. Freeman and his Sussex associates were insisting that eradicating global poverty should be the first priority and therefore economic growth must take precedence over environmental protection. The moment that one accepts the view that there are natural limits, then any notion of infinite improvement in the human condition must become impossible, or so critics on both the political left and right feared.[25]

Limits to Growth tried to anticipate that clash in moral philosophy by addressing what the "no-growth" or "equilibrium state" would require in social and ethical terms. Expanding human equality, the book reassured, would still be possible, but it "would require trading certain freedoms, such as producing unlimited numbers of children or consuming unlimited amounts of resources, for other freedoms, such as relief from pollution and crowding and the threat of collapse of the world system."[26] The critics, however, were not willing to accept that trade-off. People must be free to have all the children and consume all the resources they want. The critics would accept no limitations on freedom. Doing so, they worried, would constitute an assault on human privacy, dignity, and autonomy.

What the MIT team called for if the world was to remain humane and just was seen as nothing less than a confiscation of existing wealth, taking from rich nations like the United States and giving to poor ones like India and Liberia. Such action, responded the critics, would be impractical, immoral, and unwise. It would be impractical because it would never work; the rich would never voluntarily give up their sumptuous dinners or high-energy way of life. It would be immoral because it would require an authoritarian state, ruled by military dictators or party cadres, to carry out the redistribution, and their tyrannical power would bring an end to freedom and democracy. It would be unwise because stopping material growth would somehow stop progress in general—and progress was sacred to the West. Many sincerely believed that the unbounded spread of wealth was the best way to insure a more benevolent world. In short, economic growth was defended chiefly on grounds not that it was physically or environmentally possible but, as the Australian economist Heinz Arndt concluded, it was "desirable." What was desirable simply must be made physically possible.[27]

The economist Marc Roberts (one of the book's most unfriendly critics) defined the dominant moral perspective among his colleagues as "the classical liberal-utilitarian viewpoint," adding that it is "utterly homocentric."[28] Helping people become "better off than they had been, at least in terms of their own perceptions," is how he characterized that viewpoint. The little qualifying phrase "in terms of their own perceptions" is worth noting. If people perceive themselves as being poor, no matter how many automobiles are parked in their garages, it is not the economist's job to persuade them otherwise. In the "classical liberal-utilitarian viewpoint," nobody has the right to tell someone else to have fewer children or to consume less. Ultimately, according to this way of thinking, the earth has no intrinsic value or interest. It exists simply to satisfy human wants, no matter whether they are limited or whether they are infinite. If one believes that those wants are infinite, as economists tend to believe, then the natural environment becomes merely a warehouse of whatever will satisfy them.

Nothing in *Limits*, it should be said, required anyone to reject all homocentric thinking. The book made no plea for the rights of nature, nor did it even argue that other forms of life should be permitted to share the planet's resources. At no point did the book express any desire to preserve the wild, romantic beauty of the natural world from human domination. Instead, its authors appeared as deeply utilitarian toward nature as the economists, seeking only to prevent social collapse and calling for "a new form of human society—one that would be built to last for generations." Justice, fairness, and sustainability were the MIT team's guiding principles as much as they were for Cornucopian economists and philanthropists, but the team had lost confidence in the expansion of industrial production as the best means to achieve those principles. Neither nature's abundance nor man's technical ingenuity offered for them the old assurance. On the contrary, the limits of the earth and of human creativity were seen as sources of vulnerability and, therefore, as threats to human survival.

Economists, in contrast, along with engineers, businessmen, and others, began to insist more strenuously than ever that advancing technology could lead to a paradise for all. It could overcome nature's limits. If people, pollution, and consumption could grow exponentially, then so could technology. The business school professor Julian Simon particularly took as his mission in life celebrating in a radically homocentric worldview the promise of technology. He extolled the intelligence of people, whom he called "the ultimate resource." Carl Kaysen put that confidence in human cleverness somewhat more abstractly: "Once an exponentially improving technology is admitted into the model, along with exponentially growing population and production, the nature of its outcomes changes sharply. The inevitability of crisis ... disappears, since the 'limits' themselves are no longer fixed, but grow exponentially too."[29]

Technology, the antilimits crowd was certain, could make the earth produce more of everything. It could be made to yield more food through the miraculous ingenuity of the so-called Green Revolution, which from the 1940s on tried to keep up with population growth by increasing the yields of wheat and rice, encouraging more irrigation of arid lands, and teaching farmers around the world to use chemical pesticides and fertilizers. Technology could also stop—or at least reduce—pollution and make it possible to recycle every scrap of metal. Most important, the critics argued, technology could find substitutes for depleted nonrenewable resources. Even if the old, familiar set of resources came into short supply, manufacturers could find something else to take their place. Plastic could replace iron, just as iron had replaced wood. Noble Prize–winning economist Robert Solow went so far as to say, "the world can, in effect, get along without natural resources, so exhaustion is just an event, not a catastrophe." What he meant was that natural resources needed in the past—trees, water, soil—would no longer be needed in the future. Science, he was saying, parroting Harold Barnett some twenty years earlier, could learn to reorganize atoms and molecules into new substances and thereby create an infinite supply of resources.[30]

One of the most radical denials of the *Limits to Growth* came from two nuclear physicists, H. E. Goeller and Alvin M. Weinberg, who worked at the Oak Ridge National Laboratory in Tennessee: "We are cornucopian," they proudly declared, "even in this era of dwindling resources and in spite of dire predictions." Rather than accepting the idea of limits, they heralded what they called a future of "infinite substitutability," which would arrive, they predicted, sometime around 2300 A.D. By that point societies would have learned how to "go from ores to more common rocks." They did not, however, indicate exactly how societies were supposed to get through the next two centuries of shortages and disasters.

Indisputably, the earth's crust is loaded with highly dispersed but immense quantities of two vital resources, iron and aluminum. All we need, physicists Goeller and Weinberg were saying, is enough cheap energy to extract those extremely low-grade ores at a profit. "In the Age of Substitutability," they declared, "energy is the ultimate raw material." Given enough low-cost energy, the problem of resources could forever be solved. Where would that energy come from? Men would have to invent it. In their eyes, the most promising possibilities were those being pursued at Oak Ridge—nuclear fusion and breeder reactors that would in effect turn the technology behind hydrogen and atomic bombs into inexhaustible domestic energy powerhouses. Then there would be so much energy it would be too cheap to meter. As Weinberg put it elsewhere, "with an inexhaustible source of energy man could free himself from material want, essentially forever."[31]

For those experts or their more popularizing, business-friendly allies like Julian Simon, the environmental impact of mining low-grade land deposits or sifting through seawater or splitting or fusing atoms was an irrelevant concern. They did not ask whether doing any of that might have serious ecological effects. What they were calling for looked, in the eyes of many environmentalists, a lot like the ghastly surface coal mines of Appalachia. Harold Barnett had once praised strip mining in West Virginia for keeping resource costs low and minerals flowing into industrial production. When the big underground seams had been thoroughly exploited, the miners (with his approval) had turned to cutting off the tops of mountains and dumping the overburden into pristine river valleys, exposing the last, thin seams that could not be profitably mined with underground tunnels. It was cheap, it extended the local mining economy, but it produced what the poet Wendell Berry called "the landscaping of hell."[32]

The biggest practical challenge for self-identified Cornucopians was how soon they could achieve the miracle of nuclear power. Looked at through their eyes, all shortages would vanish when that magical technology was up and running. So long as people did not worry about the side effects of that panacea—including effects on plant and animal life, on rivers, lakes, and seas, or on the global atmosphere—there was no limit to the commodities humans could produce and consume. A new world lies forever under our feet.

Were the critics right? Certainly they were full of confidence in humankind's ingenuity, but would the future prove as rosy as they promised? Were there no material limits of any kind? Were there no serious side effects from any of the popular technological fixes? Could the world really get along without natural resources? The facts did not support the critics' extreme optimism.

Deposits of most vital resources are, the Meadows team successfully argued, not in infinite supply nor can they be found everywhere. They had been formed slowly and sporadically in the earth's upper crust and often disappeared as one dug deeper into the core. In some cases, they required thousands or even millions of years to take form through the slow circulation of water through the crust. For that reason, many were not to be found on other bodies in the solar system, where there was no water at all. Some, like the fossil fuels, were for all practical purposes nonrenewable. Like the biota that lived on them, inanimate resources had emerged under special conditions and reflected the geological history of this very special planet. No more than bison or redwoods were they inventions of the human imagination, but complex productions of an evolving earth.[33]

This much the natural sciences would confirm repeatedly, although making precise forecasts of exhaustion points would always be an elusive task. The global peaking point of petroleum extraction, for instance, was difficult to determine. In 1973, one year after *Limits* was published, this vital resource seemed about to vanish forever. The Organization of Petroleum Exporting States placed an oil embargo on the West, ending a twenty-year boom. Suddenly, it looked like oil was running out faster than anyone had expected, the Meadows pair included, and that the future might soon look very bleak. During that winter commuters were forced to scramble to find enough gasoline to get to work. But rather quickly the oil crisis was over, and it became apparent that particular shortage was caused not by depletion but by international politics. After briefly taking a nosedive in reputation, the Cornucopians saw their standing with many policymakers dramatically recover. An energy panic had flashed across the planet, then abruptly vanished, allowing people to go back to mindless consumption.

After the embargo was lifted, world oil prices dramatically fell, just as economists had predicted, indicating a return to abundance. If one uses an index of 100 for the 1990 price of oil, then in 1975, two years after the embargo, the price of oil stood at 113—but by 1992, it had fallen to only 76. Other minerals and metals showed similar drops in the years immediately falling the publication of *The Limits to Growth*.[34] Those sudden drops in commodity prices, however, did not mean that the MIT team was falsely crying wolf. The danger they saw lay many decades in the future. They had allowed for new discoveries, additional bonanza reserves, improvements in extractive technology, and temporarily fluctuating prices. The important point, they argued, along with M. King Hubbert, was that the long-term pattern for all resources must follow bell-shaped curves, first rising in abundance (and dropping in price) and then inexorably falling into scarcity and becoming more and more expensive. Short-term price fluctuations like the oil markets of 1973 could tell nothing about long-term limits or vulnerability. The dangers of fossil fuel dependence lay in the more distant future and would become truly ominous over the next half century.

Along with fossil fuel supplies, nations began to worry, and with good reason, about the dangers of nuclear power. By the end of the twentieth century, nuclear power had suffered the biggest reversal in scientific and popular acceptance of any modern industry. The market for new reactors virtually disappeared in the United States and most other countries. After a disastrous meltdown of a nuclear-power plant at Chernobyl, Ukraine, in 1986, along with mounting piles of radioactive wastes that could find no safe, or at least no publicly acceptable, form of disposal, the infinite energy promised by Goeller and Weinberg looked far from becoming reality. Thirty or forty years after *Limit's* publication, the world still had found no cheap, abundant, and environmentally safe alternative to oil, coal, and natural gas. The industrial way of life might not be in any imminent risk of collapse, but neither was its material foundation becoming more secure than before or the challenge of meeting human demands becoming less daunting.[35]

Other minerals likewise presented long-term problems of supply and safety. Copper, for example, which since the late nineteenth century had been an indispensable resource for global electrification, proved more finite than Julian Simon and other Cornucopians had supposed. By 2008 the world was consuming 15 million tons of the mineral per year. As high-grade deposits were depleted in the major supply countries, mainly located in the developing world, the affordability of copper became more doubtful. To extract copper from lower grades of ore, grades containing no more than fifty parts per million, would require prodigious torrents of energy—according to one estimate, as much as twenty times the current (2012) worldwide production of all primary energy used for all purposes.[36]

Partly because extracting a growing list of vital minerals would require tremendous amounts of energy, they were coming into short supply. The return on investment needed for their extraction threatened to fall lower and lower so that companies or governments would have to ask themselves how long they could keep mining profitably. There were few remaining pots of gold under humankind's feet. "The suggestion occasionally made that we will soon turn to [mining] common rocks," wrote the respected geologist Brian Skinner, "essentially ignoring the local concentrations we commonly call ore deposits, seems highly improbable."[37] Going to sea to find new supplies in the seabed or floating in the seawater, other scientists pointed out, would require huge energy supplies and yet produce unimpressive results. The sea does indeed contain traces of copper and other minerals, but the total supply suspended in the world's oceans amounts to a mere ten years of current land production. Faced with those earthly constraints, the Cornucopians would sometimes point toward outer space as a future source of minerals, but here again the energy needed to leave earth and return with a full payload would be enormous.[38]

So on the question of whether there would always be plenty of resources for all-out global industrialization, *Limits* had raised serious, reasonable, and enduring doubts. Most important, the book had exposed a lot of shallow thinking. It poked holes in a too-easy faith in natural or man-made abundance. Increasing numbers of citizens, along with many scientists, were convinced that immense difficulties lay ahead in finding sufficient resources. The old assumption that human ingenuity would always overcome limits was revealed as based on faith, not science. Faith by definition cannot be justified in advance; by definition it tends to run ahead of evidence. So also had American resource policy, which had been based on faith more than fact.

Many economists and technologists, nonetheless, were still not humbled by their lack of deep scientific knowledge of the earth. They were sure that they knew what the future would bring and that they had enough data on their side to make iron-clad predictions. Yet in fact they offered, like the Paley Commission, a spoonful of optimism rather than geological science. They scorned the notion that a wolf might be lurking outside, but they were not willing to open the door and take a cold, hard look. They should have held themselves to higher standards of caution and knowledge—and too often they did not.

At the same time there was a serious weakness in *Limits to Growth* that did not get sufficient attention. That weakness lay not in a lack of scientific data compared to their critics or a lack of sufficient confidence in technology. Rather, it lay in unexamined assumptions the book made about human behavior in dealing with natural limits. The authors had done almost no research into how humans actually have tended to behave over time. They simply made assertions that were not scientifically tested or rigorously documented. So, it must be said, did their critics.

The most neglected question in the whole debate was whether humans might change their attitudes and behavior and learn to come to terms with limits to growth. Predicting that outcome was impossible, but it would have helped if both sides had examined more closely the record of cultural change and adaptation that humans had established over tens of thousands of years. Knowing that record was the best—indeed the only—guide that anyone had to what people might do in the future. Pursuing more research into human adaptability would not have allowed anyone to predict the future with absolute confidence, but it might have raised the level of debate over facing limits to a more knowledgeable and insightful understanding.

The postwar situation was, of course, unprecedented and therefore the outcome was profoundly unpredictable. Humans had never before counted so many billions of their kind or experienced such organized scrambling to get more of the earth's resources into their possession. Could people once again learn to live within limits, as they had tended to do before 1492, or would they try to continue acting as they had begun doing following the news of Columbus's great discovery? The past offered a wealth of information about what had been tried before and worked or failed. Historical research into the human past could furnish data for the missing variable—the human factor. But such research, such knowledge of the past, was woefully short or ignored in the debate over *Limits to Growth*.

The MIT team gathered piles of good data on the physical world to feed their computers, but they did not do the same for the human world. Imbalanced in their thinking, they went on to make assumptions, without evidence, about how humans would likely respond to the crisis ahead. Their conclusion was expressed by the word "overshoot." It predicted that people will always tend to ignore danger signals and refuse to make changes to their way of life until it is too late to stop a catastrophic collapse. "The most probable result," *Limits* declared in its early pages, will be disaster. Although writing to prevent that outcome, they did so with deep pessimism in their hearts. Yet they offered little evidence for such a dark reading of human behavior. They had made up their mind about people and could see little hope of adaptability or foresight. As a result the book promoted an irrationally gloomy worldview.[39]

The study of human history does not provide a simple answer about whether such gloom is warranted or not. Shortcomings, failures, follies, and tragedies do litter the pages of the past, but so do successes, triumphs, heroic leadership, and substantial changes. A species that has survived as long as humans have, managing to adapt to and thrive in every part of the planet while adding substantially to its numbers and comforts over time, might not seem inescapably prone to disasters. "The most probable result" might be change and adaptation rather than overshoot. In any case further research into human behavior was needed, yet between the contending armies of scientists and economists, global ecologists and technological enthusiasts, such research into the tangled history of *Homo sapiens* never became part of the agenda.

Donella Meadows had a reputation for being the most optimistic member of the MIT team, her husband Dennis the most pessimistic. Now and then she managed to sneak in a few passages of hope to leaven the book's overall pessimism. "We have ample evidence," she wrote in 1972, "of mankind's ingenuity and social flexibility." Whatever evidence she had in mind, it did not become part of the World3 computer model. Twenty years later, in an updated edition of their project titled *Beyond the Limits*, Donella was back with more hope to offer. She wrote enthusiastically about creating a "sustainable society" that would learn to live humanely and democratically within the limits of the earth. Although the notion of "overshoot" continued to dominate their thinking about the world problematique, more emphasis was given to humankind's past record of making big changes. If humans could bring off an agricultural or an industrial revolution, Donella wrote, then they could bring off a "sustainability revolution." She warned that excessive pessimism was becoming "the single greatest problem of the current social system . . . and the deepest cause of unsustainability."[40]

Yet ten years later, in bringing out still another update titled *Limits to Growth: The Thirty-Year Update*, the MIT team was sounding gloomy again. Not enough was happening to alter the human march to catastrophe, they complained, or was happening fast enough. "History," they announced, "suggest[s] that society has limited capacity for responding to those limits with wise, farsighted, and altruistic measures that disadvantage important players in the short term."[41] Once again they gave no indication of what history they had been reading. No historian would dispute the conclusion that people's capacity to change or to be wise or farsighted has always been limited. Like the earth, those capacities are not infinite. Historians would undoubtedly agree that powerful interests have often managed to stop or postpone changes that threatened them. But in the past, historians might argue, the human capacity for cultural change has often been great enough to overcome any tendencies to overshoot and to bring about significant reforms or even revolutions.[42]

Even before the publication of *Limits to Growth*, substantial cultural change was already occurring in every country and at all levels—local, state, national, and international. Change was happening in the private as well as public sector, and change was showing up in social attitudes as well as technological innovations. Change on such a planetary scale took time; sometimes it moved slowly, sometimes more quickly. The ultimate outcome was hard to predict. Unfortunately, the MIT team was not trained to think historically and had no way of measuring and analyzing the human factor. The effect of their failure to do so was to leave a huge gap in analysis and to trap them in their darkest assumptions.

That flaw in the knowledge base was more than matched by the book's critics. They too tended to assume a fixed view of human nature, albeit a very rosy one, but like that of the Meadows it was a view not based on historical research. Collecting commodity prices over a few decades was not doing history. Making a list of past technological achievements, without examining the failures as well as the successes, or examining the social costs along with the benefits, was not doing history. A fuller knowledge of the past might have led the critics to see that markets are not infallible guides to reality, that consumer demands can change abruptly and unpredictably, that humans are not economic automatons behaving in fixed ways.

Despite this inexcusable weakness, *Limits to Growth* raised issues that deserved serious discussion and debate. Too often, however, the critics were not in the mood to take them seriously. A mere five years after *Limits* was published, the Harvard sociologist Daniel Bell concluded that its authors had been thoroughly exposed as frauds. Contemptuously, he tried to close the discussion and get back to repeating the conventional wisdom about the future of economic growth. The whole controversy, in his view, had been "a prime example of the issue-attention cycle and its deleterious effects on public policy debate ... [The] issue has now become largely exhausted." He went on to denounce the book as a misuse of science "to push a particular point of view" and repeated the familiar refrain, "economic growth is desirable, possible, and necessary." But then what did he, a sociologist, know of the physical and biological realities of nature, and what did he, as an ideologue of progress, know of the deep history of earth's many peoples?[43]

Looking back in sadness and resentment, Donella admitted, "We were indeed trying to save the world. Part of me was still in the villages of India, in the deserts and the remnants of forest, and in the choking cities. I was trying to ensure that the future would be decent for the people there and people everywhere. For the life of me I couldn't see what was wrong with that."[44]

What was wrong was that intellectual and political leaders, including Daniel Bell, Henry Wallich, and others, thought they had all the answers to what people needed and what the earth could support. Not everyone, however, was as ready as Bell to shut down the debate. It was natural scientists who tended to support *Limits to Growth*, and they would extend their research and support over the decades to come. Nor were the increasing numbers of environmentalists in the United States and around the world persuaded by the critics to reject the book. The debate was emphatically not over—in fact it had only begun.

Donella Meadows died in 2002. She left behind a long shelf of her writings, most of them written in her later years at the Sustainability Institute she established in Vermont. Dennis Meadows continued to promote computer modeling and environmental concern from an academic position at the University of Hampshire, while Jørgen Randers became president of the Norwegian Business School and deputy director general of the World Wildlife Fund. Other scientists would come along to test their data and would confirm repeatedly that exponential growth was still following a dangerous trajectory and that human institutions and values needed nothing less than a revolution.[45]

CHAPTER 9

Earth's Boundaries

BY THE LATE 1970s THE debate over limits to growth appeared to end decisively against the Meadows pair and their supporters: "Final score, Limits to Growth team, 5 points; No-Limits team, 10." Spectators sure of the outcome were seen leaving the arena early. Growth with as few impediments as possible continued to be the dominant cry in policy circles all over the world, as high-level elites increasingly spouted neoliberal, Cornucopian ideology.

But the game was not over. The Limits team continued to move quietly, subtly forward toward the rival goalposts, never giving up and eventually winning more public acceptance and scientific support. Despite repeated assurances that plenty of resources were left to dig, mine, cut down, or siphon away, the planet did not in fact seem to offer the wide-open horizons it once did. The ecological consequences of agricultural and industrial growth in particular became more, not less, criticized, and concern spread further and gained momentum. As two critics of the modern environmental movement bitterly lamented, "the idea of limits to growth still retains a hold on the public's imagination."[1]

How the environmental limits team rallied and began to move ahead on the scoreboard of scientific and popular opinion is a story that cannot be told completely or conclusively for decades to come. But it seems clear that it was the once unquestioned idea of unlimited growth that began to lose credibility back in the 1970s, although those who occupied the highest seats of political and economic power were among the last to feel the shift going on in common attitudes. It is easy to miss that shift if one looks only at, say, economics journals, business reports, or politicians' rhetoric. Despite the progrowth party's success in stirring support among themselves and top policymakers, they were in fact beginning to lose ground and finding themselves more often than before on the defensive. Over the next three decades the idea that nature puts limits on human beings spread relentlessly and—surprising even to the limits team— the strength of that idea gathered momentum, marking a historic turning point in modern culture. Henceforth the United States and other nations would never go back to old assumptions about the conquest of nature and infinite horizons that had characterized the past few centuries.

Even among high-level policymakers there was at least for a while some willingness to contemplate a no- or limited-growth future. Within a few years of the publication of *Limits to Growth*, following the inauguration of Jimmy Carter as president in 1977, the US government not only proved receptive to that book's message but set out to produce its own report on the deteriorating state of the national and global environment. Carter charged the Council of Environmental Quality, chaired by lawyer and activist (later Dean of the Yale School of Forestry and Environmental Studies) Gus Speth, and the Department of State, represented by Thomas Pickering, to gather the best governmental data available on what the environment would look like in the year 2000. Their time horizon was much shorter than the MIT team's, but their conclusions were broadly congruent.

"If present trends continue, the world in 2000 will be more crowded, more polluted, less stable ecologically, and more vulnerable to disruption than the world we live in now."[2] Those words were penned by the study's director, physicist Gerald Barney, who was no fanatical doomsayer. Earlier in his career he had worked for moderate Republicans Nelson Rockefeller and Russell Peterson and for the Pentagon before joining the Democratic president's administration. Barney's report was densely, exhaustively documented in three fat volumes. One and a half million copies were distributed, and the study was translated into eight languages. But then the Carter administration's openness to the idea of natural limits was repressed and buried by a political shift in Washington.

Only months after the Barney report appeared, Ronald Reagan defeated Carter for the US presidency and, under the slogan "It's morning in America again," won reelection in 1984. He completely repudiated the Carter administration's report and all talk of any material limits on human ambition. In Reagan's mind the world was still unspoiled and ripe with the promise of untold riches, despite evidence showing environmental degradation, resource depletion, and persistent poverty. Reagan's gaze lay beyond facts and data, in the realm of myth. Time could not alter, nor rust decay, his dream of endless wealth—a dream that animated him as much as it had F. Scott Fitzgerald's Dutch sailors seeing the new world for the first time.

During his first term in office, Reagan told an audience of southern college students: "There are no limits to growth because there are no limits of human intelligence, imagination, and wonder. A century ago, oil was nothing more than so much dark, sticky, ill-smelling liquid. It was the invention of the internal combustion engine that turned oil into a resource, and today oil fuels the world's economy. Just 10 years ago, sand was nothing more than the stuff that deserts are made of. Today, we use sand to make the silicon chips that guide satellites through space. So, remember, in this vast and wonderful world that God has given us, it's not what's inside the Earth that counts, but what's inside your minds and hearts, because that's the stuff that dreams are made of, and America's future is in your dreams. Make them come true." A bright student in the audience might have asked, why then do you call this God-given world so "vast and wonderful" if it is of such negligible importance? Might that divine gift be nature's own properties and the natural abundance of such materials as oil and silicon? Logically, the president could not both praise the gift of good land and dismiss it as completely irrelevant to human prospects.

In his second inaugural address, Reagan looked back proudly on his effort to reject environmental limits of every sort and to reassert the old "cowboy economy" of the laissez-faire frontier. "By 1980," he exulted, "we knew it was time to renew our faith, to strive with all our strength toward the ultimate in individual freedom consistent with an orderly society. We believed then and now there are no limits to growth and human progress when men and women are free to follow their dreams."[3]

What Reagan believed is easy to discover and understand—it was an old, familiar fantasy he was trying to revive. But whether the public, even those who voted for him, truly believed that fantasy is harder to say. Even while listening to such bromides, and perhaps feeling comforted by them, the public was experiencing different realities and hearing contradictory voices. Above all, the darker consequences of growth were staring them in the face every day in the form of commuter gridlock, polluted waterways, and agricultural fields drenched with chemicals needed to produce more and more food.

Whatever the official line coming from the White House or the Chamber of Commerce, most people could not ignore the fact that intense, daily battles over land and water were breaking out all over the country and engaging more and more of their attention. Whenever someone proposed a new airport, a big hydroelectric dam, or a sprawling new housing development, some group was sure to raise a protest. Environmentalists of many causes were everywhere, and in the places where most people lived, in their local neighborhoods, cities, and counties, growth had become a contentious issue that contrasted with official ideology. Skeptical about the benefits of sprawling subdivisions and proliferating highways, citizens were arming themselves with impact studies, legal advice, and community-mobilizing strategies. Unlike any generation before them, they were confronting out-of-control builders and developers, particularly when they threatened to destroy scarce wetlands, pristine forests and prairies, or agricultural land on the urban fringe. Increasingly, worried citizens were forcing "developers" to wear their once-proud label with an apology.[4]

People's public behavior, to be sure, does not always follow exactly or reliably what they privately feel in their bones, nor do their actions follow some logical consistency. Americans often seemed caught in deep ambivalence, even outright contradiction, between thought and action. A man might ride to work in a gas-guzzling automobile, for instance, while deploring the traffic jams and cursing the air pollution, even while calling himself an environmentalist. If he tried to resolve his personal conflicts by joining the cry for mass transit, powerful figures might block him. Frustrated by such inconsistencies, the pessimists might declare that nothing was happening, nothing would ever happen, or if it did, it would happen too late. The game, they worried, had already been lost.

Yet evidence from antigrowth activism suggested that for all their confusion, humans were seeking a new direction and doing so relatively quickly. Take the matter of runaway population growth. Here the established pattern of exponential increase began altering more rapidly than either the Meadows or the vast majority of demographers ever expected. Disregarding the Cornucopians' insistence that more babies means more brains, that brains are the "ultimate resource," and that population should go on increasing forever, people, after looking around them at the consequences of too many mouths to feed, began to change their assumptions and behavior. They began having fewer babies. That change happened most rapidly in rich, industrial, and overcrowded countries such as Japan and Italy, where populations even began to drop, but it also happened in the poorest countries of Africa and Asia, where in a single generation the average family size could fall from eight or more children to half that number. Some experts claimed that it was solely the level of a couple's affluence that determined reproduction habits, but wealth alone did not explain such a spreading habit of wanting fewer children. New attitudes toward family size, even among low-income families, were emerging on all sides.

Americans, like others, began accepting the view that continued population growth was really a problem needing solution, even as they tried to reassure themselves that the problem would solve itself without government help or prodding. The change did not show up in demographic data overnight. During Reagan's presidency the nation grew from 230 million to 245 million. By 2015 it would surpass 320 million. On average by that year, 35 people were living on every square kilometer in the United States. That density was still below the world average of 56 people, but where most Americans dwelt, in states like California, New York, and Illinois, population densities were at or above world norms, and such crowding was no longer considered proof of progress.

Nor were growing populations greeted with much enthusiasm elsewhere in the once beckoning Americas—in Mexico, Costa Rica, Chile, or even sparsely settled Canada. After five hundred years of heavy in-migration and high fertility, the new world had become far more crowded, and people felt it. So did citizens in Europe, Asia, and Africa. In 1979 the People's Republic of China under Chairman Mao Zedong introduced a one-child-per-family policy, and thereby averted over the next decade or so a national increase of perhaps 400 million people. While few countries were ready to follow China's forceful lead, women everywhere were voluntarily choosing to have fewer children, reflecting their desire for alternative lives beyond child-bearing and awareness of multiplying environmental constraints.[5]

In mid 2015, the world population reached 7.3 billion, with China and India together accounting for one out of three inhabitants. But by then demographers were suggesting that a leveling off might be in sight. According to recent United Nations projections the world population will almost certainly reach 9.7 billion by 2050 A.D., adding the equivalent of one and a half Chinas, and less certainly it might grow to 11.2 billion by the end of the century. The United States will by then count almost 500 million inhabitants, retaining its rank as the third largest nation in the world, with most of that increase coming through foreign immigration. At that point, however, if not before, a global stabilization seems likely to set in.[6]

One might ask whether such predictions of world population stabilization are any more reliable than the old "law" of an inevitable "demographic transition." Can anyone really foretell how big the average family will be fifty years hence, let alone one hundred years? Perhaps in fact the population will not stabilize but instead fall, and fall precipitously. Is it plausible that humans would deviate from the population patterns shown by other species? Animal populations typically rise and then fall toward extinction. This may well turn out to be the pattern followed by *Homo sapiens*, so that after rising sharply over the past few centuries, human numbers may peak and then plunge downward. Wolfgang Lutz and Sergei Scherbov of Vienna's International Institute for Applied Systems Analysis argue that a massive human population decline may indeed lie in the future, not a steady state. Europe's fertility rate has already fallen to 1.5 children per woman. Worldwide, forty-eight countries are now in the low-fertility category, including all of Europe, twenty nations in the Americas, and twenty more in Asia, including China, Japan, and Vietnam. If the world rate would fall to the same level and stay there, then by 2200 the world population would amount to only half of what it is today, and by 2300 it would be no more than one billion, a level not seen since around 1800 A.D. If that were to happen, then much of the earth's surface would no longer be required for agriculture or industry, and it would begin returning to wilderness.[7]

If human numbers do in fact level off or even decline over the next century or two, then perhaps the same might happen with other forms of growth, including growth in industrialization and consumption. Perhaps industry will go into a global retreat, and consumerism decline as a form of entertainment. And it is possible that such downward shifts might occur at a much faster rate than the MIT team, or anyone else back in the 1970s, ever imagined. Such shifts might even take place without a catastrophic crash.

Human fertility patterns are a vital index to popular attitudes and behavior. But at least as important as demographic trends and the attitudes they represent are trends within scientific research and findings. What natural scientists begin to believe and argue has usually become the norm for most people. From the time of early explorers and cartographers the scientific community has grown in influence, and now its power may be greater than that of any other group within society, even the policymakers and the captains of industry. Resistance to the power of science and scientific ideas is of course always popping up, but the resistance typically proves futile over time. Any view of nature that is inconsistent with the findings of science sooner or later loses credibility, whether it concerns the position of the earth in the cosmos or the origin of humanity or the structure of matter and energy. Thus it may be prophetic that the scientific community today tells us that we live in a world of natural limits and human vulnerability.

Even before the publication of *Limits to Growth* and the celebration of the first Earth Day, many scientists had begun moving toward that point of view. Increasingly, according to their findings, the earth is more restrictive than was once thought, more threatened, and more liable to disturbance. Scientists have been increasing human knowledge of that earth exponentially and demonstrating repeatedly that limits exist on many levels—terrestrial, oceanic, and atmospheric. To ignore those limits, they warn, would be to put at risk the planet and human life.

The limits that scientists have described, however, are not merely those emphasized in the 1970s debate over resource depletion. At that time the important limits were often reduced to a list of specific commodities needed for industrial expansion. In contrast, the limits seen by later scientists are those posed by the planet's natural systems and their capacity to sustain life. Scientists talk about boundaries that we must be careful to observe in the interest of our own survival. These include the limits of safe climate fluctuation, ecological integrity, and the hydrological cycle. The MIT team tentatively warned that "it is not known how much we can perturb the natural ecological balance of the earth." Over the subsequent three or four decades, much more came to be known about those boundaries of perturbation. Depletion still mattered, but it was the dangers of too much ecological disturbance that increasingly dominated scientific attention.

The origins of this emerging picture of planetary limits lie among nineteenth-century geologists and physicists who discovered the Ice Age and tried to understand how that geological epoch happened. Among them were Jean de Charpentier in Switzerland, Louis Agassiz in the United States, Karl Friedrich Schimper in Germany, James Croll in Scotland, John Tyndall in England, and Svante Arrhenius in Sweden (the prophet of the greenhouse effect). By piecing together the many waves of global glaciations, they began to better understand the cycles of earth and what had disrupted them in the past.

The most important figure in that new, comprehensive, integrated, and scientific picture of the earth as a single, integrated system was the Russian geochemist Vladimir Ivanovich Vernadsky (1863–1945). Building on his predecessors he traced what might be called the planet's "biography" from its origins as a hunk of hot but sterile rock hurtling through space to its current state as a home place hospitable to life. Although working in a parlous time and place, leading up to and beyond the Russian Revolution, he persisted in imagining a comprehensive science of the whole earth. Inspired by Darwinian evolution, he developed the concept of the planet as one single, integrated entity evolving in time. The making of that entity had required the collective effort of all organisms working together to capture the sun's radiant energy and transform it into "active chemical energy," through photosynthesis. Borrowing a word coined by the Alpine expert Edward Suess, Vernadsky called that living collectivity "the biosphere."

A thin crust containing all that lives, the biosphere was the power that had made the earth so wonderfully livable. The very air had been altered by changes made by its evolving organisms. They had remade the planetary atmosphere, creating its modern proportions (mostly nitrogen, but including 20 percent oxygen and only 2 percent carbon dioxide). Those proportions the biosphere had then kept constant for millions of years. The earth, in other words, had long ago developed a kind of organismic metabolism. Humans had emerged as part of that metabolism and were dependent on it for survival. "Life," Vernadsky wrote in 1926, "presents an indivisible and indissoluble whole, in which all parts are interconnected both among themselves and with the inert medium of the biosphere."[8]

Vernadsky foresaw that significant advancements would be made in our base knowledge of that geo-chemical-biological interactivity. After his death, the picture of the earth as a living planet made tremendous gains in understanding. Scientists learned much about how fluctuations of climate both affected and were controlled by the power of plant and animal life working to stabilize the earth's surface and atmosphere around a set of fluctuating norms. By the postwar period a new science of "earth systems" had begun to emerge, and it was that science that provided the intellectual foundations for the book *Limits to Growth*.

Among the leaders in earth systems science were the American ecologists Eugene Odum and G. Evelyn Hutchinson, mentors to the Meadows team. Later came the British instrument-maker James Lovelock, author of the Gaia hypothesis, a more poetic version of Vernadsky's biosphere; American paleobiologist Lynn Margulis, who showed how cooperation among organisms had affected their evolution on a planetary scale; and Dutch atmospheric chemist Paul Crutzen, who helped discover a potentially disastrous depletion of the ozone layer over the Southern Hemisphere by the release of chlorofluorocarbons, a "hole" that left organisms exposed to deadly infrared radiation. Together, those leaders described an earth that was far more integrated and interlinked in its processes than scientists had once realized.[9]

Powerful as the biosphere had been, by the late twentieth century it was understood as susceptible to damage from humans, their numbers, appetites, and technology. Vernadsky had lived too early to share that perspective. He was still able to look complacently on human intervention into the biosphere and in fact welcomed it— cheerfully calling for a new era of global management by humans as the next stage in earth's evolution, when the human mind would begin to rule and make the planet more benign than ever, a stage he called the "noosphere," from the Greek *nous*, or mind. In 1945 he wrote,

> Chemically, the face of our planet, the biosphere, is being sharply changed by man, consciously, and even more so, unconsciously. The aerial envelope of the land as well as all its natural waters are changed physically and chemically by man. In the twentieth century, as a result of the growth of human civilization, the seas and the parts of the oceans closest to shore become changed more and more markedly. Man now must take more and more measures to preserve for future generations the wealth of the seas which so far have belonged to nobody. Besides, new species and races of animals are being created by man. Fairy tale dreams appear possible in the future: man is striving to emerge beyond the boundaries of his planet into cosmic space. And he probably will do so.[10]

With the coming of the noosphere, he was confident, humans would become masters of the earth, managing it for their own purposes while achieving a benevolent reign of peace and harmony. But that was not how scientists after World War II came to see the fate of the earth.

The second half of the twentieth century brought a cosmic shower of evidence suggesting that such fairy tale dreams were not coming true. On the contrary, humans were proving far more destructive to the biosphere than Vernadsky had expected. Instead of trying to dominate the earth, said the scientists, humans must work harder to keep it in a safe and productive state. They should try to maintain the favorable environment characterizing the last ten millennia, the Holocene, which had been an unusually favorable period. Over those 10,000 years humans had invented agriculture and cities, but now those inventions were threatened. Nations must stop abusing the earth to the point of self-destruction.

The detonation of the first atomic bomb, which occurred near the conclusion of World War II, almost exactly at the time that Vernadsky's noosphere theory was published in English, ushered in that more sober, fearful view of humankind's management of the earth. From that point on the living planet seemed more fragile than before and the human species more disturbing. Besides the prospect of global nuclear war there was the growing threat of an abrupt and possibly catastrophic change in the world's climate brought on, this time, by human intervention, upsetting the ancient checks and balances. Following in the wake of those modern nightmares came another kind of disturbance—mass extinction of the planet's flora and fauna.

In 1986 a team of biologists at Stanford University, led by Peter Vitousek and including the influential environmental critic Paul Ehrlich, published the results of their survey of the state of the biosphere. Their paper became one of the key documents of an emerging earth science. Vitousek's team tried to measure the human impact on the biosphere by asking how much of the total production of photosynthesis was being diverted directly to human use or degraded by human activity. They calculated that the biosphere produces over 224 petagrams of net substance, or biomass, per year (a petagram is one trillion kilograms). Even in this time of high human numbers not much of that biomass is consumed directly by people and their domestic animals. The 5 billion people alive when they wrote consumed only 0.8 petagram of the total production. Mainly that was the amount of vegetation they ate, especially in the form of grain, while their livestock ate an additional two petagrams. Humans consumed another four petagrams in the form of wood products and fisheries, or seven petagrams in all. Seven petagrams out of 224 meant that people and their domestic animals were appropriating only three percent of the world's biomass, leaving 97 percent to support other species—or so it would seem.[11]

Indirectly, however, the earth was far more affected by humans. The scientists called this influence a process of "co-opting"—that is, destroying natural ecosystems and replacing them with cities, fields, pastures, and tree plantations, converting much more of the natural world into a humanized one. Add in the deleterious effects of pollutants on natural forests and estuaries, human-caused erosion that diminished soil productivity, and urbanization that replaced plant and animal habitat, and the human impact on nature soared. The Stanford scientists estimated that humans could be appropriating, or affecting, as much as 40 percent of all terrestrial net productivity—and with the addition of billions of more people that appropriation would keep increasing. No one could say how far it would go before it turned the planet into a monotonous and unstable desert.

The biosphere would not altogether die from those appropriations, but it would suffer grievously. It would lose much of its resilience. It biodiversity would decline rapidly, as human activities destroyed habitat and unraveled ecosystems. Such massive intervention would ultimately prove unsustainable, for people would lose vital services that the biosphere provided like retaining soil moisture, filtering water, and cleansing the air. This was no catastrophe lurking on a very distant horizon. It was happening now. "Observers," the Stanford team concluded, "who believe that limits to growth are so distant as to be of no consequence for today . . . appear unaware of these biological realities."[12]

Just as that landmark study was appearing in print, scientists from many countries were launching an ambitious joint research program to study global environmental change. Called the International Geosphere-Biosphere Programme (IGBP), it aimed to discover more fully how physical, chemical, and biological processes regulate the earth and create a single self-equilibrating system with many subsystems. They also set out to examine how far humans were disturbing those systems. The IGBP was only one of several organizations seeking to track global change; others included the International Human Dimensions Programme on Global Environmental Change (IHDP), the World Climate Research Programme (WCRP), and an international biodiversity research effort (DIVERSITAS). Then there was the Intergovernmental Panel on Climate Change (IPCC), consisting of almost two thousand scientists from every part of the world. Together those organizations would collect data on a colossal scale and, with the aid of advanced computer technology, organize that data into a new portrait of the planet.

All of the organizations came to be driven more and more by a sense of urgency. "The accelerating human transformation of the Earth's environment is not sustainable," they announced in a joint declaration issued from Amsterdam in 2001. "The *business-as-usual* way of dealing with the Earth System is *not* an option. It has to be replaced—as soon as possible—by deliberate strategies of good management that sustain the Earth's environment while meeting social and economic development objectives." More recently, the IGBP has warned, "the Earth has moved well outside the range of the natural variability exhibited over at least the last half million years. The nature of changes now occurring simultaneously in the Earth System, their magnitudes and rates of change are unprece-dented in human history and perhaps in the history of the Earth."[13]

All this was precedent for a research team led by Johan Rockstrom of the Swedish Resilience Centre in Stockholm. Drawn from many nations, the team set out to identify major critical "thresholds" that humans need to be aware of and avoid crossing, for transgressing them would set in motion potentially irreversible changes. A threshold is a crossing point. In the structure of a house it may be a stone or board that marks the opening of a door or a passage into another room or the outdoors. In physics or medicine it can mark the point of transition from one physical or physiologi-cal state to another, like the point when water begins to boil or a cancer to metastasize. Rockstrom and his team were asking what are the thresholds in planetary ecology. What are the critical transition points of global change that we should be aware of—points where the environment may abruptly jump from one state to another? Will crossing those thresholds into a new state lead to better or worse conditions for humans?

Every threshold is a passage into uncertainty. Cross it, and one enters the unknown, full of risks and dangers that cannot be foreseen. Science is largely an effort to dispel uncertainty through precise measurement. The scientific study of earth's thresholds promised to dispel some of our modern uncertainties and allow us to make better predictions and pinpoint where the thresholds lie and which are most dangerous to cross. Rockstrom and his collabo-rators chose to focus only on the most important of them—only nine of the most worrisome. Three of those thresholds, they argued, had already been crossed, with potentially grave consequences that were beginning to show up. They included change in climate, biodiversity, and the nitrogen cycle. The other six thresholds were yet to be crossed—where a door stood wide open but there was enough time to avoid plunging into the darkness beyond. Those six included the phosphorous cycle, stratospheric ozone levels, the degree of ocean acidification, the cycle of freshwater supplies, the level of atmospheric aerosols like dust and particulate matter, and the presence of chemical pollutants, including plastics, endocrine disrupters, and nuclear wastes.

The Stockholm team tried to pin down with numbers the exact boundaries for each of those processes—the point beyond which humans would enter a danger zone. For climate change, they proposed a level of 350 parts per million (ppm) of carbon dioxide in the atmosphere. It was well above the 275 ppm level that had long been the planetary norm before large-scale burning of coal and oil began. The world, the team warned, had already passed that critical point—indeed it had gone beyond 350 ppm, so that global warming was irreversibly underway. For biodiversity, they suggested a level of ten extinctions per million species per year. The natural rate of extinction had been only 0.1 to 1 extinction per 10 million species, but here they felt compelled to allow some departure from the historic norm. Ten extinctions per million species per year was greater than nature's own rate but far less than the current extinction rate, which was a hundred to a thousand times higher than what was normal in nature. Unless action was taken to reduce the rate of loss, "up to 30% of all mammal, bird, and amphibian species," they wrote, "will be threatened with extinction" in the twenty-first century.[14]

The fate of the nitrogen cycle was less familiar to the general public but no less important. The element nitrogen, an essential ingredient in making amino acids and proteins, DNA and RNA, and in the functioning of photosynthesis and food production, is crucial for life on earth. But one can have too much of a good thing. Humans have added hugely to nature's process of nitrogen fixation by cultivating leguminous soy, clover, and alfalfa crops on every continent. They have added even more by manufacturing artificial or inorganic fertilizer and applying it to agricultural fields.[15]

In the decades that followed World War I, nitrogen supplies exploded in agricultural circles. Eventually humans were taking 120 million tons of N_2 from the atmosphere, turning that gas into liquid fertilizers, and spreading them over the land and sea to increase crop yields. Nitrogen was drenching soils, running from farm fields and into waterways, creating "dead zones," or anoxic areas at the mouth of most of the world's rivers, endangering human and ecosystem health, and adding to the problem of global warming. Realistically, the Stockholm team could not recommend going back to nature's own level, so they compromised on a boundary level of 35 million tons a year. No more than that, they recommended, should be produced or applied to the land. For a nation like China, the biggest consumer of nitrogen fertilizer in the world, attaining that level would require a massive reduction in fertilizer use and lead to smaller food harvests. The reduction must be achieved, nonetheless, in order to reach a safe operating level for the planet.[16]

Trying to define earth's boundaries was sure to stir up controversies around the world. That is why the Stockholm team accepted thresholds of change that were set not only by science but also by what people could realistically accept. Setting boundaries that were not nature's involved "normative judgments of how societies choose to deal with risk and uncertainty." The team had to ask what degree of uncertainty is tolerable and how much risk might be tolerable, questions that could not be settled simply by science. Their recommendations followed what they described as a "conservative, risk-averse approach to quantifying our planetary boundaries, taking into account the large uncertainties that surround the true position of many thresholds." Above all, they argued for staying within the parameters of the known and familiar, the world of the past ten thousand years. For many farmers, economists, and policymakers, however, staying within those norms might be too restrictive.

For still others, who were more alarmed by the planet's degradation, the Stockholm boundaries might not be restrictive enough. Some wanted higher—and some wanted lower—thresholds. Some even questioned whether the idea of setting boundaries or thresholds was the right approach. Stuart Pimm, a conservation ecologist at Duke University, criticized the notion that science can determine a clear threshold for each and every environmental change, a safe level of planetary change. "It's not as if we can keep doing business as usual until we hit a planetary boundary, and all hell will break loose," he responded. "It's already breaking loose now." Why is a species extinction rate of ten or a hundred times the norm a "safe" one? Why not go back to the natural rate? Prescribing any set of boundaries might encourage a false confidence in numbers and offer a promise that the planet can be precisely steered and managed, when in truth, Pimm felt, humans are an ignorant, chaotic force and will never know the exact point when their exploitation of the earth goes too far.[17]

The undeniable appeal of the Stockholm team lay in their pragmatism. They talked about strict boundaries, but their boundaries
were designed not to polarize people too much or sound impossible to achieve. Choosing the Holocene as standard was part of that
pragmatism and was widely persuasive. Most people would have to
agree that the Holocene had been a good time for human beings.
Who would want to see that time end and another, less familiar
one begin? Setting acceptable boundaries with more or less precise
numbers could give both optimists and pessimists a unifying plan
of action. It could provide clear targets for those who wanted to save
the planet but also for those who did not want to end industrialization or repudiate everything modern.

The Stockholm team, in contrast to the Meadows, did not warn
of a dramatic "overshoot" that might lead to a collapse of civilization
nor did they call for an end to all economic growth. On the contrary, they promised that "as long as the thresholds are not crossed,
humanity has the freedom to pursue long-term social and economic
development."[18] Reassurance lay in those words "freedom" and
"development." Their levels were not meant to restrict all growth
and freedom. They would allow nations to continue their conventional pursuit of progress while not pushing humanity across earth's
crucial thresholds and into an abyss.[19]

For those in the party of growth without limits, any talk of setting
boundaries to human freedom was unacceptable. Such antago-
nists could be found all over the United States—deniers of climate
change, resource scarcity, biodiversity's importance, evolutionary
science, the whole idea of planetary thresholds—and they could be
found in other countries too. Yet earth scientists could point to many
signs of public acceptance. Extreme deniers were in the minority,
while the majority of people were ready, if cautiously so, to listen
to well-grounded scientific information and to reform their way of
life if they had "realistic" targets to follow. Even economists, who
had so widely and fiercely rejected *Limits of Growth*, began coming
around to the idea of limits. Some even began to question the old
ideal of growth in general and to call for a marriage of economics
and ecology.

Illustrative of such movement was a book titled *Scarcity and
Growth in the New Millennium* (2005). The authors, all economists
of impeccable credentials, had turned skeptical toward that great
classic in postwar natural resource economics, Barnett and Morse's
Scarcity and Growth. That earlier work had concluded with a cheerful

outlook for miners and manufacturers seeking raw materials to turn into consumer stuff. But forty years later the mood was different. The same organization that had published the earlier work, Resources for the Future, sponsored a colloquium arguing that scarcity was quite real—not scarcity as Barnett and Morse had understood the term, scarcity in market supply, but scarcity meaning an earth vulnerable to disturbances.

The new economists declared that the world faces a "New Scarcity," which they defined as "limitations on the environment's capacity to absorb and neutralize the unprecedented waste streams of humanity." Scarcity must be seen as "a complex of interrelated scarcities that cannot be considered in isolation." A sustainable economy must rest not merely on the cheap availability of critical resources but also on a healthy, stable biosphere. Talking of a "new scarcity" might seem like pouring new wine into old bottles. But it was language that economists understood, and it reflected the fact that there were economists who no longer resisted the idea of natural limits.[20]

Accepting natural limits, as the Stockholm team showed, was not the same as opposing every form of economic growth. But the idea that growth was itself unsustainable was becoming more palatable even to some distinguished economists sitting in powerful positions. Among them was Jay Forrester's colleague at MIT, the economist Robert Solow, who had been highly critical of *Limits to Growth* back in the 1970s. Three decades later he was ready to take seriously what he had once regarded as unthinkable. In a 2008 conversation with historian Steven Stoll, he declared that he had become an "agnostic" as to whether growth could or should continue: "There is no reason at all why capitalism could not survive without slow or even no growth. I think it's perfectly possible that economic growth cannot go on at its current rate forever."[21] Behind those words was the sound of conventional economic thinking cracking apart.

"Economics has been defined as the allocation of scarce resources over unlimited wants," noted Richard Norgaard of the University of California at Berkeley, one of the foremost critics of the growth ideology. Norgaard pointed out that the very first economists, including Adam Smith, had retained a sense of limits even while seeking more wealth. But on the way to modernity that early ambivalence had been replaced by an all-out devotion to economic expansion. All talk of scarcity had been banished. The professionals had become intent only on increasing the Gross National Product while ignoring the vulnerabilities and needs of the biosphere. Now, however, with so much environmental bad news, advanced thinkers like Norgaard were ready to abandon the growth ideology altogether and redirect economics toward achieving harmony with nature. Protecting "natural capital" and putting the human economy back into nature's economy were his goals.[22]

The most prominent rooster summoning the new dawn was an economist out of the American South, Herman Daly, who had advocated limits to growth even before Dennis and Donella Meadows began their careers. He had welcomed their book while excoriating the "Keynesian-neoclassical synthesis" and the Marxist variation for their common disregard of the environment. Daly was the leading theorist of the no-growth, "steady state economy." In his case the theory came out of a complicated mix of materialism and antimaterialism. On the material side he had learned from one of his teachers, the Romanian-born Nicholas Georgescu-Roegen, that the physical laws of thermodynamics say it is impossible to acquire and hoard material goods forever. Entropy, or the running down and diffusion of the sun's energy, is the inescapable law of the universe. It decrees that everything must wear out, decay, and fall apart, until one day all life on earth will vanish for lack of usable energy. The overarching purpose of economics, therefore, should be to husband fleeting resources carefully and achieve as close to a "steady state" as physically possible: Balance inputs and outputs. Teach thrift and reuse. Control wants and stabilize needs, now and as far into the future as we can see. This, said Daly, is how economics can harmonize with the laws of matter and energy.[23]

Even as Daly laid out that more sustainable kind of materialism, however, he was at heart an antimaterialist. His economic views also derived from strong religious beliefs about the sanctity of the Creation and the necessity of godly stewardship. The moral relativism and the flashy materialism of his society deeply offended him. So did the attitudes of his fellow economists, who seemed to see nothing wrong with destroying the earth to satisfy the desires of industrialist and consumer alike. At the same time Daly was offended by the worldview of scientists, who saw in nature "a mechanical product only of genetic chance and environmental necessity, with no purpose whatsoever." For him, the physical limits to growth must be acknowledged and observed, just as the scientists said. But he would do so for more than scientific reasons. Traditional religion taught that people should put moral limits on their consumption to protect God's handiwork. Any disregard of both kinds of limits, material and moral, were part of what he called "modern idolatry"—the unholy view that "man, through economic growth based on science and technology, is the true creator, and that natural wealth is just a pile of instrumental, accidental stuff to be used up in the arbitrary projects of one purposeless species. If we cannot assert a more coherent cosmology than that, then we might as well close the store and all go fishing—at least while the fish last."[24]

Daly's alternative economics came from old-fashioned Christianity and its faith in divine purpose working in the world. Yet he was not wholly traditional, for he depended on godless scientists more than he wanted to admit. It was their discoveries, not ancient religious doctrine, that was making the dream of endless progress no longer supportable. It was scientific evidence, not Christian theism, that was prompting his search for a new ethic. It was words from the IGBP's Amsterdam Declaration that inspired him more than those of the Bible: "An ethical framework for global stewardship and strategies for Earth System management are urgently needed." Church leaders might want to second that call, but the primary impetus, even the call for a new ethics, was coming from the sciences.[25]

Earth science was the most powerful advocate of a shrinking planet, one that was forcing cultural change around the world. The direction of change was toward a new ethic governing human behavior, one grounded in material self-interest and human survival but not restricted to those ends. Back in the 1930s and 1940s the American conservationist Aldo Leopold had similarly called for a new ethic—and it too had been based on science, not on religious revelation or faith in the supernatural. Ethics, he argued, are not fixed in time; they evolve with evidence. Always they move from knowledge of facts toward reinvention of values.

In Leopold's day, the facts of natural science pointed to an epidemic of land abuse on the American farm and forest. The time had come, he declared, for a new "land ethic," one that would go beyond a narrow calculus of human purposes, to protecting the whole of nature. "A thing is right," he wrote, "when it tends to preserve the integrity, stability, and beauty of the biotic community. It is wrong when it tends otherwise."[26]

Leopold died in 1948. By the twenty-first century the facts of science had increased over those he knew, and the abuse of the environment had become broader, until it affected not merely American lands but the entire earth as a single biosphere (or ecosphere). With that scaling up of damage came a scaling up of knowledge. Thus the idea of a land ethic required a scaling up to the planet as a whole. By the twenty-first century scientists and nonscientists alike were saying that humans everywhere needed nothing less than a new earth ethic.

Leopold understood that any successful ethic cannot be the work of a single author or teacher. It can only develop, he wrote, "in the minds of a thinking community." Such a community seemed to be emerging in the United States by the first decade of the twenty-first century, and indeed across a globe increasingly connected by climate issues, communications, trade, and diplomacy. It depended on the natural sciences and their expertise to inform it, but also it needed the minds of economists, political leaders, historians, philosophers, and the public at large. Where that community would end up ethically was unclear. Would it decide to abandon altogether, or merely revise modestly, long established ideas of growth and progress? Would it seek a more equitable resource distribution, practice a more global conservation, demand laws of international scope, or push economic production in a radically different direction? Answers are still to be found, but to echo Leopold, an ethic that is as big as the earth is now both an evolutionary possibility and, if one believes the scientists, an ecological necessity.

Athabasca River

A GREEN LIGHT STILL SHINES out of Second Earth, although it no longer shines along Jay Gatsby's shoreline or in the endangered mountains of Haiti or across much of the American West. These days the light comes from dense, tangled, and soaring forests that border the Amazon and its tributaries or from the boreal forests that span the northern latitudes of Canada and Alaska. Astonishingly, the hemisphere still offers immensities of both tropical and boreal forest, some of the greatest wild lands on earth. Nearly 60 percent of Canada is boreal forest, stretching from Newfoundland to the Yukon, and one million square miles of it are still undisturbed by roads or industry. Today, however, that pristine forest is beginning to draw miners, loggers, and dam builders into its remote interior where infinite riches supposedly await discovery. The Amazonian jungle is widely celebrated as a place of beauty and romance, as well as economic opportunity, but now at last civilization has also discovered the Canadian wilderness and is dreaming of what can be found there. The light coming from the north speaks of mystery, beauty, and wealth beyond reckoning. How long will it be before we discover that here also nature has limits?

Taking a walk through the boreal forest is not easy to do, for the trees grow close together, impeding the hiker's momentum and sense of direction. Swampy patches where one can sink and drown constantly block the way. Everywhere the ground heaves up and down with shallow tree roots, hummocks of moss, and granite ledges where only lichens can get a hold, while dead branches are like treacherous knives that can put out an eye or lacerate arms and legs. Mainly the trees are conifers—black spruce (*Picea mariana*) predominately, but also pine, fir, and tamarack, interspersed with hardwoods like aspen, birch, alder, and willow. The treetops are seldom more than thirty or forty feet from the ground. From high overhead the boreal forest may resemble a monotonous green pelt, but from lower down each tree, each wetland, each foot or mile of terrain differs from all the rest. Here ecological complexity and diversity are subtler than in the tropics.[1]

Like the Amazonian rainforest, the north woods of Canada are drained by magnificent rivers carrying an abundance of water to the sea—clean, fresh water on a planet where water is increasingly overdrawn and polluted. The biggest rivers include the St. Lawrence, Fraser, Saskatchewan, and Mackenzie, draining respectively to the Atlantic, Pacific, Hudson's Bay, and the Beaufort Sea. But to speak of "draining" that forest is to exaggerate: much of the rain and snow collects in glacial depressions with no outlet, forming lakes (there are more than a million of them across Canada), ponds, sloughs, and fens. Subsurface layers of rock, clay, or permafrost often prevent surface moisture from sinking into the ground or forming deep aquifers. The water table is high, making this a squishy forest, damp and redolent with decaying vegetation. The indigenous Cree called the shallow wet places "muskeg," or grassy bog. Like the bogs of Scotland or Ireland, they are filled with dead plants on their way to becoming peat, coal, or methane.

The boreal forest is a last refuge for many animals that have become endangered or extinct elsewhere. Wolf, salmon, and bear still live freely here alongside moose, caribou, lynx, and mosquito. This is a land rich in fur-bearing creatures—beaver, marten, mink, snowshoe hare—many of them recovering from centuries of overexploitation. And the birds are plentiful, forming a quarter to nearly half of the faunal biomass. More than 30 percent of North America's bird populations rely on the boreal forest for breeding. The skies are dense each spring and fall with their migrating flocks.

Among the endangered or refugee inhabitants there is also a population of mammals with big brains, the native and immigrant human communities gathered in tiny villages or small cities, adding a million or so more bellies to the demands on land, water, and vegetation. Those human societies, like the natural ecosystems, are experiencing threats to their health and way of life from an invading army of industrial corporations and workers. The boreal refuge, which has been some 10,000 years in the making, through intricate processes of evolutionary adaptation going on since the retreat of the last continental glaciers, is now under siege.[2]

One of the most dramatic conflicts in the Canadian forest is brewing along a beautiful but obscure river hidden away in the interior. It is a conflict between those who would dig up a tarry black substance to provide energy needed by modern economies, and those who would protect the northern ecosystems from such destruction and from the climate change they fear that energy consumption has already induced. One side boasts of amazing advances in science and technology, in corporate organization and labor skills. Theirs is a powerful story of economic development rivaling that of Andrew Carnegie and his steel empire. But the other, more critical side sees in that industrial triumph a growing vulnerability for the earth and its many forms of life that may prove to be our undoing.

Whichever side one prefers, this is a story richly steeped in history and politics, one that could only have unfolded within a nation that has a long history of aggressive natural resource extraction and yet also a growing desire to protect its natural legacy. Canada's history, of course, always involves the United States, other nations of the hemisphere, and indeed the whole world.

That beautiful but obscure river of the boreal is the Athabasca. Since the end of the Ice Age it has been coursing down from the Columbian Icefield in the Canadian Rockies and across the rolling plains of Alberta, traveling nearly nine hundred miles in all. Near the Saskatchewan border it joins the westward-flowing Clearwater, and at their junction the old rapacious fur industry built a trading post named Fort McMurray. Here the two rivers became one path into a bloody beaver bonanza, the dominant extractive activity in this part of Canada until World War II. Today, downstream from McMurray, which has become an oil boomtown with over 100,000 residents, the Athabasca joins the Peace River and empties into Lake Athabasca, which in turn drains into the Great Slave Lake, source of even stronger current, the Mackenzie, which flows northward until it reaches the Arctic Ocean. The Athabasca is a branch of one of the world's greatest river systems. Although only a minor branch, it is nonetheless impressive in its own right. Its current is fast and rippling, its wide expanse is breathtaking, and its high brown banks merge seamlessly with the green forest through which it runs. Near Fort McMurray those banks are streaked with black layers of oil-rich sand, telltale traces of huge subsurface deposits that the river has exposed to view. Should those deposits be exhaustively mined, and if they are, will the river survive?

Geologists call the black stuff "bitumen," another name for asphalt, tar, or pitch. It is sticky and highly viscous, like molasses on a cold morning. Before contact with white Europeans the Cree and Chipewyan learned to use the pitch for waterproofing their birch-bark canoes. In 1778 the Connecticut-born trapper Peter Pond noted those traces along the riverbanks, as did the fabled explorers Alexander Mackenzie and John Franklin. Not until after the petroleum age was born in western Pennsylvania, however, did men begin to see fabulous potential in the Alberta sands. The Geological Survey of Canada showed up on the river in the 1880s to make a first scientific investigation, and one of its employees, Robert Bell, predicted that the banks of the Athabasca "would furnish an inexhaustible supply of fuel." Bitumen is a hydrocarbon, one of the many compounds of hydrogen and carbon that include oil and natural gas. The black sands (derogatively called "tar sands") can be made, albeit with much effort, pollution, and expense, to yield a synthetic crude oil.[3]

In contrast to conventional oil that pools underground, the bitumen has fused tightly around individual grains of sand, and only intense heat can separate the two. Once the bond is broken, the bitumen itself must then be broken apart, or "upgraded," to make petroleum or other liquid fuels. In 1915 Sidney Ells, a Canadian government scientist, began experimenting in a laboratory at the Mellon Institute of Industrial Research in Pittsburgh, using very hot water to separate the bitumen from the sand, but the First World War interrupted his work. When he returned from military service he discovered that Karl Clark (also Canadian, with a doctorate in chemistry from the University of Illinois, an employee of the Alberta Research Council and the University of Alberta) had taken all his notes and was hard at work perfecting the process that Ells had envisioned.[4]

Clark won a patent in 1929 for the hot water oil separation process, but no one during the ensuing years of economic depression had money to invest and there was no profitable market for its product. The problem for investors was that each barrel of oil they might produce would require a prodigious amount of heat—and that heat could only come from burning fossil fuels, which had to be shipped in from somewhere else. The energy needed to make energy and then to transport it elsewhere was, therefore, quite expensive. At the same time synthetic oil required prodigious amounts of water—three barrels for every barrel of fuel produced—and that water could only come from the Athabasca River. So long as Alberta, like the United States, had plenty of conventional oil to mine, the laws of economics were against any development in the boreal forest.

The picture began to brighten after 1970, when, as M. King Hubbert predicted, the United States reached its peak of conventional oil production and began looking beyond its borders for new sources. Saudi Arabia was the most attractive supplier of "sweet" crude oil (an adjective applied to petroleum containing little hydrogen sulphide). It was easy to pump out of desert sands and ship anywhere on earth, and there were enormous reserves. By the early 1970s Saudi Arabia was producing over 8 million barrels a day. Then, shockingly, the Saudis joined their partners in the Organization of Petroleum Exporting Countries (OPEC) to impose an embargo on the United States and other Western nations as punishment for supporting Israel's expanding and powerful presence on Arab borders. Suddenly that Middle East source began to look more and more vulnerable, subject to intense political passions and hostilities.

The OPEC embargo of 1973 gave Canadians their first real glimmer of hope. Exhaustion of US supplies and a growing demand for oil around the world turned attention northward to those stable and safe Athabasca sands. As the price of oil soared, the old drawbacks to Alberta's bitumen diminished. And the price did indeed soar: conventional oil rose to nearly $40 a barrel, double to triple what it had been. Although it fell below that level for a couple of decades, it never returned to the old cheap price. In fact, briefly in 2009 it soared to $147 a barrel, before falling back to around $100. Every industrial nation was now experiencing a slowdown in economic growth linked to energy costs. But for Canadians, price inflation was like a morning sun rising. At prices like those, the Athabasca oil sands finally began to make economic sense, and corporations began to invade and invest.

The first company to show up was Sun Oil of Pennsylvania (SUNOCO), whose president, J. Howard Pew, was a controversial conservative who supported the John Birch Society and the American Liberty League but at the same time was a visionary in the oil business. A decade before the OPEC embargo he had acquired a subsidiary, Great Canadian Oil Sands, to start digging up and washing bitumen on a commercial scale. Eventually his company became Suncor, still today the most prominent corporate name on the Alberta energy landscape, although it has been joined by Syncrude, Shell, British Petroleum, Chevron, Marathon, Imperial, Exxon,

Koch, Phillips, Conoco, Husky, and even Petrochina—in short, most of the heavyweights in a global industry.[5] The province of Alberta owned the oil-bearing lands, having received them from the federal government in 1930. The province's prime minister began signing leases with the oil companies at very low rates and charging the lowest royalties anywhere in the world, lower than those in Alaska or neighboring Saskatchewan, mere pennies per barrel in the early stages. The province also gave the mining companies permission to divert the Athabasca River. All that remained was to find capital and invent machines to do the mining.

Since 1971 one political party has ruled Alberta—the Progressive Conservatives, who have been consistently devoted to doctrines of free enterprise, low taxes, and all-out economic development. Under the leadership of Peter Loughheed, the party repudiated Alberta's old self-image as a simple agrarian people struggling against the hostile prairie to grow wheat. Now it would see itself as modern and urban, looking to mineral resources for wealth and asserting independence from nature as well as eastern power centers like Ontario and Quebec. Eventually, it would become by far the richest province in the nation, on the strength of its fossil fuel reserves, and even take control of the whole country, putting one of its own, Stephen Harper, in office as prime minister.[6]

Unmistakably conservative in its probusiness philosophy, the Progressive Conservatives nonetheless saw themselves as forward thinking in terms of science and technology, urbanization, and energy development. Like those other "progressives" Gifford Pinchot and Theodore Roosevelt, they promoted the ideal of "conservation as development." For example, they set up an Energy Resources Conservation Board to make sure the mining companies served the public interest and made "wise use" of natural resources. The government in Alberta's capital city Edmonton saw itself as a steward of the land and yet also a partner to corporate entrepreneurs from every nation, working assiduously to get the oil out as quickly and safely as possible. That at least was public rhetoric. In practice, environmental regulations in Alberta were the loosest in Canada—and Canada overall was a nation where environmental protection had often trailed behind that of the United States.[7]

The most basic support that government could give industry was to supply reliable information on where the oil-bearing sands were located and how they had gotten there. Scientists discovered that buried beneath the boreal forest was a dramatic geological saga waiting until the twentieth century to be revealed. The oil had originated when an inland sea covered the continental interior, long before the Ice Age came and went, some 65 to 200 million years ago, during the Jurassic and Cretaceous when dinosaurs dominated the animal kingdom. Contrary to old myths, it was not the decaying bodies of dinosaurs that produced oil but rather tiny organisms in the sea proliferating and dying in warm, shallow waters. Their carcasses drifted down to form bottom sediments, until they were pushed down so far that the earth's inner heat cooked them into hydrocarbons. In later epochs, when drought and erosion covered the old seabed with hundreds of feet of sand, powerful seismic pressures forced the oil to migrate upward into the sandy layer. Find where those events had unfolded, and one found a source of energy.

Scientists discovered that oil sands lay under nearly a tenth of Alberta's territory, including the Athabasca area, covering 15,500 square miles on both sides of the river, the Cold Lake area, 8,500 square miles, and the Peace River area, 3,000 square miles—or 27,000 square miles in all. Ironically, the sands lay adjacent to one of the world's largest nature preserves, Wood Buffalo National Park, established in 1922 to protect the last free herds of bison in Canada and the endangered whooping crane.[8] Twenty-seven thousand square miles of sands is slightly larger than West Virginia. Under that mammoth tract lay 1.7 to 2.5 trillion barrels of oil. Current or foreseeable technology would allow the recovery of 300 billion barrels (BB). Still deeper, scientists discovered, lay a limestone stratum, the Carbonate Trend, that also was impregnated with oil, although how to get it out of heavy rock was anybody's guess. The United States Department of Energy has been less grandiose in its estimates of how much oil Canada has in "proved reserves." Their estimate is 173 BB, almost all of it located in the oil sands. That lower amount would still rank Canada third in the world as an oil power, behind Venezuela, which has extensive oil sands and conventional oil of its own, totalling nearly 300 BB of reserves, and Saudi Arabia, whose conventional oil reserves are calculated at 268 BB.[9]

According to the US Energy Information Administration, by 2013 the world was producing and consuming about 90 million barrels (MMB) of oil per day. Americans were consuming 18.5 MMB while producing 12.3, leaving a shortfall to be made up by imports, while Canada was producing 4.0 MMB while consuming 2.3 MMB— a much smaller amount than the United States but at a higher per capita rate. The Canadians, due to their severe winters and large distances, had long been at the top of the world in energy consumption. But they had plenty left over to export, mainly to Americans, and dreams of plenty to come. By 2013 the oil sands were yielding about 2 MMB a day, and the companies were planning to increase that output to 5 or 6 MMB by 2030.[10]

The first stage of commercial oil-sand mining took basically a "shovel" approach to getting the resource out of the ground. The first shovels were elaborate and powerful "bucket-wheel excavators," which looked like rejects from the design studios of Rube Goldberg but were actually created by efficient Germans to mine lignite. At one end of the apparatus a great turning wheel with gargantuan teeth, a set of buckets or scoops, bit into a wall of sand and then dumped each mouthful onto a conveyor belt, which carried the raw material to hot water for the separation process. The excavator crept on caterpillar trends over a cleared surface and then worked its way downward and forward, inching along day by day until it had created a gargantuan "open pit mine" stretching to the horizon. The biggest machines stood over three hundred feet tall and seemed impossible to stop, but they were rendered toothless after a mere four hours of use and their buckets had to replaced. The abrasive sands quickly wore down the hardened steel teeth.

In 1993 Suncor replaced its bucket-wheel excavators with a new system based on massive drag-line shovels and the world's largest dump trucks, similar to those used in coal mining, each powered by a 3500-horsepower diesel engine, with tires thirteen feet in diameter and built to carry four hundred tons in one load, the driver perched high in a cab like an insect riding on a dinosaur's eyebrow. Now there was only one Brobdingnagian bucket suspended from a long boom, capable of picking up one hundred tons per scoop. The machine lifted its bucket high and vomited its contents into a truck bed—four disgorgings and the truck was full. The new system was faster than the old, and the pits grew bigger than ever. The ancient forest had been logged away, the bogs drained, and the overburden left by the glaciers scraped down to the level of the oil-laden sands, waiting to be eaten. But eventually this advanced technology reached a limit.

Scientists pointed out a sobering fact to the miners: the oil sands went deep into the ground, too deep for surface-mining equipment. After going down about two hundred feet the machines would reach their limit, and production had to halt. Eighty percent of the oil sands lay beyond reach of the shovels. Some thought that was a blessing, for it would end what they regarded as the most destructive assault on the boreal forest during the entire Holocene epoch.

Few people could look on the horrible destruction done by high-tech mining and not feel some sickness inside. It was violent, ugly, and visceral. Even Karl Clark, who had no doubt that his scientific work was benefiting society, could not look on the results without anger. "It is all very wonderful," he wrote in 1965 to industry friends, "and yet, somehow, I resent the inroad into the natural state of the Athabasca River valley." He died the next year. What he would have felt fifty years later, after an upscaling of technology, is impossible to say, but his daughter writes, "It affected him deeply to see the landscape of his beloved Athabasca country scarred as the construction gangs began stripping away the overburden for the operation."[11]

The oil companies and the government of Alberta were not insensitive to this widespread repulsion. Canadians had come to love and cherish their boreal wild lands and could not rest easy while they were being obliterated. So the companies were compelled to offer that somehow, the devastated country would be reclaimed and restored to something like what it had been before. Ecological science would show the engineers and executives how restoration could be done, and they would spare no expense until it was successful. No one, to be sure, had ever brought nature back to life in this way or on this scale. There would be potentially thousands of square miles where it must be done, wherever the machines went—the draglines, backhoes, trucks, bulldozers, scrapers, graders, and all the roads and buildings, the processing plants, refineries, and pipelines they required. Their traces had to be completely removed. At the Oil Sands Discovery Centre, just outside Fort McMurray, a corporate-funded museum to educate the public about the benefits of mining, the visitor first learns about the wonders of technology before arriving at a set of exhibits on boreal ecology and the restoration needed when the mining is done. "This tiny world is a closed ecosystem," acknowledges the museum's text, an echo of earth systems thinking. We live on a small and shrinking planet with limited resources and vulnerable environments, and if we break the circle of life, we must heal it.

Healing the wounded earth meant, to begin with, the creation of tailings "ponds," or reservoirs, large enough to be seen from outer space, contained by earthen walls to keep their contents out of the Athabasca watershed. Here the sand cleaned by the bitumen washing collects and then sits until the last oil residues rise to the surface where they can be skimmed off, leaving clear water and a silicon sediment. The contents of the reservoirs also include some dangerous substances—heavy metals like mercury, for example, that can leak into the river and poison drinking water in downstream communities. Those towns are inhabited mainly by the Cree people who, it is charged, have been dying at high, unprecedented rates from cancer. Ducks may die too when they land on the reservoirs and get trapped in the oily residues. When and if those problems are solved, and the water in the tailings reservoirs is recycled and used once again in the hot water separation process, there remains the challenge of turning the pale, sterile sand into green forest and rich, organic muskeg.

The uncomfortable truth is that reclamation probably cannot succeed within any single human lifetime, or perhaps for centuries, not until nature succeeds in applying its own methods of regeneration. The companies, led by Syncrude, cannot wait that long and retain public confidence, so they have devised a strategy that is still in the early stages of experimentation. Near an old mine site close to the river stands a model of man-made, accelerated reclamation, a "park" named Gateway Hill that Syncrude offers as proof of its commitment and determination to "return the land back to nature." Or, as another roadside sign explains, "Our policy is to return the land to a stable, safe condition of supporting biologically self-sustaining communities of plants and animals. This includes creating a landscape that sustains a varied and integrated mosaic of land uses." In the 1980s the company began reclaiming 5,600 acres of mined-over land, with plans to reclaim 11,400 acres more. In 2008 the government of Alberta certified that this project had succeeded in redeeming a small corner of the mining fields from man's destruction.[12]

Gateway Hill boasts a hiking trail winding through a thriving set of aspens, the early succession trees of the boreal forest. It looks over a smoothly contoured artificial lake, a large hay meadow with mowing machines, and a small fenced compound where six bison are kept for viewing. This carefully nurtured mosaic has returned the earth from sterility to a practical, recreational, and suburban tidiness—but it is not boreal forest or muskeg. No one knows how to bring back the full complexity of nature or replicate all the relationships or services found in the natural ecosystem. And no company has promised to reclaim the entire oil sands area, the thousands and thousands of square miles of land that they plan to strip and drain, or to fill in all those 200-foot-deep pits with sand, gypsum, and a dressing of a top soil. All that would cost a fortune. The companies will be gone as soon as the oil is gone, and only nature can complete the healing.

The companies reassure the public that reclamation will not be necessary over those acres where the oil sands are too deep for surface mining. For those lands they have devised a new technology that will leave more of the surface undisturbed: *in situ* processing that looks more like conventional oil pumping, with a field of derricks, pipes, and haul roads threading through the boreal forest. This process will mean drilling deep into the ground and injecting hot steam directly into the subsurface sands, freeing the bitumen and pumping it to the surface. It will require prodigious amounts of energy to generate that steam, inject it hundreds of feet down, and make the sluggish bitumen flow. The energy needed to do that must come from natural gas piped into northeastern Alberta from distant fields. An obscure government report reveals that this process will require one joule of energy to produce 1.4 joules of usable fuel. That is substantially more energy than needed to produce conventional oil. Whether it will be a good return on investment depends on the world market for the end product, gasoline or diesel fuel. Whether it will be good for the planet is a matter of ecological judgment, demanding assessment of where all the carbon freed from the earth will go.[13]

The answer is that after combustion the freed carbon escapes into the atmosphere as carbon dioxide, a greenhouse gas. Some of the carbon the oceans may absorb, some may find its way back into the soil through photosynthesis, but much will stay in the air and, once again, change the climate of the earth. Bitumen mining and upgrading produces substantially more CO_2 than conventional oil. This is the stark truth that neither government nor industry wants to confront. They say that the world needs more oil and that conventional supplies are running out, that we are forced to mine bitumen, but they do not add that we are making a Faustian bargain in doing so. In order to become more rich and powerful, we must pay the devil his due—a hotter and more tumultuous planet.

Soon the challenge of reclaiming a few thousand acres of strip-mined land may seem relatively inconsequential in the fuller global picture. The tough challenge is how we can live safely with carbon combustion. Carbon is the very marrow of our being, the basis of all life, the stuff that forests are made of. But carbon can also become a pollutant as serious as any we have known. Burning carbon on an industrial scale is pushing us beyond a safe equilibrium point, say the scientists, beyond a zone that has allowed us to thrive since our emergence out of the African savannah, and is thrusting us into an unfamiliar future that may or may not be good for humans or life in general.

Albertans are a car-happy people, burning more oil than the Canadian average on their wide and numerous highways. Edmonton, for example, is a sprawling city of low density, where scenic parkways are a local art form. Many of the roads lead to one of the world's largest indoor shopping malls, a destination where one can surf in a heated, man-made sea while winter storms rage outside. If mining bitumen for gasoline will make the province's severe winters less severe—and there is every chance it will—then can Albertans be blamed for regarding climate change as a good thing? Global temperature increase, however, will mean the expansion of the prairie northward and a migration of the boreal forest out of Alberta, toward what is now tundra and ice, the home of the polar bear. But Alberta's expanding prairie may turn out to be drought-prone and thin-soiled, and no good for growing wheat or corn.

With the migration of the forest northward will come the opening of Canada's Arctic coast to year-round, ice-free shipping, creating the Northwest Passage from east to west that John Franklin and others lost their lives trying to find. The extreme northern territory of Nunavut may become the Alberta of the future, finding fossil fuel deposits of their own, drilling in offshore waters and ripping up newly discovered deposits of bitumen. So the world advances, we might say, becoming ever different, offering new opportunities for the fortunate few.

Albertans may welcome some or all parts of that scenario, but why would anyone in Nova Scotia, Florida, or China want to see things turn out that way? Is it in their interest, or their grandchildren's interest, to bring on rapid and possibly radical climate change over the course of this century? Unlike Canadians, they may become poorer in too many ways to count. Their best interest might seem to lie in cutting back on the carbon they emit into the atmosphere and hanging on to the climate that they have. They might want to see the boreal forest stay right where it is, intact ecologically and storing lots of carbon in its roots and branches and in the muskeg.[14]

The bitumen-mining oil companies and their government supporters are sure that reaction will not stop them. They expect world demand for their product to double or triple within a few decades, and to meet that demand they must find new ways to move their carbon to international markets. Railroad cars have not turned out to be a safe way to do that—they have caught on fire and endangered towns they have passed through. Therefore, the companies have decided to build pipelines underground to pump their product to refineries and shipping ports thousands of miles away, mixing the bitumen with light oil to make it flow a little faster. Two such pipelines have been proposed, but both have met with fierce resistance, not so much because of their future effects on global climate but because of possible soil and water contamination by leaks and spills of the places they would pass under.

One pipeline, named Keystone XL, which would pump 830,000 barrels a day, would stretch down the Great Plains toward Nebraska and Kansas, eventually linking to Port Arthur, Texas, on the Gulf of Mexico. Another pipeline, the Northern Gateway, would cross the Rocky Mountains and come down the Skeena River valley to Kitimat, British Columbia, a port opening onto the Pacific Ocean. That pipeline would carry 525,000 barrels of bitumen per day, enough to fill 225 supertankers a year, all presumably heading to Asia. Those who want those pipelines built are rich, powerful, and (if public opinion polls are credible) supported by clear majorities of North American voters. But federal, state, and provincial governments must give their approval and grant the power of eminent domain to allow the pipelines to proceed. Stopping the pipelines would force a big restraint on future oil-sands development—not stopping it altogether but keeping production down to the current 2 million barrels a day instead of allowing a future 6 million. The companies try to rally support by claiming that Venezuela's state oil company will grab the business if they do not.[15]

The critics of oil-sands mining, wherever it occurs in the hemisphere, are worried not about booming today's economy but safeguarding tomorrow's planet. James Hansen, who in 2013 retired as head of the US National Aeronautics and Space Administration's Goddard Institute for Space Studies, has warned in the strongest terms that all-out development of the oil sands would be "game over" for those who seek to prevent climate change. The world would be hooked on carbon combustion for centuries to come, without any workable plan for getting the carbon out of the air and back into the ground. Joining him in opposition is Bill McKibben, a writer and speaker of uncommon eloquence who has called climate change the most dangerous threat facing civilization everywhere. The dislocations and damage it will cause, he warns, might throw humans back into a dark age of impoverishment, disease, and anarchy. Both men understand that they are fighting against the most influential set of economic interests the world has ever seen, and that the public is slow to awaken to the dangers inherent in its consumption of energy.[16]

Oil in some form remains abundant, especially in the Americas, and some would say, too abundant for our own good. The oil sands, promise the oil companies, have enough to keep us running for three hundred years. They laugh at the *Limits to Growth* calculation back in 1972 that petroleum reserves would last only until around 2022.[17] That three-hundred-year supply, the companies do not say, would require staying at today's level of consumption. It does not allow for any growth in the rate of consumption, while in fact the industry is hoping to increase that rate by 200 to 300 percent in the next fifteen years alone. If the oil industry gets its wishes and generates exponential growth in consumption, then their supply will all be gone within far less than three centuries from now. And when that happens, nations will be forced to find a way to downsize their appetite and to adjust once more to the sun's daily energy flux—or figure out how to build safe nuclear power plants and dispose of their radioactive wastes.

Jacques Cartier, one of Canada's first European explorers, took one look at the boreal forests of Labrador and declared that here was "the land that God gave to Cain." It was too desolate, he thought, offering no soil, no potential for farms or villages, fit only for the man who murdered his brother Abel. That was the voice of a disappointed seeker. More recent explorers have, in contrast, found in the northern forests an unspoiled Eden and have moved in with force, seeking to own and transform. How all of us and our descendants henceforth will respond to that green light shining out of the north, shining there as it does in few remaining places, will determine earth's future.

Epilogue

"The Pale Blue Dot" photograph of Earth (*see color plate*)

Life on a Pale Blue Dot

THE AMERICAN SPACECRAFT VOYAGER I is a unique traveler in earth annals. Launched from Cape Canaveral, Florida, in August 1977, it resembles a giant metallic insect weighing 1,200 pounds. The most striking part of its anatomy is a dish antenna, bulging like a great round mouth for communicating with its human creators. Long booms stick out in all directions like legs and feelers, and on them are strapped various scientific instruments, a generator, and cameras. This strange creature was sent out to gather data on the planets Jupiter and Saturn, along with their moons, and has continued into interstellar space. Still on mission decades after liftoff, the craft is now 12 billion miles from home and traveling at 38,000 miles per hour.[1]

Back in 1990, as Voyager I approached the edge of our solar system, nearly 4 billion miles from earth, it received a command to turn its photographic equipment around and take pictures of what it was leaving behind. One of the cameras took sixty images—and one of those images, snapped on Valentine's Day, featured the earth. The subject, however, had to be identified by experts because few amateurs looking at it would immediately say, "That's us. That's where we are in the cosmos." To the untrained eye the photo shows a vast darkness streaked with rainbow colors refracting from the metallic skin of the spacecraft. (See Plate 5.) Almost invisible is a tiny pale blue dot accidentally highlighted in a vertical orange stripe. The dot covers a mere 0.12 of a pixel in a mosaic of 640,000 pixels—one tiny, ambiguous dot that is Mother Earth.[2]

Originally, no one on the NASA team had planned to waste energy by taking those backward looking photographs, which would contribute nothing to their scientific agenda. But then the most popular voice of science in the nation, Carl Sagan, author of many books and host of the widely viewed television documentary *Cosmos*, pressured the mission's leader Edward Stone to collect some images that might inform and impress the public mind. Stone agreed, and his visual imaging team, led by Candace Hansen of the Jet Propulsion Laboratory and Carolyn Porco of the University of Arizona, sent the signal that made the historic pictures.

These would not be the first photographs of the earth taken from space. Astronauts on earlier manned expeditions to the Moon had brought out their cameras and created memorable images too. The so-called Blue Marble picture, taken in December 1972 from the Apollo 17 spacecraft, became one of the most widely distributed icons in the history of photography.[3] Taken at a distance of 28,000 miles from earth, it shows our home planet as resplendent as a child's playground marble, its bright swirling blue and white colors created by the oceans and clouds that dominate the globe. There is land in the photo too, and a faint suggestion of life. The continent of Africa peeks through the clouds, all tawny soil and green forest, the birthplace of *Homo sapiens*.

But what we do not see in the Blue Marble photograph, or the one of a Pale Blue Dot, is that planet called in these pages Second Earth. The photos say that humankind has arrived at a different era with new ways of thinking about humanity and our place in the cosmos. Now the earth is one unitary whole and yet smaller and more vulnerable than we ever imagined. From the perspective of Voyager I, that tiny pinpoint of light suggests that here is your beginning and here is possibly your limit, at least as far into the future as we can see. It is not a picture to inspire grandiose visions.

Photographs, art critics say, are constructs of feelings, not unmediated truths. What we feel when we see an image varies in meaning from person to person as it touches individual emotions. True enough, but there can be no denying that the Pale Blue Dot is a record of fact with little human intervention. From 4 billion miles away the earth is undeniably a very small speck in the solar system. If we could see ourselves from even farther out, from Voyager I's current position in space, the tiny speck would completely vanish in the boundless space of a hundred billion galaxies.

Faced with such an unmediated truth, the cosmic minuteness of the place we call home, humans may have trouble absorbing the information. But the factual record will not go away. We may try to cling desperately to our geocentric and anthropocentric past, even try to reassert tattered religious traditions and insist that we earthlings must be the favored children of God, that the whole cosmos exists for our benefit, and that we stand in the center of everything. The facts reported by a robot camera, nonetheless, do not support those claims and cannot be evaded. Inevitably we are being forced to make a change in consciousness as big as or bigger than the ones Darwin and Copernicus set in motion—further decentering ourselves in the universe. Earlier changes induced by heliocentric astronomy and evolutionary biology, powerful though they were, could not in the end offset the message of Second Earth and its promise of natural abundance. It is impossible to say exactly when that promise and the confidence it induced began to lose ground. But it seems to be ending right now: when the factual record shouts our vulnerability, when we look bleakly into the darkness of outer space while fearing that earth's oceans will inexorably rise and flood our cities.

Christopher Columbus and his three small wooden ships reached the Bahamas in October 1492, just shy of five hundred years before the Voyager I's photos were taken. The discovery of a new world helped ignite cataclysmic upheavals in science, technology, cultural and economic development, and globalization. It ignited multiple revolutions: the dramatic expansion of knowledge through science, the rise of modern capitalism, the industrialization of production, the exploitation of new sources of energy, and the invention of such modern political ideologies and institutions as liberalism, communism, and democracy. All of those revolutions fed on an enormous expansion in the natural resource base. New ideas and institutions, this book has argued, do not emerge out of a material vacuum. They are not self-generated, nor free and independent of the natural world. They evolve as the earth evolves and as people move from place to place, encountering new possibilities or new limitations, responding to new information and opportunity.

What new ideas and institutions will emerge on the earth as we are now beginning to understand it? A decisive material fact of our time is that our home planet is ecologically shrinking because of our growing technology, population, and consumption. While its average diameter still measures 8,000 miles and its surface area is still about 200 million square miles, earth's capacity to support life has not increased, in fact has diminished. The global systems that have long sustained the evolution of life and human civilization are being seriously disturbed by our numbers and activities. Those systems can no longer sustain the demands we make on them. Ideas and institutions are being intensely challenged by that predicament, and eventually they will crack apart.

Now we can see with blinding clarity one further fact: the earth is only a tiny rock floating in a universe of countless rocks big and small, of great gaseous spirals gyrating across the heavens, of tumultuous magnetic storms, and of empty space and more space. Yet for all the size and grandeur of the universe, there is no place for us humans to go but where we are. We are stuck on our little rock. We can send out a spacecraft like Voyager I, but we cannot ride on it. This time technology does not open up immense, profitable frontiers of natural resources, untapped oceans filled with fish, deep deposits of coal or uranium, or atmospheres rich in oxygen.

It may be that the earth is not the only rock in the universe providing some or all of the conditions of life. But it is the only one we absolutely know we could survive on. Mercury and Venus are incredibly hot and toxic to us. Mars, on the other hand, is frigid and bombarded with ultraviolet radiation, making it nearly impossible for any form of life to evolve or survive there. All the outer planets are more unlivable yet. As for the rest of the universe, whatever favorable environments it may contain are completely out of reach. We cannot get to them any time soon or perhaps ever.

It took Columbus a couple of months or so to cross the Atlantic Ocean by sail, leaving Spain on August 3, 1492, sighting the Bahamas on October 12, and making landfall on Cuba on October 28. A couple of months would not get us very far into outer space. Even if we could travel by the speed of light (186,000 miles per second, 670 million miles per hour), we would need more than four years to reach the nearest solar system, Proxima Centauri. But we cannot get to the next solar system in a mere four years, for the fastest we can travel is a mere fraction of the speed of light. Voyager I, the fastest moving craft we have ever launched, will take 80,000 years to reach Proxima Centauri. And if it does in fact arrive, it will surely be silent when it gets there. Will there be any one left on earth to listen?

With manifest disappointment, the astronomer Carl Sagan admitted, "the Earth is the only world known so far to harbor life. There is nowhere else, at least in the near future, to which our species could migrate. Visit, yes. Settle, not yet. Like it or not, for the moment the Earth is where we make our stand."[4] That acknowledgment by a self-confessed space enthusiast, so eager to explore and travel beyond the earth, should end all science fiction fantasies about space colonization. Any visiting of other planets will likely come far into the future, if ever. Even sending out a tiny number of scientific visitors beyond the Moon or Mars is a hopeless idea. But if we could do so, would putting a man or woman on another planet for a few hours or even days really be worth the immense cost? Perhaps a hundred or two hundred years from now, we may change our mind. By then we may have the technical and economic means to send an entire colony of men and women all the way to Proxima Centauri ... but then what? Will they find there an inhabitable planet? Or will they have to go on to the next solar system or the next? How many more centuries may it take before a successful band of immigrants can send home a glowing report from another earth?

Sagan, while admitting the difficulties confronting any human expansion beyond this planet, glimpsed the cultural consequences of seeing the earth from outer space. He was right: they are and will be shattering. Perhaps we should speak not merely of cultural consequences but of "counterconsequences." A broader awareness of our position in the cosmos may return us, in some ways, to where we were more than five centuries ago. We may experience a radical undoing of those ideas and institutions that have come to define our life on earth. If we realize that we cannot easily leave our home planet, we might find ourselves returning to ancient ways of thinking about land, water, other forms of life, climate, and the earth as a dwelling place.

Perhaps the chief goal animating modern life, first in Europe and the Americans and now globally, has been to achieve infinite growth in money and possessions. This goal has found its most powerful expression in the doctrines and institutions of capitalism, especially during the past century or so in Britain, the United States, Japan, and now China. What will happen to that quest for endless growth? The prospects for pursuing it on a shrinking, vulnerable planet are fading fast, forcing us to rethink the purpose of human existence.

No people will be more shocked by a turn away from that modern way of thinking than those who have lived longest by it. Nations that have been used to living by the simplest of means right down to the present should not find it so hard to understand that abundance is not endless, whereas people in Western societies, especially the United States, which have been so firmly devoted to the ideology of capitalism and so blessed in natural abundance, may find it nearly impossible to adjust.

How will the role and ethos of modern science fare henceforth in the universe it has helped us discover? Rather than pushing society toward growth and conquest, as it so often has done in the past, science may find a new purpose—restoring the resilience of earth systems and finding ways to live more sustainably within their limits. Already this may be happening as science increasingly turns itself into an agent of environmental protection. That looks like cultural adaptation at work, reflecting a radical shift in material conditions, although we cannot predict how far it will go, or whether science will continue to enjoy the exalted position it has held over the past few centuries.

The ideals of liberty and democracy may also face unprecedented challenges and may not survive as we have known them. Is a society that allows a high degree of personal freedom and individualism sustainable when the material horizons begin to shrink and ecological systems to unravel? Answers are not yet apparent, but it is possible that the future may bring new social hierarchies into existence, or more authoritarian governments that promise to move quickly to enforce limits; it may even be that mass democracy will be dismissed as unworkable. On the other hand, our descendants over the next few centuries might choose to redefine democracy in less fragmented, individualistic terms—not as a political culture devoted to freeing the individual from all restraint, but instead as a culture that embraces restraint for all.[5]

Already a creeping fear that social coercion is gaining ground has polarized American politics. The split between increasingly angry parties, one libertarian and one communitarian, may reflect that we live at the beginning of a postabundance world and are feeling the tensions that will stir.

Above all, the recent fact-based discoveries of our miniscule place in the cosmos and the ongoing environmental crisis on our little planet seem likely to diminish the importance of being "Human." For centuries we have celebrated ourselves as an exceptional species, separate from and free to transform the natural world around us. Now that view seems illusory and self-destructive. We are less important than we thought. All the religions, ideologies, and economic doctrines invented by us, Sagan writes, all the kings and peasants, all the saints and sinners, all the "superstars" and "supreme leaders" in our history, now shrink in significance. We cannot avoid seeing ourselves as one flawed species among many, joined with others on a mote of dust hurtling through space. "The folly of human conceits," to use Sagan's words, may be the hardest truth of our time to absorb.[6]

Over the past five centuries the study of human history made great advances, although often expressed with anthropocentric certitude. History was commonly understood to be the record of our species' triumphant march toward progress, wealth, moral enlightenment, and dominance of the planet. We were on our way to what some have recently begun calling the Anthropocene, an epoch in which the whole earth is managed and controlled by our brains. If the term Anthropocene means that we humans wield enormous influence on earth, it is hard to deny its appropriateness. If, however, it means that we have established a permanent empire and may now live as gods, the term may be an illusion. Our triumphs have ironically brought us to the point of seeing our own insignificance.

The very idea of history is, with fits and starts, going through a metamorphosis. The history we write in the future may start not with the rise of human civilizations, but with the deeper origins of the universe, putting off until late in the story the appearance of a tiny mammal on a tiny planet that thought itself supremely important.[7] The little one evolved a consciousness and learned to keep records and reflect on the changes it experienced. For a brief moment it spread out to occupy all the landmasses on its home planet, circling around an obscure star. On the last of those landmasses, lying enticingly in the Western Hemisphere of their globe, humans expanded as fast and furiously as they could. They wrote down every detail of their exploits and dreamed of achieving an infinite splendor. But then one day their brains discovered the sobering truth that they face many limits. The universe, while infinite, is not infinite for them.

NOTES

PROLOGUE

1. For a recent appraisal see Maureen Corrigan, *So We Read On: How The Great Gatsby Came To Be and Why It Endures* (New York: Little, Brown, 2014).
2. F. Scott Fitzgerald, *The Great Gatsby* (New York: Charles Scribner's Sons, 1925), 182.
3. Fitzgerald, *The Great Gatsby*, 182.
4. Classic exemplars of this interpretation include Francis Jennings, *The Invasion of America: Indians, Colonialism, and the Cant of Conquest* (Chapel Hill: University of North Carolina Press, 1975); Tzvetan Todorov, *The Conquest of America: The Question of the Other*, trans. Richard Howard (New York: Harper & Row, 1984); and David Harvey, *Spaces of Global Capitalism: A Theory of Uneven Geographical Development* (London: Verso, 2006).
5. See, for example, David Landes, *The Wealth and Poverty of Nations: Why Some Are So Rich and Some So Poor* (New York: Norton, 1998); Daron Acemoglu and James Robinson, *Why Nations Fail: The Origin of Power, Prosperity, and Poverty* (New York: Crown, 2012); and Jan de Vries, *The Industrious Revolution: Consumer Behavior and the Household Economy, 1650 to the Present* (New York: Cambridge University Press, 2008).
6. Paul Crutzen and Eugene Stoermer, *Global Change Newsletter* 41 (May 2000): 17–18. See also Will Steffen, Jacques Grinevald, Paul Crutzen and John McNeill, "The Anthropocene: Conceptual and Historical Perspectives," *Philosophical Transactions of the Royal Society* A369 (2011): 842–67; and Dipesh Chakrabarty, "The Climate of History: Four Theses," *Critical Inquiry* 35 (Winter 2009): 197–222. Geologists have not yet decided whether to accept the term "Anthropocene" as equivalent to the Holocene or Pleistocene in stratigraphy.
7. Although the focus of this book is mainly on the United States and its antecedents in Europe, the dream of a new world paradise has South American and Middle Eastern non-European echoes. See, for example, Sergio Buarque de Holonda, *Visão do Paraíso: Os motivos edênicos no descobrimento e colonização do Brasil* (1959; reprint, São Paulo: Publifolha, 2000); and Thomas D. Goodrich, *The Ottoman Turks and the New World: A Study of Tarih-i Hindi-i Garbi and Sixteenth-Century Ottoman Americana* (Weisbaden: O. Harrassowitz, 1990).

CHAPTER 1

1. A provocative thesis suggests that the Chinese admiral Zheng He's fleets discovered the Americas seventy-one years before Columbus, after sailing around the Cape of Good Hope and into the Atlantic Ocean. The evidence for that claim is scanty, but it begins with a Venetian cartographer's chart of 1424,

showing four islands in the western Atlantic that may have been Puerto Rico and Guadeloupe and that presumably were charted by Zheng's fleet of ships and somehow passed on to Venice. See Gavin Menzies, *1491: The Year China Discovered America* (New York: Harper, 2002). Even if true, that feat of discovery would not invalidate the fact that it was Europeans, not Asians, who took control of the Western Hemisphere and gained enormous wealth and power as a consequence.

2. Still the best one-volume account of the "Discoveries" is Samuel Eliot Morison, *The Great Explorers: The European Discovery of America* (New York: Oxford University Press, 1978). For a general introduction to the voluminous literature, see Peter Mancall, "The Age of Discovery," in *The Challenge of American History*, ed. Louis Masur (Baltimore: Johns Hopkins University Press, 1999), 26–53.

3. John P. Snyder, "Map Projection in the Renaissance," in *The History of Cartography*, vol. 3: *Cartography in the European Renaissance, part 1*, ed. David Woodward (Chicago: University of Chicago Press, 1987), 371. See also Rodney W. Shirley, *The Mapping of the World: Early Printed World Maps, 1472–1700* (London: Holland Press, 1987), 178–79. For the father's contributions, see Andrew Taylor, *The World of Gerard Mercator: The Mapmaker Who Revolutionized Geography* (London: HarperCollins, 2004), esp. 197–208 on the now controversial "Mercator projection."

4. Colin McEvedy and Richard Jones, *Atlas of World Population History* (New York: Penguin Books, 1978), 18, 57, 122, 167, 181, 183, 206, 270.

5. All discussions of this matter must start with Alfred Crosby, *Ecological Imperialism: The Biological Expansion of Europe, 900–1900* (New York: Cambridge University Press, 1986), which explains European success in acquiring the Americas by lack of disease experience among the native peoples. Others have similarly argued for a biological rather than military debacle—a 90 to 95 percent death rate from diseases among the Indians. That estimate has led some to become high counters, most prominently among them Henry F. Dobyns, *Their Numbers Became Thinned: Native American Population Dynamics in Eastern North America* (Knoxville: University of Tennessee Press, 1983). See also William M. Denevan, ed., *The Native Population of the Americas in 1492* (Madison: University of Wisconsin Press, 1976), and Russell Thornton, *American Indian Holocaust and Survival: A Population History* (Norman: University of Oklahoma Press, 1987). A persuasive challenge comes from David Henige, *Numbers from Nowhere: The American Indian Contact Population Debate* (Norman: University of Oklahoma Press, 1998). For a critique of the theory that microorganisms introduced by Europeans were sufficient to defeat the Indians, see Paul Kelton, *Epidemics and Enslavement: Biological Catastrophe in the Native Southeast, 1492–1715* (Lincoln: University of Nebraska Press, 2007); and David S. Jones, "Virgin Soils Revisited," *William and Mary Quarterly* 3rd ser., 60 (October 2003): 703–42.

6. Douglas Ubelaker, "North American Indian Population Size, AD 1500–1985," *American Journal of Physical Anthropology* 77:3 (November 1988): 288–94; and Shepard Krech III, *The Ecological Indian: Myth and History* (New York: Norton, 1999), 87–94. See also Massimo Livi Bacci, *A Concise History of World Population*, 4th ed. (Oxford: Blackwell, 2007), 43–48.

7. For this list of cultivars I am indebted to Angus Wright, an expert on Latin American agricultural history and author of *The Death of Ramon Gonzalez: The*

Modern Agricultural Dilemma, rev. ed. (Austin: University of Texas Press, 2005), which discusses in detail the deep legacy of Mexico's farming and peasant culture.

8. Charles C. Mann, *1491: New Revelations of the Americas Before Columbus* (New York: Knopf,2005), 64– 65.

9. Arguing the case for Amazonian lost worlds is Mann, *1491*, 280–311. On the prevalence of *terra preta*, which are anthropogenic soils in the now forested region, see Bruno Glaser and William I. Woods, eds., *Amazonian Dark Earths: Explorations in Space and Time* (Berlin: Springer-Verlag, 2004). Such soils are estimated to cover less than 10 percent of the Amazonian basin. The main target of these and other Amazonian civilization theorists is Betty Meggers, in *Amazonia: Man and Culture in a Counterfeit Paradise*, rev. ed. (Washington, DC: Smithsonian Institution, 1996), who argues that nature has always put a limit on agricultural development in the Amazon region. On the rise and fall of Cahokia, see William I. Woods, "Population Nucleation, Intensive Agriculture, and Environmental Degradation: The Cahokia Example," *Agriculture and Human Values* 21 (2004): 151–57.

10. For a contrary argument, see William M. Denevan, "The Pristine Myth: The Landscape of the Americas in 1492," *Annals of the Association of American Geographers* 82 (September 1992): 369–85. He argues that the entirety of North and South America was at the time of contact a man-made "garden." More plausibly one can say that the new world was not all wilderness, but large areas remained essentially wild, with little or no human management, or they returned to a state of wildness after Indian population losses.

11. Van der Donck, *Description of the New Netherlands*, trans. Jeremiah Johnson, *Collections of the New York State Historical Society*, 2nd ser., vol. I (1841), 185.

12. Besides the *Description*, Van der Donck wrote a *Remonstrance of New Netherland*, protesting the West Indies Company's power and influence over the colony. See Russell Shorto, *The Island at the Center of the World* (New York: Doubleday, 2004), 204, 228.

13. In 1609 the English-born Henry Hudson commanded a mostly Dutch crew in a search for the Northwest Passage, a water route to Asia over the top of North America. The river named after him turned out, disappointingly, not to be that passage, and he went on to die, two years later, in Hudson Bay at the hands of his own men. See Peter Mancall, *Fatal Journey: The Final Expedition of Henry Hudson—A Tale of Mutiny and Murder in the Arctic* (New York: Basic Books, 2009).

14. Adriaen Van der Donck, *A Description of New Netherland*, ed. Charles T. Gehring and William A. Starna, trans. Diedrik Willem Goedhuys (Lincoln: University of Nebraska Press, 2008), 2, 5.

15. Van der Donck, *Description* (Goedhuys trans.), 12–15, 19–22.

16. Van der Donck, *Description* (Goedhuys trans.), 49–60.

17. Van der Donck, *Description* (Goedhuys trans.), 64, 71.

18. The city of Yonkers, New York, takes its name from *Jongkeer* Van der Donck and, with the city of the Bronx, sits on what was once his estate. His sawmill gave its name to the Saw Mill River and Saw Mill River Parkway.

19. For environmental changes that have occurred over the past four centuries, see Theodore Steinberg, *Gotham Unbound: The Ecological History of Greater New York* (New York: Simon & Schuster, 2014); and Eric W. Sanderson, *Mannahatta: A Natural History of New York City* (New York: Abrams, 2009).

CHAPTER 2

1. Raynal, *Histoire philosophique et politique, des Établissmens & du commerce des Européens dans les deux Indies* (Amsterdam: n.p., 1770). The original reads: "Il n'y a point eu d'événement aussi intéressant pour l'espece humaine en général & pour les peuples de Europe en particulier, que la découverte du nouveau monde & le passages aux Indes par le Cap de Bonne-Espérance. Alors a commencé une révolution dans le commerce, dans la puissances des nations, dans les moeurs, l'industrie & le gouvernement de tous les peoples."

2. *Nicolas Copernicus Minor Works*, vol. 3, ed. Pawel Czartoryski (London: Macmillan, 1985), "Copernicus and the Money Question," 169–215.

3. Copernicus, *On the Revolutions*, ed. Jerzy Dobrzycki, trans. Edward Rosen (1543; Baltimore: John Hopkins University Press, 1978), Book One, chap. 2–3. On Columbus's impact on Copernicus, see Thomas Kuhn, *The Copernican Revolution: Planetary Astronomy in the Development of Western Thought* (Cambridge, MA: Harvard University Press, 1957), 124.

4. Charles Darwin, *Journal of Researches into the Natural History and Geology of the Countries Visited during the Voyage of H.M.S. Beagle Round the World* (London: John Murray, 1845). It was later republished as *The Voyage of the Beagle*.

5. Edmund Russell, *Evolutionary History: Uniting History and Biology to Understand Life on Earth* (New York: Cambridge University Press, 2011), 103–131.

6. Jason Moore, "The *Modern World-System* as Environmental History? Ecology and the Rise of Capitalism," *Theory and Society* 32 (June 2003), esp. 327–57 on silver and sugar in the Americas.

7. Standard accounts of the chain of revolutions in early modern Europe include R. R. Palmer, *The Age of the Democratic Revolution: A Political History of Europe and America, 1760–1800* (Princeton, NJ: Princeton University Press, 1959–64); and E. J. Hobsbawm, *The Age of Revolution: Europe, 1789–1848* (New York: Praeger, 1962, 1969), both of which ignore the legacy of Columbus and the discovery of the new world. Two exceptions are J. H. Elliott, *The Old World and the New* (Cambridge: Cambridge University Press, 1970), and Roger Schlesinger, *In the Wake of Columbus: The Impact of the New World on Europe, 1492–1650*, 2nd ed. (Wheeling, WV: Harlan Davidson, 2007). See also Hugh Honor, *The New Golden Land: European Images of America from the Discoveries to the Present Time* (London: Allen Lane, 1975).

8. Webb, *The Great Frontier* (1951, 1952; reprint, Austin: University of Texas Press, 1964), 12, 105.

9. Webb, *The Great Frontier*, 12.

10. Webb, *The Great Frontier*, 17. Webb's population figure for Europe may underestimate the impact in territorial gain. A more recent estimate by the economic historian Jan de Vries omits Russia and the Ottoman Empire, leaving a European population of only 61.6 million in 1500. See De Vries, *European Urbanization, 1500–1800* (London: Methuen, 1984). Even then, only a few nations along the Atlantic coast acquired most of the Americas' land and natural wealth.

11. Webb, *The Great Frontier*, 3–6, 13.

12. Webb, *The Great Frontier*, 27.

13. Webb, *The Great Frontier*, 21, 27, 418.

14. For biographical details, see Joe B. Frantz, "Remembering Walter Prescott Webb," *Southwestern Historical Quarterly* 92 (July 1988): 16–30; and Necah Stewart

Furman, *Walter Prescott Webb: His Life and Impact* (Albuquerque: University of New Mexico Press, 1976).

15. Webb, *The Great Frontier*, 15.

16. Geoffrey Barraclough, *History in a Changing World* (Oxford: Blackwell, 1955), 144–52. See also the assessment by British Empire historian Peter Marshall, "The Great Frontier," *Past & Present* 7 (April 1955): 55–62; and world historian William H. McNeill, *The Great Frontier: Freedom and Hierarchy in Modern Times* (Princeton, NJ: Princeton University Press, 1983).

17. Kenneth Pomeranz, *The Great Divergence: China, Europe, and the Making of the Modern World Economy* (Princeton, NJ: Princeton University Press, 2000), 3–27.

18. Pomeranz, *The Great Divergence*, 11, 23. Besides the windfall of new world resources, he emphasizes the development of the British coal industry (59–62, 66–68). For critical appraisals see Jan de Vries, "Are Coal and Colonies Really Crucial? Kenneth Pomeranz and the Great Divergence," *Journal of World History* 12 (Fall 2001): 407–46; Philip C. C. Huang, "Development or Involution in Eighteenth-Century Britain and China? A Review of Kenneth Pomeranz's 'The Great Divergence: China, Europe, and the Making of the Modern World Economy,'" *Journal of Asian Studies* 61 (May 2002): 501–38; and Gale Stokes, "The Fates of Human Societies: A Review of Recent Macrohistories," *American Historical Review* 106 (April 2001): 522–24. See also E. L. Jones, *The European Miracle: Environments, Economies, and Geopolitics*, 3rd ed. (New York: Cambridge University Press, 2003).

19. Earl J. Hamilton, *American Treasure and the Price Revolution in Spain, 1501–1650* (Cambridge, MA: Harvard University Press, 1934), 34.

20. Hamilton, *American Treasure*, 45.

21. Pomeranz, *The Great Divergence*, 274–78.

22. Crosby, *Ecological Imperialism*, 5.

23. McEvedy and Jones, *Atlas*, 18.

24. Thomas Jefferson, First Inaugural Address, March 4, 1801, in *Thomas Jefferson: Writings*, ed. Merrill Peterson (New York: Library of America), 494.

CHAPTER 3

1. *To the Hebrides: Samuel Johnson's Journey to the Western Isles of Scotland and James Boswell's Journal of a Tour to the Hebrides*, ed. Ronald Black (Edinburgh: Birlinn, 2007). Smith, in contrast to many natural historians of his day who were worried about land degradation, emphasized the resilience and stability of nature and concluded that entrepreneurs could not cause any serious environmental problems needing government intervention. See Fredrick Albritton Jonsson, "Rival Ecologies of Global Commerce: Adam Smith and the Natural Historians," *American Historical Review* 115 (December 2010): 1351. See also Jonsson, *Enlightenment's Frontier: The Scottish Highlands and the Origins of Environmentalism* (New Haven, CT: Yale University Press, 2013).

2. Adam Smith, *An Inquiry into the Nature and Causes of the Wealth of Nations*, 5th edition, ed. Edwin Cannan (New York: Modern Library, 1937), lvii, 3–6.

3. Smith, *Wealth of Nations*, 13–14, 423, 631.

4. Smith, *Wealth of Nations*, 94.

5. Smith, *Wealth of Nations*, 95.

6. Smith, *Wealth of Nations*, 590. It is not clear whether Smith read the first edition of Raynal's popular work or a later edition, or whether he met the Enlightenment *philosophe* on his European travels.

7. Smith, *Wealth of Nations*, 531–32.

8. On Adam Smith's distinction between agriculture and industry, see Colin Duncan, *The Centrality of Agriculture: Between Humankind and the Rest of Nature* (Montreal: McGill-Queen's University Press, 1996).

9. Thomas Robert Malthus, *An Essay on the Principle of Population*, ed. Philip Appleman (1798; reprint, New York: Norton, 1976), 20.

10. Malthus, *An Essay on the Principle of Population*, 120.

11. This language is from the King James Version.

12. Malthus, *An Essay on the Principle of Population*, 44–46. On the Edenic myth and narratives of its "recovery," see Carolyn Merchant, *Reinventing Eden: The Fate of Nature in Western Culture* (New York: Routledge, 2003).

13. Carey, in his paean to free trade, declared: "The earth is a great machine, given to man to be fashioned to his purpose. The more he fashions it the better it feeds him, because each step is but preparatory to a new one more productive than the last; requiring less labour and yielding larger return." In *The Harmony of Interests: Agricultural, Mechanical and Commercial*, 2nd ed. (New York: Myron Finch, 1852), 123. For an analysis of Carey's shaky science, see Steven Stoll, *The Great Delusion: A Mad Inventor, Death in the Tropics, and the Utopian Origins of Economic Growth* (New York: Hill & Wang, 2008), 144–48.

14. Anthony Wrigley, *Continuity, Chance and Change: The Character of the Industrial Revolution in England* (Cambridge: Cambridge University Press, 1988), 5–6. See also Wrigley, "The Limits to Growth: Malthus and the Classical Economists," *Population and Development Review* 14, Supplement (1988): 30–48. A brilliant account of the shift to coal as a major energy source is Richard G. Wilkinson, *Poverty and Progress: An Ecological Perspective on Economic Development* (New York: Praeger, 1973), 112–37.

15. Vaclav Smil, *Energy Transitions: History, Requirements, Prospects* (Santa Barbara: Praeger, 2010), 86–89.

16. W. Stanley Jevons, *The Coal Question: An Inquiry Concerning the Progress of the Nation and the Probable Exhaustion of Our Coal Mines*, 2nd ed. (New York: Macmillan, 1866), vi, 1, 177.

17. Jevons, *The Coal Question*, 241, 242, 375.

18. Jevons, *The Coal Question*, 177–78. Jevons rejected the notion that increased efficiency in fuel use would make the resource last longer; on the contrary, according to what has become known as the "Jevons paradox," efficiency only leads to more consumption.

19. John Stuart Mill, *Principles of Political Economy with Some of Their Applications to Social Philosophy* (London: John W. Parker, 1848), Vol. II, 309. On the limits that nature puts on economic production, see Vol. I, 30, 36.

20. Mill, *Principles of Political Economy*, Vol. II, 311.

FIELD TRIP: NANTUCKET ISLAND

1. For the island's history see Nathaniel Philbrick, *Away Off Shore: Nantucket Island and Its People, 1602–1890* (Nantucket: Mill Hill Press, 1994); Frances Karttunen, *The Other Islanders: People Who Pulled Nantucket's Oars* (New Bedford: Spinner

Publications, 2005); Alexander Starbuck, *The History of Nantucket* (1924; Rutland, VT: Charles E. Tuttle, 1969); and Obed Macy, *The History of Nantucket,* 2nd ed. (1880; Clifton, NJ: A. M. Kelley, 1972). A good popular introduction to regional geology is Dorothy Sterling, *The Outer Lands: A Natural History Guide to Cape Cod, Martha's Vineyard, Nantucket, Block Island, and Long Island* (Garden City, NY: Natural History Press, 1967). See also Sara Winthrop Smith, *Nantucket: A Brief Sketch of Its Physiography and Botany* (New York: Knickerbocker Press, n.d.).

2. The Earth's surface covers 197 million square miles (510 million square kilometers), of which 139 million (361 million sq. km.) are the seas, or 70 percent. The Atlantic and the Pacific, both opened for travel and use by Columbus's voyages, cover 30 and 60 million square miles respectively, with the Southern and Arctic oceans adding another 13 million. The linked continents of North and South America extend over 16 million square miles, or a mere 16 percent of the size of those oceans. On the need for more attention to marine ecology and history, see W. Jeffrey Bolster, "Putting the Ocean in Atlantic History: Maritime Communities and Marine Ecology in the Northwest Atlantic, 1500–1800," *American Historical Review* 113 (February 2008): 19–47; and "Opportunities in Marine Environmental History," *Environmental History* 11 (July 2006): 657–97.

3. William Bradford, *Mourt's Relation: A Journal of the Pilgrims at Plymouth,* ed. Dwight Heath (Cambridge, MA: Applewood Books, 1986), 6, 12. European-based crews had killed tens of thousands of North Atlantic whales before the eighteenth century.

4. Farley Mowatt, *Sea of Slaughter* (Toronto: McClelland and Stewart-Bantam, 1984), 13. An excellent overview of the global extinction crisis, which began some centuries back and has accelerated dramtically in recent decades, is Elizbeth Kolbert's *The Sixth Extinction: An Unnatural History* (New York: Henry Holt, 2014). See especially Chapter VI, "The Sea Around Us."

5. Elizabeth Little, in her pamphlet series "Nantucket Algonquian Studies," published by the Nantucket Historical Association, has examined the Indians' and the early white settlers' relationship to the island's ecology.

6. Daniel Vickers, "The First Whalemen of Nantucket," *William and Mary Quarterly* 40 (October 1983): 560–83; and David Lowenthal, "The Common and Undivided Lands of Nantucket," *Geographical Review* 46 (July 1956): 399–403. A sweeping account of early whaling in the North Atlantic appears in John F. Richards, *The Unending Frontier: An Environmental History of the Early Modern World* (Berkeley: University of California Press, 2003), 574–616.

7. Thomas A. Jefferson, Marc A. Webber, Robert L. Pitman, *Marine Mammals of the World* (London: Academic Press/Elsevier, 2008), 74–78; Richard Ellis, *Men and Whales* (New York: Knopf, 1991), 27–32.

8. Foster Rhea Dulles, *Lowered Boats: A Chronicle of American Whaling* (New York: Harcourt, Brace, 1933), 46.

9. Dulles, *Lowered Boats,* 63–64.

10. For general background see Eric Jay Dolin, *Leviathan: The History of Whaling in America* (New York: Norton, 2007); and David Moment, "The Business of Whaling in America in the 1850s," *Business History Review* 31 (Autumn, 1957): 261–91.

11. Edouard A. Stackpole, *The Sea-Hunters: The New England Whalemen during Two Centuries, 1635–1835* (Philadelphia: Lippincott, 1953), 473.

12. Hector St. John de Crèvecœur, *Letters from an American Farmer* (1782; New York: Signet, 1963), 137, 153–54. See also Lisa Norling, *Captain Ahab Had a Wife: New England Women and the Whalefishery, 1720–1870* (Chapel Hill: University of North Carolina Press, 2000).

13. Edward Byers, *The Nation of Nantucket: Society and Politics in an Early American Commercial Center, 1660–1820* (Boston: Northeastern University Press, 1987), 6–11, 201–94; Robert C. Ellickson, "A Hypothesis of Wealth-Maximizing Norms: Evidence from the Whaling Industry," *Journal of Law, Economics, & Organization* 8 (Spring 1989), 96.

14. Lance E. Davis, Robert E. Gallman, and Karin Gleiter, *In Pursuit of Leviathan: Technology, Institutions, Productivity, and Profits in American Whaling, 1816–1906* (Chicago: University of Chicago Press, 1997), 441–43; Dulles, *Lowered Boats*, 189–90.

15. James L. Dunlap, "Nantucket's Master Mason: Christopher Capen," www.nha. org/history/hn/HNcapen.htm.

16. Herman Melville, *Moby Dick; or, The Whale* (1851; New York: Norton, 1967), 381–85.

17. For the history of whale science, see D. Graham Burnett, *The Soundings of the Whale: Science and Cetaceans in the Twentieth Century* (Chicago: University of Chicago Press, 2012).

18. Ernest Thompson Seton, *Lives of Game Animals* (1929), cited in Donald Worster, *An Unsettled Country: Changing Landscapes of the American West* (Albuquerque: University of New Mexico Press, 1994), 66–69.

19. Farley Mowatt, *A Whale for the Killing* (New York: Penguin, 1972), 234. See also Friends of the Earth, *The Whaling Question: The Inquiry by Sir Sydney Frost of Australia* (San Francisco: Friends of the Earth, 1979), 34.

20. Tim D. Smith, Randall Reeves, Elisabeth A. Josephson, Judith N. Lund, and Hal Whitehead, "Sperm Whale Catches and Encounter Rates during the 19th and 20th Centuries: An Apparent Paradox," in *Oceanic Past: Management Insights from the History of Marine Animal Populations*, ed. David J. Starkey, Poul Holm, and Michaela Barnard (London: Earthscan, 2008), 159; N. A. Mackintosh, *The Stocks of Whales* (London: Fishing News, 1965).

21. Hal Whitehead, "Estimates of the Current Global Population Size and Historical Trajectory for Sperm Whales," *Marine Ecology Progress Series* 242 (October 2002): 295–304. A new approach based on genetics may greatly expand estimates of whale populations before hunting, and therefore the scale of the killing. See Stephen R. Palumbi and Joe Roman, "The History of Whales Read from DNA," in *Whales, Whaling, and Ocean Ecosystems*, ed. James A. Estes et al. (Berkeley: University of California Press, 2006), 102–15; and Joe Roman and Stephen R. Palumbi, "Whales before Whaling in the North Atlantic," *Science* 301 (July 25, 2003): 508–10.

22. Alexander Starbuck, *History of the American Whale Fishery*, vol. 2 (1878; New York: Argosy-Antiquarian, 1964), 142–43, 600–1. See also Everett S. Allen, *Children of the Light: The Rise and Fall of New Bedford Whaling and the Death of the Arctic Fleet* (Boston: Little, Brown, 1973).

23. Charles M. Scammon, *The Marine Mammals of the North-western Coast of North America* (1874; New York: Dover, 1968), 242–43. According to S. F. Harmer, "Sperm whaling reached its zenith in 1837, more than twenty years before it had petroleum as a competitor. The decline from that year to 1860 was due to

the destruction of the whales in excess of their rate of reproduction." Quoted in Francis Ommanney, *Lost Leviathan* (New York: Dodd, Mead, 1971), 92.

24. My interpretation differs somewhat from that of a team of economists (Lance Davis et al., *In Pursuit of Leviathan*, 131–49), who argue that the whalers did not damage the whale population. By "damage" they seem to mean total extinction.

25. Crèvecœur, *Letters from an American Farmer*, 136.

26. Edward Bellamy, *Six to One: A Nantucket Idyll* (New York: G. P. Putnam's, 1877), 11, 28.

27. Quoted in James D. Alsop, "Island Refashioning: The Nantucket Agricultural Society, 1856–1880," *New England Quarterly* 77 (December 2004): 568.

28. Alsop, "Island Refashioning," 571.

29. Alsop, "Island Refashioning," 585.

30. Clay Lancaster, *Holiday Island: The Pageant of Nantucket's Hostelries and Summer Life from Its Beginnings to the Mid-Twentieth Century* (Nantucket: Nantucket Historical Association, 1993); Dona Brown, *Inventing New England Regional Tourism in the Nineteenth Century* (Washington, DC: Smithsonian Institution Press, 1995), 105–34. For an example of the popular tourist guide, see Isaac H. Folger, *Hand-Book of the Island of Nantucket* (Nantucket: Folger & Rich, 1878).

31. Walter Beinecke Jr., obituary, *New York Times*, May 25, 2004; Jane Holtz Kay with Pauline Chase-Harrell, *Preserving New England* (New York: Pantheon Books, 1986), 62.

CHAPTER 4

1. George Perkins Marsh, "Watershed," *Johnson's New Universal Encyclopedia* (New York: A. J. Johnson, 1881), Vol. IV, Part II, 1299. The story of Marsh's introduction to the watershed concept is told in David Lowenthal, *George Perkins Marsh: Prophet of Conservation* (Seattle: University of Washington Press, 2000), 19. Other watershed thinkers included John Wesley Powell, explorer of the Colorado River and director of the US Geological Survey from 1881 to 1895. He called the watershed a "hydrological basin," but it was a similar idea to Marsh's—a bounded, limited area of land within which living things were linked and interdependent.

2. Harold A. Meeks, *Time and Change in Vermont: A Human Geography* (Chester: Globe Pequot Press, 1986), 14–17, 92–95. The peak of land clearing for sheep came before 1850, and by 1870 the land was beginning to revert to forest. On Marsh's family origins and settlement in Woodstock, see Lowenthal, *George Perkins Marsh*, 8–11, 16–17. See also Richard W. Judd, *Common Lands, Common People: The Origins of Conservation in Northern New England* (Cambridge, MA: Harvard University Press, 1997), especially 1–39 and 94–95, which argues that Marsh owed an intellectual debt to farmers and naturalists.

3. Leading studies of the Whig Party do not mention Marsh and his role in Congress. See Michael F. Holt, *The Rise and Fall of the American Whig Party: Jacksonian Politics and the Onset of the Civil War* (New York: Oxford University Press, 1999); and Daniel Walker Howe, *The Political Culture of the American Whigs* (Chicago: University of Chicago Press, 1979). Marsh was a maverick within his party—too critical of economic development at times and not one who idealized the business class.

4. Marsh, *Man and Nature*, 43.

5. Marsh, *Man and Nature*, 36, 44.

6. Marsh, *Man and Nature*, 228.

7. Marsh, *Man and Nature*, 158, 187. His chief authority on the climatic effects of deforestation was the French chemist Jean Baptiste Boussingault (174–78).

8. For the contrast between Marsh's awe before pristine nature and "the Italian distrust of unpeopled land," see Marcus Hall, *Earth Repair: A Transatlantic History of Environmental Restoration* (Charlottesville: University of Virginia Press, 2005), 28–32. Other important perspectives on Marsh can be found in a special issue of *Environment and History* 10 (May 2004).

9. Before 1850 Americans had "improved" about 114 million acres, mostly through deforestation. Between 1850 and 1859, the amount of land clearing had risen another 40 million acres. See Michael Williams, *Americans and Their Forests: A Historical Geography* (New York: Cambridge University Press, 1989), 118–20.

10. Marsh, *Man and Nature*, 353.

11. Georges-Louis Leclerc, Comte de Buffon, *Des Époques de la Nature*, cited in Clarence Glacken, *Traces on the Rhodian Shore: Nature and Culture in Western Thought from Ancient Times to the End of the Eighteenth Century* (Berkeley: University of California Press, 1967), 666.

12. Karl Marx and Friedrich Engels, *Communist Manifesto* (Chicago: Charles H. Kerr, 1910), 18.

13. In the second edition of his book, Marsh cited the Milanese priest Antonio Stoppani on the "anthropozoic era." Paul Crutzen, "Geology of Mankind," *Nature* 415 (January 2002): 23.

14. Marsh, *Man and Nature*, 36.

15. *The Journal of Henry David Thoreau* (New York: Dover, 1962), Vol. XIV, 161, 306–7.

16. Marsh, *Man and Nature*, 203–4. On silviculture, or tree planting, see 269–79.

17. Lowenthal, *George Perkins Marsh*, 303. On the 1890 census, see Frederick Jackson Turner, "The Significance of the Frontier in American History," American Historical Society, *Annual Report for 1893* (Washington, DC: Government Printing Office, 1894), 199–227.

18. Marsh, *Man and Nature*, 244.

19. Charles S. Sargent, *Report on the Forests of North America (Exclusive of Mexico)* (Washington, DC: Government Printing Office, 1884), 493.

20. Franklin B. Hough, "On the Duty of Governments in the Preservation of Forests," *Proceedings of the American Association for the Advancement of Science*, Portland Meeting, August 1873.

21. On the establishment of the Adirondack state park, see Roderick Nash, *Wilderness and the American Mind*, 4th ed. (New Haven, CT: Yale University Press, 2001), 116–21.

22. See my book *A Passion for Nature: The Life of John Muir* (New York: Oxford University Press, 2008), 319–22.

23. Muir, "God's First Temples: How Shall We Preserve the Forests?" Sacramento *Daily Union*, February 5, 1876, 8.

24. Gifford Pinchot, *Breaking New Ground* (1947; reprint, Seattle: University of Washington Press, 1972), xxiii, 4. See also Char Miller, *Gifford Pinchot and the Making of Modern Environmentalism* (Washington, DC: Island Press, 2001), esp. 55–56.

CHAPTER 5
1. Patten, *The New Basis of Civilization* (New York: Macmillan, 1907), 25–26.
2. See Joan F. Kenny, Nancy L. Barber, Susan S. Hutson, Kristin S. Linsey, John K. Lovelace, and Molly A. Maupin, "Estimated Use of Water in the United States in 2005," *U.S. Geological Survey Circular* 1344 (Washington, DC: Government Printing Office, 2009).
3. Williams, *Americans and Their Forests*, 7.
4. On the transition from wood to coal see US Bureau of the Census, *The Statistical History of the United States from Colonial Times to the Present* (Stamford, CT: Fairfield Publishers, 1965), 356–60; and Sean Patrick Adams, "The U.S. Coal Industry in the Nineteenth Century," Economic History Association, https://eh.net/encyclopedia/article/adams.industry.coal.us.
5. The United States holds 28 percent of the world's remaining coal reserves, far more than any other country. See the US Energy Information Administration website, www.eia.gov/todayinenergy.
6. "A total of 76 billion tons of coal remain (64 billion bituminous and 12 billion anthracite) in Pennsylvania. The coal mined first was the thickest and most easily accessible. The remaining coal seams are thinner and more difficult and expensive to recover. Much of what remains will be very difficult to utilize in the foreseeable future." William E. Edmunds, *Coal in Pennsylvania* (Harrisburg: Pennsylvania Geological Survey, 2002), 17.
7. Alfred D. Chandler Jr., "Anthracite Coal and the Beginnings of the Industrial Revolution in the United States," *Business History Review* 46 (Summer 1972): 178–81; Christopher F. Jones, "A Landscape of Energy Abundance: Anthracite Coal Canals and the Roots of American Fossil Fuel Dependence, 1820–1860," *Environmental History* 15 (July 2010): 449–484.
8. Pennsylvania's bituminous fields underlie nearly the entire western half of the state, and deposits continue southward all the way to Alabama. Until 1970 Appalachia produced 70 percent of the nation's total output, but today, according to the US Geological Survey, it supplies only 43 percent of the total, most of the rest coming from the Northern Plains (see map at http://pubs.usgs.gov/mf-maps/mf-2330/milici1.pdf).
9. Cited by Joel Tarr, "Search for a 'Sink' for an Industrial Waste: Iron-Making Fuels and the Environment," *Environmental History Review* 18 (Spring 1994): 14. Tarr argues that the "by-product" or "retort" oven captured some of the pollutants for use, but then it polluted the rivers with ammonia, cyanide, and phenolics. America's changing perception of pollution is discussed in Adam Rome, "Coming to Terms with Pollution: The Language of Environmental Reform, 1865–1915," *Environmental History* 1 (July 1996): 6–28.
10. Brian Black, *Petrolia: The Landscape of America's First Oil Boom* (Baltimore: Johns Hopkins University Press, 2000), 194. See also the same author's *Crude Reality: Petroleum in World History* (Lanham, MD: Rowman & Littlefield, 2012).
11. Chad Montrie, *Making a Living: Work and Environment in the United States* (Chapel Hill: University of North Carolina Press, 2008), 75.
12. Western Virginia's history of coal is well covered in Ronald D. Eller, *Miners, Millhands, and Mountaineers: Industrialization of the Appalachian South, 1880–1930* (Knoxville: University of Tennessee Press, 1982); and *Uneven Ground: Appalachia since 1945* (Lexington: University Press of Kentucky, 2008). The classic account of Eastern Kentucky's fall into industrialization is Harry M. Caudill, *Night Comes to the Cumberlands: A Biography of a Depressed Area* (Boston: Little, Brown, 1963).

13. Paul Salstrom, *Appalachia's Path to Dependency: Rethinking a Region's Economic History, 1730–1940* (Lexington: University Press of Kentucky, 1994), 126–27; Dwight B. Billings and Kathleen M. Blee, *The Road to Poverty: The Making of Wealth and Hardship in Appalachia* (New York: Cambridge University Press, 2000), 8–16, 197.

14. See Harold L. James and Paul K. Sims, eds., "Precambrian Iron-Formations of the World," *Economic Geology* 68 (November 1973): 913–14. Today the production of 2000 pounds of iron requires 3600 pounds of pelletized ore, 750 pounds of limestone, 125 pounds of natural gas, 249 pounds of coal, and 3350 pounds of air. William F. Hosford, *Iron and Steel* (New York: Cambridge University Press, 2012), xx.

15. I take this phrase from the title of Eric Rauchway's book, *Blessed Among Nations: How the World Made America* (New York: Hill and Wang, 2006), although the riches of coal and iron do not figure among his list of national assets. The phrase originally occurred in a 1915 speech by President Woodrow Wilson, who extolled the nation's natural resource endowment: "Think of the great reservoir of hope . . . that there is in this great land of plenty" (cited, Rauchway, 147).

16. Albert H. Chester, "The Iron Region of Northern Minnesota," *Eleventh Annual Report of the Geological and Natural History Survey of Minnesota* (Minneapolis: 1882), 154–167; Francis N. Stacy, "The Iron Mines That Give Us Leadership: The Most Extraordinary Deposits in the World in the Mesabi Range," *The World's Work* VIII (September 1904): 5235–5243. Stacy writes: "For this revolution in mining, we have, of course, to thank Nature first. Geology has done more to make it possible than the human inventor" (5237).

17. Chicago was the nation's epicenter for a new landscape of agricultural production, including wheat, corn, beef, and pork. See William Cronon, *Nature's Metropolis: Chicago and the Great West* (New York: Norton, 1991). Equally important was the landscape of industrialization, whose epicenter was Pittsburgh, Pennsylvania.

18. Svante Arrhenius, *Worlds in the Making: The Evolution of the Universe*, translated by H. Borns (New York: Harper, 1908), 54. See also Spencer R. Weart, *The Discovery of Global Warming* (Cambridge, MA: Harvard University Press, 2003); and Libby Robin, Sverker Sörlin, and Paul Warde, eds., *The Future of Nature: Documents of Global Change* (New Haven, CT: Yale University Press, 2013), 303–12.

19. Marsh, *Man and Nature*, 37, 42.

20. Thomas J. Misa, *A Nation of Steel: The Making of Modern America, 1865–1925* (Baltimore: Johns Hopkins University Press, 1995), describes those technological and social impacts.

21. John Van Dyke, "Editor's Note," *Autobiography of Andrew Carnegie* (Boston: Houghton Mifflin, 1920), vii; Carnegie, "The Gospel of Wealth," *The Gospel of Wealth and Other Timely Essays* (New York: Century, 1900), 15.

22. Misa, *A Nation of Steel*, 5–28.

23. Paul Krause, *The Battle for Homestead, 1880–1892: Politics, Culture, and Steel* (Pittsburgh: University of Pittsburgh Press, 1992); David Nasaw, *Andrew Carnegie* (New York: Penguin, 2006), 405–27; Joseph Frazier Wall, *Andrew Carnegie* (New York: Oxford University Press, 1970), 537–82.

24. Angela Gugliotta, "How, When, and for Whom Was Smoke a Problem in Pittsburgh?" in *Devastation and Renewal: An Environmental History of Pittsburgh*

and Its Region, ed. Joel Tarr (Pittsburgh: University of Pittsburgh Press, 2003), 110–25.

25. Carnegie, "The Natural Oil and Gas Wells of Western Pennsylvania," *Macmillan's*, January 1885, reprinted in Carnegie, *The Empire of Business* (New York: Doubleday, Page, 1902), 280–81.

26. Angela Gugliotta, "'Hell with the Lid Taken Off': A Cultural History of Air Pollution—Pittsburgh" (PhD dissertation, University of Notre Dame, 2004), 102, 180.

27. Nasaw, *Andrew Carnegie*, 942–49.

28. Wall, *Andrew Carnegie*, 540–41.

29. Carnegie, "The Gospel of Wealth," 4–5.

CHAPTER 6

1. The classic account of conservation in the Roosevelt era is Samuel Hays, *Conservation and the Gospel of Efficiency: The Progressive Conservation Movement, 1890–1920* (Cambridge, MA: Harvard University Press, 1959), which focuses on "the technological spirit" behind the movement. For other perspectives see Douglas Brinkley, *The Wilderness Warrior: Theodore Roosevelt and the Crusade for America* (New York: HarperCollins, 2009); and Paul Russell Cutright, *Theodore Roosevelt: The Making of a Conservationist* (Urbana: University of Illinois, 1985).

2. Theodore Roosevelt, "Opening Address by the President: Conservation as a National Duty," *Proceedings of a Conference of Governors in the White House*, Washington, DC, May 13–15, 1908 (Washington, DC: Government Printing Office, 1909), 8. The full proceedings can be found at the Library of Congress's American Memory digital collection, "The Evolution of the Conservation Movement, 1850 to 1920," http://memory.loc.gov/ammem/amrvhtml/conshome.html.

3. "Conservation," *Oxford English Dictionary* Online (Oxford: Oxford University Press, 2000), www.oed.com.

4. "Journal of Travels to Europe, Including Egypt and the Holy Land. Near Cairo, Dec. 13, 1872," *Theodore Roosevelt's Diaries of Boyhood and Youth* (New York: Charles Scribner's Sons, 1928), 290–91.

5. John Reiger, *American Sportsmen and the Origins of Conservation*, 3rd ed. (Corvallis: Oregon State University Press, 2001), 146–74.

6. For criticism of the class bias in wildlife conservation, see Louis Warren, *The Hunter's Game: Poachers and Conservationists in Twentieth-Century America* (New Haven, CT: Yale University Press, 1997); and Karl Jacoby, *Crimes Against Nature: Squatters, Poachers, Thieves, and the Hidden History of American Conservation* (Berkeley: University of California Press, 2001).

7. Theodore Roosevelt, "First Annual Message," December 3, 1901, *The Works of Theodore Roosevelt* (New York: Charles Scribner's Sons, 1926), vol. 15, 103.

8. According to Kathleen Dalton, "Roosevelt's conservation campaign had been a constant war between the executive branch and Congress. His edicts, vetoes, outbursts of frustration, and executive power grabs bespoke how difficult it had been to get anything done within the prevailing political climate." *Theodore Roosevelt: A Strenuous Life* (New York: Knopf, 2002), 248.

9. Donald Worster, *Rivers of Empire: Water, Aridity, and the Growth of the American West* (New York: Pantheon Books, 1985), 160–69, 172–73. See also Hays, *Conservation and the Gospel of Efficiency*, 9–15; Brinkley, *The Wilderness Warrior*, 422–26.

10. "First Annual Message," *The Works of Theodore Roosevelt*, vol. 15, 103.

11. "The New Nationalism," Osawatomie, Kansas, August 31, 1910, *The Works of Theodore Roosevelt*, vol. 17, 15.

12. Gifford Pinchot, *Breaking New Ground*, 325–26. See also Whitney R. Cross, "W J McGee and the Idea of Conservation," *The Historian* 15 (Spring 1953): 148–67.

13. Ward was best known for his two-volume work, *Dynamic Sociology* (1883, 1887). His views resemble closely what James C. Scott has called "high modernist ideology," defined as "a strong, one might even say muscle-bound, version of the self-confidence about scientific and technical progress." *Seeing Like a State: How Certain Schemes to Improve the Human Condition Have Failed* (New Haven, CT: Yale University Press, 1998), 4.

14. For a fuller discussion of Ward's ideas, see my book *A River Running West: The Life of John Wesley Powell* (New York: Oxford University Press, 2001), 445–49.

15. McGee, "The Conservation of Natural Resources," *Proceedings of the Mississippi Valley Historical Association for the Year 1909–1910* (Cedar Rapids, IA: Torch Press, 1911), 376.

16. For this agency's brief career and objectives, see Hays, 105–9; and Donald Pisani, "Water Planning in the Progressive Era: The Inland Waterways Commission Reconsidered," *Journal of Policy History* 18:4 (2006): 389–418. While integrated water planning did not succeed in Theodore Roosevelt's day, it did come back during the New Deal administration of Franklin Roosevelt and gain influence in later decades. See also WJ McGee, "Water as a Resource," *Annals of the American Academy of Political and Social Science* 33 (May 1909): 37–50.

17. Pinchot, *Breaking New Ground*, 346.

18. On the marginalized role of women in the shift toward a more "expert" conservation, see Adam Rome, " 'Political Hermaphrodites': Gender and Environmental Reform in Progressive America," *Environmental History* 11 (July 2006): 440–63. See also Shen Hou, *The City Natural: Garden and Forest Magazine and the Rise of American Environmentalism* (Pittsburgh: University of Pittsburgh Press, 2013), 185–86, which traces the aesthetic side of conservation, which aimed to restore beauty and grace to the urban environment, as well as save rural and wild places.

19. Worster, *A Passion for Nature*, 418–31.

20. The full story is told in Robert Righter, *The Battle Over Hetch Hetchy: America's Most Controversial Dam and the Birth of Modern Environmentalism* (New York: Oxford University Press, 2005).

21. Andrew Carnegie, "The Conservation of Ores and Related Minerals," *Proceedings of a Conference of Governors*, 14–25.

22. Carnegie, "The Conservation of Ores and Related Minerals," 23–24.

23. Carnegie, "The Conservation of Ores and Related Minerals," 24.

24. See James Penick, *Progressive Politics and Conservation: The Ballinger-Pinchot Affair* (Chicago: University of Chicago Press, 1968), and Char Miller, *Gifford Pinchot and the Making of Modern Environmentalism* (Washington, DC: Island Press, 2001), 206–17.

25. Theodore Roosevelt, *African Game Trails* (New York: Charles Scribner's Sons, 1910), 407–8.

26. Pinchot, *The Fight for Conservation* (1910; rpt., Seattle: University of Washington, 1967), 20, 42, 128, 146. See also Brian Balogh, "Scientific Forestry and the

Roots of the Modern American State: Gifford Pinchot's Path to Progressive Reform," *Environmental History* 7 (April 2002): 198–225.

27. Otis Graham, *Towards a Planned Society: From Roosevelt to Nixon* (New York: Oxford University Press, 1976). If we mean by planning the implementation of a "national growth policy," then it began with Theodore Roosevelt and his conservation agenda.

28. John Kenneth Galbraith, *The New Industrial State* (New York: Houghton Mifflin, 1967), 71, 173.

29. Steinberg, *Down to Earth: Nature's Role in American History* (New York: Oxford University Press, 2002), 156.

30. Muir, "Hetch Hetchy Valley," in *The Writings of John Muir*, vol. 5: *The Yosemite* (Boston: Houghton Mifflin, 1916), 286.

31. Similar questions were raised by Grant McConnell, "The Conservation Movement—Past and Present," *Western Political Quarterly* 7 (September 1954): 463–78.

32. Madison, "On the Safety of Multiple Interests: Ambition Will Counteract Ambition," Federalist Paper 51, February 6, 1788, *The Debate on the Constitution, Part Two*, ed. Bernard Bailyn (New York: Library of America, 1993), 164.

33. See Paul Hirt, *A Conspiracy of Optimism: Management of the National Forests since World War Two* (Lincoln: University of Nebraska Press, 1994).

FIELD TRIP: IMPERIAL VALLEY

1. Anyone interested in the history of this place must start with William deBuys, *Salt Dreams: Land and Water in Low-Down California*, with photographs by Joan Myers (Albuquerque: University of New Mexico Press, 1999).

2. Eliot Blackwelder, "Origin of the Colorado River," *Bulletin of the Geological Society of America* 45:3 (1934): 551–66.

3. House of Representatives, *Reports of Explorations and Surveys, to Ascertain the Most Practicable and Economical Route for a Railroad from the Mississippi River to the Pacific Ocean*, 33rd Cong., 2d sess., 1854–55, H. Exec. Doc. 91, pt. 5, 249. For a later, more cautious appraisal, see Thomas H. Means and J. Garnett Holmes, "Soil Survey Around Imperial, Cal.," US Department of Agriculture, Bureau of Soils, Circular no. 9, January 10, 1902.

4. House Committee on Public Lands, *Colorado Desert*, Report to Accompany H.R. 417, 37th Cong., 2d sess., 1862, H. Rept 87, 2. Wozencraft's life is chronicled in Dan Thrapp, *Encyclopedia of Frontier Biography* (Lincoln: University of Nebraska Press, 1991), Vol. III, 1599–1600.

5. Chaffey quoted in *The Valley Imperial* (n.p.: Imperial County Historical Society, 1991), 21.

6. J. A. Alexander, *The Life of George Chaffey* (Melbourne: Macmillan, 1928), 291–92.

7. The rate of annual river flow is taken from H. T. Cory, "Irrigation and River Control in the Colorado River Delta," *Transactions of the American Society of Civil Engineers*, 76, Paper No. 1270 (1913), 1205. Later estimates would soar to 17 million acre-feet per year, encouraging overdevelopment of the watershed.

8. Theodore Roosevelt, "Message from the President of the United States, *Imperial Valley or Salton Sink Region*," 59th Cong., 2d sess., 1907, S. Doc. 212, 6–7.

9. George Kennan, *The Salton Sea: An Account of Harriman's Fight with the Colorado River* (New York: Macmillan, 1917), chaps. 3–5; Edgar F. Howe and Wilbur Jay Hall, *The Story of the First Decade in Imperial Valley, California* (Imperial, CA: Edgar F. Howe and Sons, 1910), chap. 8; and H. T. Cory and William P. Blake, *The Imperial Valley and the Salton Sink* (San Francisco: J. J. Newbegin, 1915), chaps. 10–11.

10. Department of Commerce, *Thirteenth Census of the United States* (Washington, DC: Government Printing Office, 1913), V and VI; *Fourteenth Census* (1922), VI: 3; *United States Census of Agriculture: 1945* (1946), I: 33.

11. *The Valley Imperial*, 7. For more critical views see Benny Joseph Andres Jr., "Power and Control in Imperial Valley, California: Nature, Agribusiness, Labor and Race Relations, 1900–1940," PhD dissertation, University of New Mexico, 2003, esp. chaps. 4–5; and William T. Vollman's unique and vivid saga *Imperial* (New York: Viking, 2009).

12. Imperial Irrigation District, *The Boulder Dam All American Canal Project,* November 1924, 23. See also Phil Swing, *Colorado River Hearings and Miscellaneous Documents, vol. I* (Washington, DC: Government Printing Office, 1924); and Beverley Moeller, *Phil Swing and Boulder Dam* (Berkeley: University of California Press, 1971).

13. Worster, *Rivers of Empire*, 202–12; Paul Taylor, "Water, Land, and Environment in Imperial Valley," *Natural Resources Journal* 13 (January 1973): 1–35.

14. Norris Hundley, *The Great Thirst: Californians and Water, 1770s–1990s* (Berkeley: University of California Press, 1992), 203–32.

15. Among the weaker voices were those of Indians and Mexicans, whose traditional claims long were ignored. See Alfonso Cortez-Lara and Maria Rosa Garcia-Acevedo, "The Lining of the All-American Canal: The Forgotten Voices," *Natural Resources Journal* 40:2 (2000): 261–80; Evan R. Ward, *Border Oasis: Water and the Political Ecology of the Colorado River Delta* (Tucson: University of Arizona Press, 2003); and Eric I. Boime, "'Fluid Boundaries': Southern California, Baja California, and the Conflict Over the Colorado River, 1848–1944," PhD dissertation, University of California, San Diego, 2002.

16. Tom Waller, "Expertise, Elites, and Resource Management Reform: Resisting Agricultural Water Conservation in California's Imperial Valley," *Journal of Political Ecology* 1:1 (1994): 13–41; and Steven P. Erie and Pascale Joassart-Marelli, "Unraveling Southern California's Water/Growth Nexus: Metropolitan Water District Policies and Subsidies for Suburban Development, 1928–1996," *California Western Law Review* 36:2 (2000): 267–90.

17. Hundley, *The Great Thirst*, 392–97. See also Robert Gottlieb and Margaret Fitzsimmons, *Thirst for Growth: Water Agencies as Hidden Government in California* (Tucson: University of Arizona, 1991), chap. 4; Brent M. Haddad, *Rivers of Gold: Designing Markets to Allocate Water in California* (Washington, DC: Island Press, 2000), 63–94; and A. Dan Tarlock, "From Natural Scarcity to Artificial Abundance: The Legacy of California Water Law and Politics," *Hastings West-Northwest Journal of Environmental Law and Policy* 1:1 (1994): 71–84.

18. For the full text see Bureau of Reclamation, "Record of Decision: Colorado River Water Delivery Agreement," www.usbr.gov/lc/region/g4000/crwda/crwda_rod.pdf.

19. Thomas R. Karl, Jerry M. Melillo, and Thomas C. Peterson, eds., *Global Climate Change Impacts in the United States* (New York: Cambridge University Press,

2009), 9. The range of their projections reflects different rates of CO_2 emissions. See also Angela Jardine, Robert Merideth, Mary Black, and Sarah LeRoy, *Assessment of Climate Change in the Southwest United States: A Report Prepared for the National Climate Assessment* (Washington, DC: Island Press, 2013); and Jonathan Overpeck et al., "Dry Times Ahead," *Science* 328 (June 25, 2010): 1642–43.

20. For current California snowpack reports, see Doug Carlson et al., "Sierra Nevada Snowpack Is Virtually Gone," April 1, 2015, California Department of Water Resources, pdf newsrelease, http://www.water.ca.gov/news/newsreleases/2015/040115snowsurvey.pdf.

21. William deBuys, *A Great Aridness: Climate Change and the Future of the American Southwest* (New York: Oxford University Press, 2011), 132. See also James Lawrence Powell, *Dead Pool: Lake Powell, Global Warming, and the Future of Water in the West* (Berkeley: University of California Press, 2008); and the US Bureau of Reclamation, *Colorado River Basin and Supply Study* (December 2012).

22. Although desalination of seawater is now going on in Tampa, Yuma, and San Diego, and a few other cities around the world, the scale is nowhere large enough to make up for a major decline in western rivers. Then there are the environmental constraints. According to a National Academy of Science study, "Possible environmental impacts of desalination are impingement and entrainment of organisms when seawater is taken in, ecological impacts from disposing of salt concentrates, and increased greenhouse gas emissions from increased energy use, among other concerns." See *Desalination: A National Perspective* (Washington, DC: National Academies Press, 2008), 3, 108–46.

23. For an insightful discussion of Wright's novel see George L. Henderson, *California and the Fictions of Capital* (New York: Oxford University Press, 1999), 183–95.

24. Marcia Keith, "Water Inputs in California Food Production," Water Education Foundation, Sacramento CA, 1991, 26. The beef industry prefers much lower figures, but this study seems to be the most unbiased one available. Imperial Valley, because of its higher temperatures and evaporation rates, uses more water than the California average.

CHAPTER 7

1. Osborn, *Our Plundered Planet* (Boston: Little, Brown, 1948), vii.

2. Osborn, *Our Plundered Planet*, 196. See also Osborn's book *The Limits of the Earth* (Boston: Little, Brown, 1953), in which he writes: "Man is becoming aware of the limits of his earth. The isolation of a nation, or even a tribe, is a condition of an age gone by" (3).

3. Vogt, *Road to Ruin* (New York: William Sloane, 1948), 14–15.

4. For relevant background to this period, see Jackson Lears, *Fables of Abundance: A Cultural History of Advertising in America* (New York: Basic Books, 1994); Robert Collins, *More: The Politics of Economic Growth in Postwar America* (New York: Oxford University Press, 2000); and Lizabeth Cohen, *A Consumer's Republic: The Politics of Mass Consumption in Postwar America* (New York: Knopf, 2003).

5. *Historical Statistics of the United States*, Millennium Edition Online (New York: Cambridge University Press, 2000), Tables Dc531, Df343.

6. Colin McEvedy and Richard Jones, *Atlas of World Population History* (New York: Penguin Books, 1978), 342, 350; *Historical Statistics of the United States*, Table Aa2.

7. Christian Pfister, "The '1950s Syndrome' and the Transition from a Slow-Going to a Rapid Loss of Global Sustainability," in *The Turning Points of Environmental History*, ed. Frank Uekoetter (Pittsburgh: University of Pittsburgh Press, 2010), 90–118.

8. M. King Hubbert, "Our Energy Resources," *Physics Today* 2 (April 1949): 19–20. See also Hubbert, "Nuclear Energy and the Fossil Fuels" (1956), www.hubbert-peak.com/hubbert/1956/1956.pdf; and Kenneth Deffeyes, *Hubbert's Peak: The Impending World Oil Shortage* (Princeton, NJ: Princeton University Press, 2008).

9. *Resources for Freedom* (Washington, DC: Government Printing Office, 1952), I:1–5.

10. John Kenneth Galbraith, "How Much Should a Country Consume?" in *Perspectives on Conservation: Essays on America's Natural Resources*, ed. Henry Jarrett (Baltimore: Johns Hopkins University Press, 1958), 89–99. Galbraith's *The Affluent Society* is one of the period's most important works of social criticism.

11. Samuel Ordway Jr., *Resources and the American Dream* (New York: Ronald Press, 1956 rev. ed.), 3.

12. Ordway, *Resources and the American Dream*, 5, 6, 8. Italics in the original.

13. Ordway, *Resources and the American Dream*, 26.

14. Barnett and Morse, *Scarcity and Growth: The Economics of Natural Resource Availability* (Baltimore: Johns Hopkins University Press, 1952). For a critical overview see Richard Norgaard, "Scarcity and Growth: How Does It Look Today?" *American Journal of Agricultural Economics* 57 (November 1975): 810–14.

15. Barnett, "The Myth of Our Vanishing Resources," *Transaction* 4 (June 1967): 6–89. See also Gardner Brown Jr. and Barry Field, "Implications of Alternative Measures of Natural Resource Scarcity," *Journal of Political Economy* 86 (April 1978): 229–243.

16. The story of postwar environmentalism in the United States has been told from many different perspectives. See Stephen Fox, *John Muir and His Legacy: The American Conservation Movement* (Boston: Little, Brown, 1961); Samuel Hays, *Beauty, Health, Permanence: Environmental Politics in the United States, 1955–1985* (New York: Cambridge University Press, 1987); Michael Egan, *Barry Commoner and the Science of Survival: The Remaking of American Environmentalism* (Cambridge, MA: MIT Press, 2009); Thomas Robertson, *The Malthusian Moment: Global Population Growth and the Birth of American Environmentalism* (New Brunswick, NJ: Rutgers University Press, 2012); and Jacob Hamblin, *Arming Mother Nature: The Birth of Catastrophic Environmentalism* (New York: Oxford University Press, 2013).

17. David M. Potter, *People of Plenty: Economic Abundance and the American Character* (Chicago: University of Chicago Press, 1954). The book was a revised version of Potter's 1950 Walgreen lectures at the University of Chicago.

18. Potter, *People of Plenty*, 59.

19. Potter, *People of Plenty*, 82. The United States in 1949 boasted a per capita income of $1453, far higher than that of the United Kingdom ($773), Norway ($587), France ($482), West Germany ($320), the USSR ($305), Japan ($100), or China ($27). The other nations in the Americas, except for Canada, had remained as poor or poorer than the Europeans.

20. Central Intelligence Agency, *The World Factbook*, especially Country Comparison: GDP Per Capita (PPP), https://www.cia.gov/library/publications/the-world-factbook/rankorder/2004rank.html.

21. Robert Collins, "David Potter's People of Plenty and the Recycling of Consensus History," *Reviews in American History* 16 (June 1988): 326–28.

22. Jackson Lears, "Reconsidering Abundance: A Plea for Ambiguity," in *Getting and Spending: European and American Consumer Societies in the Twentieth Century*, ed. Susan Strasser, Charles McGovern, and Matthias Judt (Cambridge: Cambridge University Press, 1998), 450–51.

23. Potter, *People of Plenty*, 142–65. Jackson Lears writes, "twentieth-century advertising iconography redefined the source of abundance from the fecund earth to the efficient factory" (*Fables of Abundance*, 18). For Potter the same cultural traits, not natural abundance, had produced both the American farm and factory.

24. Potter, *People of Plenty*, 117, 124, 129.

CHAPTER 8

1. Donella Meadows, "Chapter One—How the Limits to Growth Happened," February 16, 2011, 1–2. I wish to thank Dennis Meadows for providing a copy of this unfinished and unpublished manuscript, along with copies of other valuable materials. I am also indebted to Jørgen Randers for assistance.

2. Donella Meadows, "Chapter One," 3.

3. The definitive history of this pivotal event is Adam Rome, *The Genius of Earth Day: How a 1970 Teach-In Unexpectedly Made the First Green Generation* (New York: Hill & Wang, 2013).

4. Executive Committee of The Club of Rome, "Commentary," in Donella H. Meadows, Dennis L. Meadows, Jørgen Randers, and William W. Behrens III, *The Limits to Growth: A Report for the Club of Rome's Project on the Predicament of Mankind* (New York: Signet Book/New American Library, a Potomac Associates Book, 1972), 195.

5. Jay Forrester, *World Dynamics* (Cambridge MA: Wright-Allen, 1971), 13–17.

6. The history of the Club of Rome, its meetings with Jay Forrester, and the club's subsequent development are well covered in Peter Moll, *From Scarcity to Sustainability: Futures Studies and the Environment: The Role of the Club of Rome* (Frankfurt: Peter Lang, 1991), esp. chaps. 1–2.

7. Forrester, "World Dynamics and the Club of Rome," *From the Ranch to System Dynamics: An Autobiography* (1992), www.friends-partners.org/GLOSAS/Peace%20Gaming/System%20Dynamics/Forrester's%20papers/Forrester-Ranch.html.

8. Donella Meadows, "Chapter One," 8.

9. Meadows et al., *Limits to Growth*, 27–29.

10. Meadows et al., *Limits to Growth*, 26–29. For the international reaction to the book, see Mauricio Schoijet, "*Limits to Growth* and The Rise of Catastrophism," *Environmental History* 4 (October 1999): 515–30; Elke Seefried, "Towards the Limits to Growth? The Book and Its Reception in West Germany and Britain, 1972–73," German Historical Institute/London *Bulletin* 33 (May 2011): 3–37; Keith Suter, "The Club of Rome Revisited," Australian Broadcasting Corporation radio talk, 1999, www.abc.net.au/science/slab/rome/default.htm; and Ugo Bardi, "The Story of the Limits to Growth," chap. 2, *Revisiting*

the Limits to Growth (manuscript awaiting publication). I am grateful to Bardi, professor of physical chemistry at the University of Florence, for generously providing a copy of his manuscript.

11. Meadows et al., *Limits to Growth*, 70–72.
12. Meadows et al., *Limits to Growth*, 76–78.
13. Meadows et al., *Limits to Growth*, 89.
14. Donald Worster, *Nature's Economy: The History of Ecological Ideas*, rev. ed. (New York: Cambridge University Press, 1994), Part Six.
15. Hutchinson, "The Biosphere," *Scientific American* (September 1970): 53. Quoted in Meadows et al., *Limits to Growth*, 78.
16. A notable dissenter among environmentally active natural scientists was Barry Commoner, who disagreed about the cause and shape of the environmental threat. It was not consumption, in general, he insisted, and it was emphatically not population growth that was endangering the earth. The environmental crisis (in his view) was caused simply by the addition of new chemical substances—phosphate detergents and leaded gasoline were his leading examples—created by private corporations in pursuit of profits. Corporate capitalism was, in Commoner's view, the great polluter, implying that in a socialist world there would be no crisis. See, for example, Commoner, "Economic Growth and Ecology—A Biologist's View," *Monthly Labor Review* 9 (November 1971): 9–13.
17. "The Worst Is Yet to Be?" *Time* 99 (January 1, 1972), 40.
18. Robert Gillette, "The Limits to Growth: Hard Sell for a Computer View of Doomsday," *Science* 175 (March 10, 1972): 1091.
19. Donella Meadows, "Chapter One," 14.
20. Cover and inside promotional quotes, Meadows et al., *Limits to Growth*.
21. Kaysen, "The Computer That Printed Out 'Wolf,'" *Foreign Affairs* 50 (July 1972): 668; Passell, Roberts, and Ross, review in *New York Times Book Review*, April 2, 1972; Wallich, "More on Growth," *Newsweek* (March 13, 1972): 86; Nordhaus, "World Dynamics: Measurement without Data," *The Economic Journal* 83 (December 1973): 1157, 1183. Nordhaus, however, later wrote "economists have for the most part ridiculed the new view of growth, arguing that it is merely Chicken Little Run Wild. I think that the new view of growth must be taken seriously and analyzed carefully." See his "Resources as a Constraint on Growth," *American Economic Review* 64 (May 1974): 22.
22. Forrester, "World Dynamics and the Club of Rome."
23. Galbraith, "How Much Should a Country Consume?" *Perspectives on Conservation*, ed. Henry Jarrett (Baltimore: Resources for the Future/Johns Hopkins Press, 1958), 92; Boulding, "The Shadow of the Stationary State," *The No-Growth Society*, ed. Mancur Olson and Hans Landsberg (New York: Norton, 1973), 98; Boulding, "The Economics of the Coming Space Ship Earth," *Environmental Quality in a Growing Economy*, ed. Henry Jarrett (Baltimore: Resources for the Future/Johns Hopkins University Press, 1966), 3–14.
24. Heilbroner, "Ecological Armageddon," *New York Review of Books*, April 23, 1970, 3, 9. For a fuller statement of his views, see *An Inquiry into the Human Prospect* (New York: Norton, 1975).
25. H. S. D. Cole, Christopher Freeman, Marie Joboda, and K. L. R. Pavitt., ed. *Thinking about the Future: A Critique of The Limits to Growth* (London: Chatto & Windus, 1973), 10. This University of Sussex group complained vaguely about

the "political bias" of the American environmentalists, but their chief criticism was that "the MIT group is underestimating the possibilities of continuous technical progress" (10).

26. Meadows et al., *Limits to Growth*, 184.
27. Heinz Arndt, *The Rise and Fall of Economic Growth: A Study in Contemporary Thought* (Cheshire: Longman, 1978), 144–51.
28. Roberts, "On Reforming Economic Growth," in Olson and Landsberg, *The No-Growth Society*, 124.
29. Kaysen, "The Computer That Printed Out 'Wolf,'" 664. Julian Simon's influential book, *The Ultimate Resource*, was published by Princeton University Press in 1981, and was followed in 1984 by *The Resourceful Earth*, coauthored by Herman Kahn. For a more thorough discussion of Simon's life and work, especially his confrontations with the environmental scientist Paul Ehrlich, see Paul Sabin, *The Bet: Paul Ehrlich, Julian Simon, and the Gamble over Earth's Future* (New Haven, CT: Yale University Press, 2013). On the bet that Simon refused to take with Ehrlich, see Alan Weisman, *Countdown: Our Last, Best Hope for a Future on Earth?* (New York: Back Bay Books/Little, Brown, 2013), 403.
30. Solow, "The Economics of Resources or the Resources of Economics," *American Historical Review* 64 (May 1974): 118.
31. Goeller and Weinberg, "The Age of Substitutability," *Science* 191 (February 20, 1976): 683–89. See also H. E. Goeller and A. Zucker, "Infinite Resources: The Ultimate Strategy," *Science* 223 (February 3, 1984): 456–62. Ironically, Weinberg once called nuclear power, in a phrase that haunted him for the rest of his life, "a Faustian bargain," i.e., a dangerous pact made with the Devil to gain power and wealth.
32. Wendell Berry, "The Landscaping of Hell: Strip-Mine Morality in East Kentucky," in *The Long-Legged House* (New York: Audubon/Ballantine, 1969), 12–29. For both legal, scientific, and visual dimensions of the new mining practices, see Mark Squillace, *The Strip Mining Handbook* (Washington, DC: Environmental Policy Institute, 1990); Tom Butler, *Plundering Appalachia: The Tragedy of Mountaintop Removal Coal Mining* (n.p.: Earth Aware Editions, 2009); and R. K. Tiwary, "Environmental Impact of Coal Mining on Water Regime and Its Management," *Water, Air, and Soil Pollution* 132 (November 2001): 185–99.
33. Bardi, "Mineral Resources as Limits to Growth," chap. 8, *Revisiting the Limits to Growth*.
34. Joel Cohen, *How Many People Can the Earth Support?* (New York: Norton, 1995), 53–55.
35. Among the enthusiastic prophets were Passell, Roberts, and Ross, who in their 1972 review of *Limits* (see note 21) wrote, "A virtually infinite source of energy, the controlled nuclear fusion of hydrogen, will probably be tapped within 50 years." Forty-three years later such an energy source had not yet materialized.
36. Bardi, "Mineral Resources as Limits to Growth," chap. 8, in *Revisiting the Limits to Growth*.
37. Brian J. Skinner, *Earth Resources*, 2nd ed. (Englewood Cliffs, NJ: Prentice-Hall, 1976), 14.
38. The most persistent advocate of outer-space mining is the Arizona scientist John S. Lewis. See, for example, his *Mining the Sky: Untold Riches from the Asteroids, Comets, and Planets* (New York: Perseus, 1997). He has not told us,

however, where the energy will come from to harvest those riches, or which resource needs can or cannot be economically filled in this way. The idea is still in the realm of science fiction, including, for example, the 1979 film *Alien*, directed by Ridley Scott.

39. For sociological catastrophism see William R. Catton Jr., *Overshoot: The Ecological Basis of Revolutionary Change* (Urbana: University of Illinois Press, 1980).

40. Donella Meadows, Dennis Meadows, and Jørgen Randers, *Beyond the Limits: Confronting Global Collapse, Envisioning a Sustainable Future* (Post Mills, VT: Chelsea Green, 1992), 233.

41. Donella Meadows, Jørgen Randers, and Dennis Meadows, *Limits to Growth: The 30-Year Update* (London: Earthscan, 2004), xvii. The concept of "sustainable development" was made popular by the so-called Bruntland Report, published as *Our Common Future*, by the World Commission on Environment and Development (Oxford: Oxford University Press, 1987), 64. This report defined the phrase as "development that meets the needs of the present without compromising the ability of future generations to meet their own needs." See also Ulrich Grober, *Sustainability: A Cultural History*, trans. Ray Cunningham (Totnes, UK: Green Books, 2012).

42. Jared Diamond identifies two behaviors that have saved societies in the past: a willingness to embrace long-term planning and to reconsider their core values. See *Collapse: How Societies Choose to Fail or Succeed* (New York: Viking, 2005), 522.

43. Daniel Bell, in *Prospects for Growth: Changing Expectations for the Future*, ed. Kenneth D. Wilson (New York: Praeger, 1977), 14, 17, and 21.

44. Donella Meadows, "Chapter One," 3.

45. The most thorough recent appraisal is by Graham Turner, "A Comparison of *The Limits to Growth* with 30 Years of Reality," *Global Environmental Change* 18 (August 2008): 397–411. Turner updates the MIT team's data and corroborates their projections: "The global system is on an unsustainable trajectory unless there is substantial and rapid reduction in consumptive behavior in combination with technological progress" (410). See also Charles Hall and John Day Jr., "Revisiting the *Limits to Growth* after Peak Oil," *American Scientist* 97 (May–June 2009): 230–37; "30 Years Beyond the Limits—An Interview with Jørgen Randers," *Plausible Futures Newsletter* (2007): online journal, http://plausiblefutures.com/30-years-beyond-the-limits-an-interview-with-j%C3%B8rgen-randers/; and Debora MacKenzie, "Doomsday Book," *New Scientist* 911 (January 7, 2012): 41.

CHAPTER 9

1. Bjørn Lomborg and Olivier Rubin, "Limits to Growth," *Foreign Policy* 133 (November–December 2002): 43.

2. Gerald Barney et al., *Global 2000 Report to the President: Entering the 21st Century* (Washington, DC: Government Printing Office, 1980), I: 1. On the Carter administration's reaction to environmental constraints, see Sabin, *The Bet*, 103–15.

3. Ronald Reagan, "Remarks at Convocation Ceremonies at the University of South Carolina in Columbia, 20 Sept. 1983"; Second Inaugural Address, January 21, 1985, *The Public Papers of President Ronald W. Reagan*. Ronald Reagan Presidential Library, http://www.reagan.utexas.edu/archives/speeches/publicpapers.html#.

4. A penetrating analysis of popular attitudes toward economic growth is Bret Wallich's *At Odds with Progress: Americans and Conservation* (Tucson: University of Arizona Press, 1991).
5. See http://en.wikipedia.org/wiki/List_of_countries_by_population_density.
6. United Nations, Department of Economic and Social Affairs, Population Division, *World Population Prospects: The 2015 Revision, Key Findings and Advance Tables*, Working Paper No. ESA/P/WP.241, 2015. See also United Nations Department of Economic and Social Affairs, "World Population to 2300" (New York, 2004), 1–2.
7. Wolfgang Lutz and Sergei Scherbov, "Explanatory Extensions of IIASA's World Population Projections: Scenarios to 2300," Interim Report IR-08-022 (Laxenburg: International Institute for Applied Systems Analysis, 2008); and Lutz et al., *The End of World Population Growth in the 21st Century: New Challenges for Human Capital Formation and Sustainable Development* (London: Earthscan, 2004).
8. Vernadsky, "The Biosphere," excerpts reprinted in Libby Robin, Sverker Sörlin, and Paul Warde, ed., *The Future of Nature: Documents of Global Change* (New Haven, CT: Yale University Press, 2013), 161–73. For an updated version of Vernadsky's perspective, see James Lovelock, *Gaia: A New Look at Life on Earth* (New York: Oxford University Press, 1979).
9. Rejecting the concept of the "biosphere" as too narrowly focused on living organisms, Canadian scientists Ted Mosquin and Stanley Rowe have suggested a new focus in earth science on "the enveloping Ecosphere—that web of organic/inorganic/symbiotic structures and processes that constitute Planet Earth." See their paper "A Manifesto for Earth," *Biodiversity* 5:1 (2004), available online at www.ecospherics.net/pages/EarthManifesto.pdf.
10. Vernadsky, "The Biosphere and the Noosphere," *American Scientist* 33 (January 1945): 9–10. See also "The Transition from the Biosphere to the Noosphere," reprinted in *21st Century* (Spring–Summer 2012): 10–31. The French philosopher and Jesuit priest Pierre Teilhard de Chardin expanded on Vernadsky's concept in *The Phenomenon of Man* (1955). See also Brian Thomas Swimme and Mary Evelyn Tucker, *Journey of the Universe* (New Haven, CT: Yale University Press, 2011).
11. Peter Vitousek, Paul Ehrlich, Anne Ehrlich, and Pamela Matson, "Human Appropriation of the Products of Photosynthesis," *BioScience* 36 (June 1986): 369. On the Ehrlichs' contribution to environmental thinking, see Alan Weisman, *Countdown*, 399–413.
12. Vitousek et al., "Human Appropriation," 373. Other scientists point to the difficulties of measuring this impact exactly and estimate it more loosely at anywhere from 10 to 55 percent of terrestrial production: Stuart Rojstaczer, Shannon Sterling, and Nathan Moore, "Human Appropriation of Photosynthesis Products," *Science* 294 (December 21, 2001): 2549–52. See also Peter Vitousek, Harold Mooney, Jane Lubchenco, and Jerry Melillo, "Human Domination of Earth's Ecosystems," *Science* 227 (July 25, 1997): 494–99, and related articles in the same issue.
13. Berrien Moore III et al., "2001 Amsterdam Declaration on Earth System Science," www.igbp.net/about/history/2001amsterdamdeclarationonearthsystemscience.4. 1b8ae20512db692f2a680001312.html. (emphasis in the original). Will Steffen et al., *Global Change and the Earth System: A Planet Under Pressure: Executive Summary,*

Stockholm, Sweden: IGBP Secretariat, Royal Swedish Academy of Sciences (2004), 4.

14. Johan Rockstrom et al., "A Safe Operating Space for Humanity," *Nature* 461 (September 24, 2009): 473–74.

15. The best account of this pivotal invention is Vaclav Smil, *Enriching the Earth: Fritz Haber, Carl Bosch, and the Transformation of World Food Production* (Cambridge, MA: MIT Press, 2000). See also Interagency Working Group on Harmful Algal Blooms, Hypoxia, and Human Health of the Joint Subcommittee on Ocean Science and Technology, "Scientific Assessment of Hypoxia in U.S. Coastal Waters" (Washington, DC, 2010).

16. Rockstrom et al., "A Safe Operating Space," 474; Hanqin Tian et al., "Food Benefit and Climate Warming Potential of Nitrogen Fertilizer Uses in China," *Environmental Research Letter* (2012), http://iopscience.iop.org/1748-9326/7/4/044020/article.

17. Rockstrom et al., "A Safe Operating Space," 473; Pimm, quoted by Sophia Li, "Has Plant Life Reached Its Limits?" *New York Times*, September 20, 2012.

18. Rockstrom et al., "A Safe Operating Space," 475.

19. The danger of "overshoot," however, has resurfaced in discussions of "the human footprint," defined as the collective load or demand made by all nations on "natural capital," that is, the ecological services and natural resources of the earth. That footprint, according to one calculation, overshot the earth's capacity in the 1980s and has continued to grow larger. See Mathis Wackernagel et al., "Tracking the Ecological Overshoot of the Human Economy," *Proceedings of the National Academy of Science* 99 (July 9, 2002): 9266–71.

20. R. David Simpson, Michael A Toman, and Robert U. Ayres, "Scarcity and Growth in the New Millennium: Summary," *Scarcity and Growth Revisited: Natural Resources and the Environment in the New Millennium* (Washington, DC: Resources for the Future, 2005), 2, 22.

21. Steven Stoll, "Fear of Fallowing: The Specter of a No-Growth World," *Harpers Magazine* 315 (March 2008): 92.

22. Richard Norgaard, "Optimists, Pessimists, and Science," *BioScience* 52 (March 2002): 288. Exemplary of the new economic thinking are Juliet B. Schor, *Plenitude: The New Economics of True Wealth* (New York: Penguin, 2010); and Robert Costanza et al., *An Introduction to Ecological Economics*, 2nd ed. (Boca Raton, FL: CRC Press, 2015).

23. Herman Daly, "Introduction to the Steady-State Economy," *Economics, Ecology, Ethics: Essays Toward a State-State Economy* (New York: W. H. Freeman, 1980), 1–32.

24. Herman Daly, *Beyond Growth: The Economics of Sustainable Development* (Boston: Beacon Press, 1996), 22.

25. Moore et al., "Amsterdam Declaration."

26. Leopold, "The Land Ethic," *Sand County Almanac* (1949; reprint, New York: Oxford University Press, 1968), 201–26.

FIELD TRIP: ATHABASCA RIVER

1. James A. Larsen, *The Boreal Ecosystem* (New York: Academic Press, 1980); Ken Drushka, *Canada's Forest: A History* (Durham, NC: Forest History Society, 2003).

2. Over 300 bird species are at home in the Canadian boreal forest, and several million water birds spend at least part of their year there. See the Boreal

Songbirds Initiative's website (www.borealbirds.org). Among the human residents, 600 First Nation (or Indian) communities have ties to the boreal, or the subarctic cultural area, most of them speaking languages of the Algonquian family. "Aboriginal Peoples," *The Canadian Encyclopedia* (www.thecanadianencyclopedia.ca/).

3. The role of science in developing the Canadian North is addressed in Stephen Bocking, "Science and Spaces in the Northern Environment," *Environmental History* 12 (October 2007): 867–94; and in Morris Zaslow, *The Opening of the Canadian North, 1870–1914* (Toronto: McClelland and Stewart, 1971).

4. S. C. Ells, "Research Touches the North," *Canadian Geographical Journal* 24 (June 1942): 256–67. See also J. M. Parker and K. W. Tingley, *History of the Athabasca Oil Sands Region, 1890 to 1960's*, vol. 1: *Socio-Economic Developments*, Alberta Oil Sands Environmental Research Program, September 1980; James M. Parker, "The Long Technological Search," in John W. Chalmers, ed., *The Land of Peter Pond*, Occasional Publication No. 12 (Edmonton: Canadian Circumpolar Institute Press, 2003), 141–69; Donald Wetherell and Iren Kmet, *Alberta's North: A History, 1890–1950* (Edmonton: Canadian Circumpolar Institute Press, 2000), 352–61; and Graeme Wynn, *Canada and Arctic North America: An Environmental History* (Santa Barbara, CA: ABC-Clio, 2007), 323–44.

5. A current map of mineral leases in the Athabasca region is available from the Oil Sands Discovery Centre: www.history.alberta.ca/oilsands/resources/docs/discovery-centre-handout.pdf.

6. Useful for understanding the province's unique politics are Geo Takach, *Will the Real Alberta Please Stand Up?* (Edmonton: University of Alberta Press, 2010); and Michael Payne, Donald Wetherell, and Catherine Cavanagh, eds., *Albert Formed—Alberta Transformed* (Edmonton and Calgary: University of Alberta Press and University of Calgary Press, 2005). On Alberta's changing self-image see P. J. Smith, "Alberta Since 1945: The Maturing Settlement System," in L. D. McCann, ed., *Heartland and Hinterland: A Geography of Canada* (Scarborough, ON: Prentice-Hall Canada, 1982), 295–302.

7. Among the many critical histories of Alberta bitumen mining, the most comprehensive, particularly on the government-corporate nexus, is Andrew Nikiforuk, *Tar Sands: Dirty Oil and the Future of a Continent*, rev. ed. (Vancouver: Greystone, 2010). See also Robert Boschman and Mario Trono, eds., *Found in Alberta: Environmental Themes for the Anthropocene* (Waterloo, ON: Wilfred Laurier University Press, 2014), Part Two, "Bituminous Sands," 85–169.

8. Wood Buffalo National Park, where some 6,000 bison are currently protected, covers 44,800 square kilometers, or 13,000 square miles, about half the size of the oil-sands country. Less than 8 percent of the boreal forest is protected from development, although citizen groups are pushing for much more. Nancy Langston, "Paradise Lost: Climate Change, Boreal Forests, and Environmental History," *Environmental History* 14 (October 2009): 646.

9. US Energy Information Administration, www.eia.gov/countries/country-data.cfm.

10. US Energy Information Administration.

11. Mary Clark Sheppard, ed. *Athabasca Oils Sands: From Laboratory to Production: The Letters of Karl A. Clark, 1950–1966* (Sherwood, AB: Geoscience Publishing, 2005), 306; and Sheppard, ed., *Oil Sands Scientist: The Letters of Karl A. Clark, 1920–1949* (Edmonton: University of Alberta Press, 1989), 89.

12. On the pros and cons of reclamation, see Bridget Mintz Testa, "Reclaiming Alberta's Oil Sands Mines," *Earth Magazine* (February 2010), American Geosciences Institute, Issue Archive (www.earthmagazine.org); Government of Alberta, Alberta's Oil Sands, Reclamation" (www.oilsands.alberta.ca), and Jennifer Grant, Simon Dyer, and Dan Wonillowicz, "Fact or Fiction? Oil Sands Reclamation," May 2008, Pembina Institute, Publications (www.pembina.org).

13. In the 1950s some Canadians were keen to detonate nuclear bombs underground to free the oil from the sands. See William Marsden, *Stupid to the Last Drop: How Alberta Is Bringing Environmental Armageddon to Canada* (Toronto: Knopf, 2007), 14–22. On the energy costs of *in situ* mining see Nikiforuk, *Tar Sands*, 312.

14. According to Matt Carlson, Jeff Wells, and Dina Roberts, "The Boreal Forest globally stores more carbon than any other region of the globe, perhaps two or three times as much carbon as is stored in the tropics." *The Carbon the World Forgot: Conserving the Capacity of Canada's Boreal Forest Region to Mitigate and Adapt to Climate Change*, Boreal Songbird Initiative and Canadian Boreal Initiative (Seattle: 2009), 2.

15. On local attitudes toward the pipeline crossing the United States, see Steven Mufson's *Keystone XL: Down the Line* (Kindle Single electronic text; TED Book Conferences, 2013). On reaction to the British Columbia pipeline, see Paul Bowles and Henry Veltmere, ed., *The Answer Is Still No: Voice of Pipeline Resistance* (Halifax and Winnipeg: Fernwood Publishing, 2014).

16. Hansen, "Game Over for the Climate," *New York Times*, May 9, 2012; Karl Taro Greenfeld, "Bill McKibben's Battle against the Keystone XL Pipeline," *BloombergBusinessweek*, February 28, 2013. See also McKibben, *The End of Nature* (New York: Random House, 1989), and Elizabeth Kolbert, *Field Notes from a Catastrophe: Man, Nature, and Climate Change*, rev. ed. (New York: Bloomsbury, 2015).

17. Meadows et al., *Limits to Growth*, 66.

EPILOGUE

1. National Aeronautics and Space Administration, National Space Science Data Center, Voyager I, http://nssdc.gsfc.nasa.gov/nmc/spacecraftDisplay.do?id=1977-084A.

2. Download the image at http://eoimages.gsfc.nasa.gov/images/imagerecords/52000/52392/PIA00452.tif.

3. See www.nasa.gov/images/content/115334main_image_feature_329_ys_full.jpg.

4. Carl Sagan, *Pale Blue Dot: A Vision of the Human Future in Space* (New York: Ballantine, 1994), 7.

5. For a political philosopher's perspective on these issues, see William Ophuls, *Ecology and the Politics of Scarcity: The Unraveling of the American Dream* (New York: W.H. Freeman, 1992).

6. Sagan, *Pale Blue Dot*, 6–7.

7. See, for example, David Christian's *Maps of Time: An Introduction to Big History* (Berkeley: University of California Press, 2004), which begins nearly 14 billion years ago with the Big Bang. Not so "deep" in time but still expanding the usual historical perspective to include evolution and the natural world is J. R. McNeill and William H. McNeill, *The Human Web: A Bird's Eye of World History* (New York: Norton, 2003).

INDEX

abundance: Communist ideology and, 36; cultural explanations of, 153–56, 185; early European accounts of the Americas and, 22–23; exploitation of, 19–20, 35, 58–62, 85, 91, 111; fossil fuels and visions of, 50–52; government management of, 108, 112; industrialization and, 36, 50, 91; labor costs and, 149; limits of human ingenuity and, 6–7, 25, 35–36, 172, 185; limits of nature's endowments and, 6, 8, 35, 40, 42, 46–50, 52–54, 78, 81, 85, 92–93, 100, 107–9, 140–41, 144–45, 147–48, 151, 155, 161–80, 183–86, 189, 198–99, 203, 221–22; maritime trade and, 58–63; mineral wealth and, 29, 93–95; perceptions and, 5–7; as richness of experience and relationships, 154; "Second Earth" and, 5–7, 13–16, 18–19, 24, 29, 31–35, 37–40, 42, 44–45, 49–50, 55–58, 70, 73, 91, 140, 143, 147, 156, 178, 203, 220–21; slavery and, 20; spontaneous activity of nature and, 54–55; substitutability seen as means of preserving, 173–74; sustainability and, 35; technology viewed as means of preserving, 173–75; trade and, 19–20, 23, 32, 38, 43

Adirondack Mountains, 87, 95

Africa: decline in birth rates in, 187; early modern population data from, 16; European colonization of, 7, 33, 39; *homo sapiens* origins in, 213, 220; raw materials exported from, 144; slavery and, 6, 20, 31, 39

Agassiz, Louis, 189

agriculture: climate change and, 195–96; deforestation and, 22, 82, 86, 98; environmental impacts from, 183, 186, 195–96; European practices in North America and, 22; experiments in, 70–71; the Frontier and, 89, 98; *Genesis* account of, 82; Green Revolution and, 173; human productivity increased by, 43, 45–46; Indians' practice of, 17–18, 22; international trade and, 131; law of diminishing returns and, 49; Marsh on, 82, 98;

nitrogen fertilizer and, 195–96; slavery and, 31; Smith on, 43, 45–46; sustainable forms of, 70–71; water usage and, 82, 89, 128–30, 133–35

Alaska: boreal forests in, 18, 203; dry landscape in, 132; mineral wealth in, 38; oil royalties in, 208; Russian exploration of, 23; U.S. acquisition of, 85

Alberta (Canada): automobiles in, 213–14; bitumen deposits in, 205–14; bitumen extraction methods in, 210–13, 252n14; climate change and, 214; conventional oil deposits in, 207; Cree Indians in, 211–12; environmental devastation in, 210–11; geological history of, 209; oil pipelines in, 214–15; oil royalties in, 208; Progressive Conservative Party in, 208; promises of ecological restoration in, 211–12; state ownership of bitumen fields in, 208; wealth of, 208

All-American Canal, 129

Alsop, James, 71

Amazon River basin, 15, 19, 203–4

American exceptionalism, 152–53, 155–56

American Indians. *See* Indians

American Museum of Natural History, 117

American Revolution, 41, 46, 61

Amsterdam Declaration (International Geosphere-Biosphere Programme; 2001), 194, 200

anthracite coal, 93

Anthropocene, 7, 225

Apollo 17 space mission (1972), 220

Appalachia: coal mining and deposits in, 95–97, 102, 121, 174, 237n18; environmental devastation in, 174; poverty and isolation in, 96

Arctic region: climate change and, 99, 214; early European maps and, 13; whales and, 65–66, 68

Arizona, 111–12, 123, 130, 133

Arndt, Heinz, 172

Arrhenius, Svante August, 99, 132, 189

Printed in the USA/Agawam, MA
October 17, 2022

799894.033